We Were Going to Win, or Die There

WITH THE MARINES AT GUADALCANAL, TARAWA, AND SAIPAN

We Were Going to Win, or Die There

WITH THE MARINES AT GUADALCANAL, TARAWA, AND SAIPAN

by

940.545973
ELR

Lieutenant Colonel Roy H. Elrod, USMC

Edited by Fred H. Allison

Number 10 in the North Texas Military Biography and Memoir Series

University of North Texas Press

Denton, Texas

10 9 8 7 6 5 4 3 2 1

Permissions:
University of North Texas Press
1155 Union Circle #311336
Denton, TX 76203-5017

The paper used in this book meets the minimum requirements of the
American National Standard for Permanence of Paper for Printed Library
Materials, z39.48.1984. Binding materials have been chosen for durability.

Library of Congress Cataloging-in-Publication Data

Names: Elrod, Roy H., 1919-2016, author. | Allison, Fred H., 1950– editor.
Title: We were going to win, or die there : with the Marines at
    Guadalcanal, Tarawa, and Saipan / by Lieutenant Colonel
    Roy H. Elrod, USMC ; edited by Fred H. Allison.
Other titles: North Texas military biography and memoir series ; no. 10.
Description: Denton : University of North Texas Press, [2017]
    | Series: North Texas military biography and memoir
    series ; no. 10 | Includes bibliographical references.
Identifiers: LCCN 2017024792 | ISBN 9781574416893 (hardback : alk. paper)
Subjects: LCSH: Elrod, Roy H., 1919-2016. | Marines—United
    States—Biography. | United States. Marine Corps. Marine Regiment,
    8th—Biography. | World War, 1939-1945—Campaigns—Pacific
    Ocean—Personal narratives, American. | Guadalcanal, Battle of, Solomon
    Islands, 1942-1943—Personal narratives, American. | Tarawa, Battle
    of, Kiribati, 1943—Personal narratives, American. | Saipan, Battle of,
    Northern Mariana Islands, 1944—Personal narratives, American.
Classification: LCC VE25.E47 A3 2017 | DDC 940.54/5973092 [B] —dc23
LC record available at https://lccn.loc.gov/2017024792

*We Were Going to Win, or Die There: With the Marines at Guadalcanal, Tarawa, and
Saipan* is Number 10 in the North Texas Military Biography and Memoir Series

The electronic edition of this book was made possible by
the support of the Vick Family Foundation.

Contents

Preface

n the course of my duties as the oral historian for the U.S. Marine Corps History Division, I interviewed marines of all ranks and varied time periods. I was made aware of retired Marine Lieutenant Colonel Roy H. Elrod in an unusual manner: through family friends from Muleshoe, Texas. This is where I grew up and coincidentally, where Roy grew up, but about thirty years apart. In 2012, when we met, Roy and I lived within five miles of each other but more than 1,500 miles from Muleshoe, in Fredericksburg, Virginia. I was impressed when I met Roy. Here he was ninety-three years old, he lived alone in a modern, large brick home, and he drove his Hummer (!) where he needed to go. His wife of sixty-three years, Malda, had passed away in 2008.

I was simply amazed at his vitality and mental acuity. Spread out on his dining room table were scrapbooks, letters, photographs, and various documents pertaining to his Marine Corps career. When he talked to me about his World War II experiences, I realized his story had to be captured.

The first interview occurred in October 2012. We met on numerous occasions after. We talked about the war and combat in the Pacific, but also about his life growing up in Muleshoe, and his life after the war, and after he retired from the Marine

Corps in 1961. The interviews were recorded, most were audio only, although a few sessions were videotaped. All the sessions were transcribed. All together about thirty hours of interviews were recorded and transcribed. There were other times, at social events, when we chatted informally, and he would say something that I had not heard in the interviews. I would jot it down to be added to the overall body of information on his experiences.

I edited the transcripts to make the story as it appears in the book. I provided annotated notes at the beginning of each chapter, and endnotes throughout. I selected the most descriptive and compelling parts and omitted others for brevity's sake. In some instances I rearranged the narrative sequence to make a linear story line. I selected pertinent parts of his large collection of letters he wrote to relatives during the war to highlight and emphasize key aspects of his commentary and inserted them at appropriate locations. The letters were a truth-teller, written at the time and place of the events. They are reliable where memory, whether you are twenty-five or ninety-five, is not. One drawback to the letters, however, is that Roy, as do most military men who write letters home from a combat arena, painted a fairly rosy picture of his situation. This was to protect his loved ones. But there were instances when the letters revealed genuine feelings or descriptions of his situation at the time that he wrote them. Besides their historical witness, the secondary benefit of the letters, as well as the photos, scrapbook clippings, and documents is that they served to keep Roy's memory fresh. Another check on his memory was the Marine Corps official records at the History Division. I checked dates, locations, and names against Roy's account. I came to realize that his memory was amazingly accurate, considering.

I believe that his story is valuable beyond recounting one marine's experiences. It carries a historical authenticity that perhaps other memoir-type accounts do not have. Through Lieutenant Colonel Elrod's experiences, the reader can learn about life in the Marine Corps of the World War II-era. And about the heroic marines that endured miserable conditions, maiming, and death to defeat a relentless and merciless enemy at iconic Pacific battles.

Introduction

"When I raised the logs I saw inside their dugout . . . one of the Japanese was lying on his stomach with his rifle and bayonet up, pointed to the entrance. I could see the gunner just to his left, who was still in front at the firing position. They were on full alert. . . . I was holding the M-1 in my right hand like a pistol, and the two logs with my left hand. When I lifted the logs, the Japanese soldier who was right under me turned his head around, but he didn't get his weapon around. As he turned his head, I put a round in his forehead; the muzzle of the rifle was no more than four or five inches from his head. I immediately then put two rounds in the gunner's head because he was beginning to swing around in the hole. That took care of that machine gun position." Roy H. Elrod, USMC

Roy H. Elrod, born in 1919, came from the small West Texas town of Muleshoe. He was raised on a farm operated by his widowed mother. He managed to save enough money, even in the midst of the Depression to attend Texas A&M, however he did not finish. As the war clouds gathered, he joined the Marine Corps in 1940. This was the "Old Corps," before the World War II expansion grew it ten times its former size. After boot camp he was assigned to the recently re-activated Eighth Marine Regiment, or "Eighth

Marines" as marines say. He was assigned to a 37-mm anti-tank gun crew. After the Japanese attacked Pearl Harbor and the war began, the Eighth Marines were the first Marines to head to the Pacific. They thought they would be the first to fight, but instead they went to Samoa and guarded these isolated but strategic islands, awaiting a Japanese attack that never came.

In the meantime, the First Marine Division assaulted Guadalcanal and engaged the Japanese in that bloody and pivotal fight. Three months later in November the Eighth Marines arrived to reinforce the First Marine Division. They were just in time because the Japanese had recently landed fresh troops. The fight in November and December was fierce as the Americans began an offensive that eventually doomed the Japanese. Roy Elrod by this time had been commissioned and commanded a platoon of 37-mm guns. Operating his platoon of 37-mm guns along the front lines to support marine infantry, he earned a Silver Star and a battlefield promotion to first lieutenant.

In January 1943, hungry, battle fatigued, and sick, the Eighth Marines went to New Zealand for rest and recovery. The New Zealanders, who believed that the marines had delivered them from a very real Japanese threat, made life very good for the marines. The marines also trained and prepared for the next battle.

This turned out to be on tiny Betio Island, part of the Tarawa atoll in the Central Pacific. Tarawa is famous for the bordering reef that prevented landing craft from reaching the beach. Marines had to wade in a half mile or so, while the Japanese ripped them with defensive weaponry that bristled ashore. Elrod got his four 37-mm guns ashore, his marines towing and manhandling them half a mile through the deadly surf. It is doubtful if any other 37-mm guns made it ashore the first day. The battle for Tarawa lasted only seventy-six hours, but theses were hours of non-stop fighting. Surviving without a wound, Roy considered himself remarkably fortunate.

Recovery and re-training after Tarawa occurred on the big island of Hawaii. Here, Elrod was promoted to captain and given command of a platoon of half-track trucks, mounted with a 75-mm cannon and machine guns. With this platoon he made his third amphibious landing, this time at Saipan, another vicious melee with an enemy that gave, and received, no quarter. His half-tracks prowled the front lines, supporting marine riflemen by blasting into Japanese caves and dugouts.

Just as the Eighth Marines were about to be relieved at the front, a Japanese artillery round exploded within yards of Elrod's position. He was riddled with shrapnel; the war ended for him there. Six months of recovery and rehabilitation followed. When out of the hospital at San Diego, one of his first acts was to drive to Texas and marry his high school sweetheart, Malda. The marriage lasted sixty-three years.

This is an account of the World War II experiences of Roy H. Elrod. They are in many ways unique, but in many ways they are not. They represent what many, many marines experienced during World War II in the Pacific.

CHAPTER ONE

Muleshoe to Texas A&M: Growing Up in Texas, 1920s and 1930s

Roy H. Elrod hailed from Muleshoe, Texas. Muleshoe, situated on the western edge of the high plains of Texas, or the Panhandle, was in many ways still a frontier. The town became the county seat of Bailey County, named for Peter J. Bailey, who fought at the Alamo. The Panhandle was the last holdout of the ferocious Comanche Indians who had terrorized settlers since Europeans had arrived in that part of North America. The U.S. Army finally subdued them in 1874, and they were relegated to an Oklahoma reservation. Bailey County was not officially a county until 1918, the year before Roy Elrod was born. He was the fourth baby registered in the new county. Extensive settlement did not occur until an efficient means of pumping water from the bountiful underground Ogallala aquifer was available. When Elrod was growing up there in the 1920s and 1930s, it was still sparsely settled, in transition from ranch grassland to modern irrigated farms. This wide-open, wind-swept prairie lay vacant for miles. On the family farm, raised by a single mother but within a network of extended family, he developed a powerful work ethic, a fierce sense of self-reliance and independence, and a knack for improvisation.

Elrod attended Texas A&M University for two school years, 1936–1938. College at that time, although incredibly less expensive than today, was still a financial struggle. He had saved money from working in high school and continued to work while a college student. Texas A&M, founded by the Morrill Act of 1862, was one of the nation's senior military colleges. At the time Elrod attended, as well as today, A&M had an extremely proud tradition. During World War II, A&M supplied over 14,000 officers to the military. This was more than the combined total from the U.S. Naval Academy and West Point. Although Elrod was not commissioned while at A&M, his two years spent there prepared him in many ways for life as a combat marine in World War II.

I was born on June 23, 1919, in a small farm house about four miles north of Muleshoe, Texas.[1] My grandmother delivered me and I was the first child of Nina (Wallace) and Roy Elrod. This land had been part of the XIT ranch.[2] The

---

1 Muleshoe is situated along the western side of the Texas panhandle. The first settlers did not arrive in that area until the late nineteenth century. This was due partly to the lack of rainfall and vegetation to support agricultural activities.

2 The XIT was at one time the largest ranch in the world, under fence. Three million acres of Texas panhandle land had been sold to Chicago investors in 1881 if they would fund the building of a new Texas state capitol. They did and it ended up costing $3,000,000. Later the XIT was divided into smaller tracts and sold to

Spanish referred to this area as the Llano Estacado, or Staked Plains, and is part of the Great Plains. When a person stands there, he sees no distinctive land forms, for there are no trees or bushes of any consequence. My grandfather had moved to Muleshoe from Rocky Ford, Colorado, in 1914 to start a demonstration farm for the Coldern Land Company. Although the farm was successful, he didn't like living in that area and wanted to go back to Colorado. He had two daughters, my mother and her sister. While in Muleshoe they married brothers, and they remained there.

My mother had a good bit of education, more than the average young woman of that time. She had graduated high school in Rocky Ford before coming to Muleshoe and had even gone to business college in Dallas for a year. I doubt my father had more than two or three years of school. According to my mother, he was the last working cowboy on the YL Ranch. He could obviously read and write, but I have few memories of my father. He died of cancer in 1923 when I was four years old.

When my father became ill and realized that he wasn't going to live too much longer he bought some land and put it all in my mother's name. This is the farm I grew up on. He actually never lived on it. It was about four miles north of Muleshoe on the Friona Highway. It was 240 acres, and it was still in the unbroken buffalo grass sod. This sod was a unique kind of vegetation, since it put down roots very deep and the roots were very thick and tough. The early settlers cut up blocks of that and used it for building blocks to build what they called "soddies," small houses

---

ranchers and farmers. The land that Roy grew up on was on the southern border of XIT land.

that they lived in until they could get lumber. There was absolutely no natural timber in the area. These early pioneers heated their stoves and cooked using buffalo chips or cow chips for fuel.

We never lived in a soddie. Our first house had been a cowboy bunkhouse at an XIT line camp, called East Camp. These line camps were for two or three cowboys to live at, and a chuck wagon would bring them supplies about once a month. I don't have many memories of my father, but I have a vivid memory of the day I went along with my father and his brother, my uncle, in a flatbed wagon out to this line camp. When we got up to the house, there was a squatter family in the house, and they didn't want to move. My father called them out and held them against the side of the house at the point of a rifle while my uncle brought all their belongings out and put them in the wagon, and they hauled them off the property. I have always thought in my own mind that my father took me with them on this errand for one of two reasons: if he got in trouble he could tell the judge that he didn't intend to kill these people in front of this four-year-old boy, or he took me along to show me how a real man handled his problems. I still have the rifle my father used. It was his .30-.30 saddle gun.

Evidently my father was a good planner. When he realized he was dying, he also bought a life insurance policy. My mother said he made one premium payment on it before he died. When he died she received a lump sum of $10,000, which in those days was like the income for three years. She received $50 a month for twenty years, so really we were fine. She always had a tenant farmer on the farm. The tenant farmer got sixty percent and she got forty percent from whatever he produced. My mother was a very staunch Methodist, and we never missed a church service. She was also a very hardheaded and determined woman. It was her way or the highway. Nobody ran over her.

My mother, my little sister, and I lived at the East Camp house for only five or six months. We moved in with my Aunt Faye and my Uncle Carl [mother's sister and father's brother] on their property about a mile away. They had a big two-story house and plenty of room. My uncle did most of the work on building our house. It was a very nice house. It had plaster walls inside, and the outside was a weatherboard with stucco over it.

That road where we lived, that went into Muleshoe, was first graded when I was probably six or seven years old. Before that it had been just a wagon road. There were hardly any roads in that area at all. My father had a Model T, but my mother traded it for a 1925 Dodge coupe—the ugliest thing I had ever seen in my life. It was huge. It was a little lower than the Model T, but all the Model Ts had made these ruts that served for roads in that part of the country. With the Dodge we would get hung on high center. I learned how to dig a little hole and get under the car and jack it up with the jack at an angle so when it got high enough it would lift the car up and drop it back, and then after one or two times of this it was back far enough to get traction and could get out. My mother got to be a genius at getting up and out of the ruts.

I started shooting guns at an early age. How young, I don't know, but I am sure it was with some of my uncles. I do remember the Christmas when I was eight and my mother bought me a .22 rifle. She took me out and set five bottles up on the fence. I'm sure I wasn't shooting from very far, but I eventually hit one of the bottles. I was quite pleased with myself. She took the rifle then and shot the necks off the four remaining bottles.

She said, "That's what you're supposed to do." She would let me go out and hunt birds and rabbits and any other little animals. She gave me four or five bullets, and she expected me to bring in four or five rabbits, ground squirrels, or birds. If I failed and only brought in three or so, then the next time I was only allowed three bullets. So, I soon learned to shoot with a rifle. This little Stevens Crack Shot was a very accurate gun. Once or twice I managed to line up two sparrows and killed both with one bullet. It was my mother's way or no way. She could shoot the eye out of a rabbit. As a result I became a very good rifle shot. My mother showed me the proper position and sight alignment, but it was up to me to make a good shot.

I rode horses as far back as my memory goes. I got my own horse when I was five. He was a half Shetland and half Morgan and was pony-size. He and I became pretty good friends. As I grew older I rode further and further away from home. One of my favorite things to do when I was a boy was to take long pony rides. My mother would make me a lunch. I took a two-gallon canvas water bag. Those canvas water bags seeped just enough and the evaporation of the water that seeped and the dry air would keep the water cool. If we went by a windmill or a place like that, I would drink and get some water for my horse by pouring it into my hat. At that time probably three-fourths of the land was just like it was left by the Indians and the buffalo. I used to find buffalo skulls scattered all around over the area, and also buffalo wallows.[3]

---

3 Elrod related that these were made when the buffalo were on the South Plains. In the spring their hair would begin to molt, so they would lie down on their sides and kick around and around to rub that hair off. These buffalo wallows were just the length of a buffalo from his shoulder to the end of his hind feet. As this was

As a boy, I used to go out with my uncles when they did work around the farms. I worked on the windmills, worked on fences and other things, and I became quite convinced that I never wanted to have anything to do with a farm. But when I was eleven, with the Depression going on, it seemed like a good idea for me to find work. I got a job—on a farm. I went to work for a farmer named Churchill, working ten hours a day, six days a week for seventy-five cents a day during the summer. I mainly drove teams, but I also built fences and all the normal things around the farm. From the very beginning I didn't get along very well with him. He was from Connecticut or someplace up north, and I was a Confederate and did not like a Yankee. They were "damn Yankees." I had four great-grandfathers who had been in the Confederate Army. Churchill wanted to treat me like a hired hand, but I didn't feel like I was a hired hand. On most of the ranches and farms, the help ate right with the family. He had a big root cellar, and he expected me to eat my lunch there. I didn't think that was right. He lived there with his wife and two little girls and his father, who was an old sick man. They raised turkeys, and they had a shed where the turkeys were kept. Churchill had part of the shed screened off for his father to live in. It had a bed in it and some little pieces of furniture. I didn't think it was right, the way he treated his father. So, Churchill and I never got along, and I didn't work there very long.

Fortunately, after three or four weeks my grandfather needed someone to drive a truck delivering ice for his ice house.

---

done they gradually killed the grass there. When the rains came it would make mud holes and in the summer when the flies were bad, the buffalo would get in there and kick around again to get mud up over their backs as protection against the flies. These buffalo wallows were scattered all over the place.

I had been working for seventy-five cents a day for Churchill, and my grandfather paid me a dollar, so this was moving forward. Working at the ice house allowed me to spend lots of time with my maternal grandfather, Wallace. I was at an impressionable age, twelve to fifteen years old, and he had a big influence on me. He was born and spent his entire life on the western frontier. He had made the first land rush in Indian Territory, now Oklahoma. He was at an age he liked to talk about the past, and I liked to listen. My grandfather didn't have much education, but he was a very bright old man. One time we were talking, and he said, "Roy, there's only one thing that a man has to do, and that's die. Everything else is a matter of choice." As I've grown older I have come to realize that was really a fact. In my own life, I realized the things I did were not done by somebody else or forced by somebody else. They were things I made my own choice about. It taught me to not blame other people for my shortcomings. Another thing my grandfather said was, "Don't ever get into a fight you don't intend to win. But, don't go looking for trouble. There will be enough trouble coming along on its own. If you have a serious difference with somebody, don't waste your time with argument. Hit the guy. Don't try to knock him down. Try to kill the son-of-a-bitch." This was the attitude that those old gents had.

One time a fellow from the federal government came to the ice house and wanted to know why Wallace was not complying with the NRA's [National Recovery Administration] policies.[4]

---

4   The National Recovery Administration was a New Deal program instituted in 1933 by the federal government but declared unconstitutional in 1935 by the Supreme Court because they deemed it violated separation of branches provisions

Now most everyone at that time was a staunch Democrat. But not everybody liked FDR [President Franklin Delano Roosevelt]. My grandfather always called him that "son-of-a-bitch Roosevelt." They did not like the WPA [Works Progress Administration] and other New Deal programs. They came out with the NRA the last year that I worked in the icehouse. But this young man came to my grandfather's icehouse and said, "Mr. Wallace, I'm here from the NRA, and you will have to. . . ." He never finished that sentence. My grandfather jumped up and grabbed him by the throat slammed him against the side of the building two or three times and explained to him that if he didn't get away very quickly that it would be the last of him. After that, apparently, the NRA decided it didn't affect the Wallace ice business because no one ever came back. Texans didn't like to be told.

I started high school the year I was thirteen. We only had eleven grades in Texas at that time—seven grades of elementary school and four of high school. In the summer before I started high school, I would walk into town to the swimming pool. I would cut across backyards, and as I went by this one house, here was this girl I had never seen. She was in a pretty yellow dress out on the back porch shaking crumbs out of a tablecloth. A light went off in my head: "That's for me." Her name was Malda Chandler, and I later married her. We dated all through high school. She was actually born in southern Virginia. Her father died when she was five, and her mother was a Texan. She lived with her mother in South Texas until her mother died

---

of the Constitution. The NRA aimed to assist businesses and labor overcome the ravages of the Great Depression.

when she was twelve. She moved to Muleshoe when she was thirteen and lived with her older sister and her family.

For a date Malda and I would go to Dee's Hot Shot café for a hamburger and a Coke for about fifty cents. We went to Clovis, New Mexico, if we wanted to see a movie. The theater in Muleshoe closed about the time speaking movies came out.

I kept delivering ice for my grandfather until I was fifteen years old. By this time, he was seventy-five and he decided to close his ice business. That summer, the summer before my senior year, I started working for a farmer driving a tractor at night. I would meet him at the field along a road at sundown. We would fill the tractor with fuel, do whatever else needed to be done, fill the planter with seed if I was planting. Then I would drive the tractor all night, and I would meet him at daylight. I hated it. I hated it with a passion. But again, I was getting a dollar a day, or night. This was when tractors were first coming in. They had iron wheels with big lugs on them. They didn't have any springs, and it was a rough ride. The seat was on a flexible piece of metal, and it had a little bounce. Driving one of those things was not a walk in the park.

The next summer I started doing the same thing. Well, one day I was sleeping after driving that tractor all night, and my stepfather called me. He said there had been a big hailstorm in Muleshoe, and this contractor was hiring extra help. So, I quickly got up and got my clothes on and walked the four miles into town and applied for a job. I was hired at 25 cents an hour, which was big money.

All the houses then were roofed with cedar shingles, not a shake but a thin cedar shingle, and in that dry weather they became very brittle, and a hailstorm could be pretty destructive. So, every house in town had leaks. This one contractor, Sylvan Robinson, was about the only contractor around, and he put me to work repairing these roofs. A lot of the time my job was crawling around the attic with pieces of wire, and any place I could see daylight through the roof, I would stick that wire through. A man working on the roof would come along and fix the hole. After we finished repairing these roofs, he let all the extra help go except me. I worked that whole summer in construction. I worked six days a week, twenty-five cents an hour. I had been saving my money up all through the year. I was planning to start college in September 1936.

No one in my family had been to college except a few who had gone to the normal college in Canyon, Texas.[5] All through high school I had perfect attendance, all four years. I finished third in my class. I was the highest boy, and my girlfriend Malda was the salutatorian. I had scored high enough in high school that I had a $300 scholarship to a small college down near Fredericksburg, Texas. That would probably have covered my expenses the first year. I had my mind set on going to Texas A&M, though. I had always been interested in military-type things. There were several veterans of World War I in Muleshoe. Most of them didn't talk much about the war, but we knew they were there. All through my early life I read about the Civil War and about World War I. So, I had always been interested in the military, and I knew about A&M and I liked the A&M uniform too.

---

5 He is referring to West Texas State Normal College. A "normal college" was established specifically to give aspiring teachers a formal education. This college later became West Texas State University which later became West Texas A&M.

Sometime in the summer of 1936 I submitted my high school transcript. Actually, there was very little paperwork and I was accepted. When it came time to go down in early September, my mother's brother, Uncle Wayne, drove me down. He and I were not particularly close friends. We made a non-stop drive down. I got out of the car, and he turned and left.

I was let out at the steps of the administration building in a drizzling rain. I discovered that I enjoyed the weather in that part of Texas. There was a lot more rain, and there were trees. I found that I liked trees. The only trees in Muleshoe were those my father planted around the courthouse and a few planted around houses. I was very impressed with Texas A&M. I had never been that close to buildings of that type and size. There was a line there of new students that were checking in. I became chatty with an Italian boy named Novelli, who was standing in line beside me. When we got in to the powers that be, they asked me my major, and I said, "Geology." I had absolutely no idea what geology was. I had read a book in the summer by a man named Roy Chapman Andrews about his activities in the Gobi Desert.[6] He had found some of the first dinosaur fossilized eggs and other things. He had mentioned that he was a geologist. Well, it was not the geology that I was interested in, it was his discoveries and explorations. That is probably what influenced me to select geology.

---

6   Roy Chapman Andrews gained national fame as an explorer for the American Museum of Natural History in New York City. He began his career at the museum in 1906 by sweeping floors and assisting in the taxidermy department. By 1934 he had become the museum's director. Andrews wrote several books about his explorations and is best remembered for the series of dramatic expeditions he led to the Gobi of Mongolia from 1922 to 1930.

At that time the freshmen were referred to as "fish." There were about 1,100 of us in the freshmen class and approximately 4,000 students in the entire college. Most all the boys were like I was. It was the middle of the Depression, and money was hard to come by. There were a few boys whose families had money, but the vast majority of us were barely getting by. Since A&M at that time was all-male, one of the requirements was to be in Army ROTC [Reserve Officer Training Corps]. Since I had no real preference, I was assigned to B Battery, Field Artillery. We lived in accordance to what military units we were in, very similar to the way they lived at the service academies.

I didn't keep any civilian clothes there. I just wore my uniform all the time. If we had a laboratory class, we had white coveralls. I learned to take care of the uniform, to polish brass, polish my shoes—that sort of thing. I enjoyed the military aspects of A&M. We still had the old eight-man squad drill. Each person in the squad had to perform slightly differently when different maneuvers were made. We had to learn each of these, so that no matter what part of the squad we were in we could perform correctly.

All of our activities were related around the military. In addition to our regular college classes, we had military science and military training. We marched to the mess hall in formation. The corporals handled the training of the freshmen. They were the enforcers. We were continually taken out and put through the manual of arms and so forth by the corporals. Every morning we also had to fall out at reveille for roll call. They had us rehearse the various yells. They don't call them cheers there at A&M. They call them yells. We had to learn all the school songs. We had a Regular Army colonel who was the senior military instructor. He was one reason I put the army out to pasture, because he was very unimpressive. He was overweight with very slender legs. He always wore riding breeches with leather puttees. Among the students his name was "Bird-legs Lewis."

For the first forty days we were not allowed to have dessert at lunch or dinner. Dessert was called "cush," and it was held over our head as a motivator. If we messed up they would add another day until cush; we always knew how many days until cush. In the mess halls the waiters were students. They had that as their extra jobs. I had to have an extra job, and I was assigned to the landscape arts department. That's a very fancy sounding name for what I really did which was push a rotary lawnmower, clean drainage ditches, and other chores using various hand tools. We reported to a man named Charley, who assigned us, and we were paid fifty cents an hour and were only allowed to earn $15 a month. At that time, room, board, and tuition was $32.50 a month. With the money I had saved and the $15 from working I managed to squeak by. My first year at A&M I spent a total of $425. I hadn't learned about second hand textbooks and other ways to save money.

There was a lot of hazing and so forth. The freshmen were required to introduce themselves to anyone they met on the college whose name they did not know. Upperclassmen all had a substantial paddle, and one of the things they expected was that you would go tell one upperclassman from another something that he knew would annoy or irritate him. So, he would tell you, "Assume the position!" You would bend over, and they whacked you across the butt with the paddle. So, we all had bruised butts all the time and that went on all year.

I was only seventeen then, and actually I had absolutely no business being in college at that time. I was a lousy student. If I liked the class, I behaved myself and actually studied a little bit. If I didn't like the professor or didn't enjoy the class, I was in continual trouble. The most difficult thing for me was for the first time in my life I was around other people, 24-7. I had spent so much time alone growing up in West Texas on the farm, so this was very difficult for me to get accustomed to.

I always got a good grade in military science. I suppose I had an inclination for the military. My other studies though were not so good. There were a couple of classes that I liked, and I liked my English instructor, so I made pretty good grades there. I think I had as many failures that first year as I had passing grades.

I only got away from campus a few times that first year. This young lady, Malda Chandler, that I had dated through high school was working for an insurance company in Dallas. I went and saw her a few times. After we had graduated from high school, her older sister with whom she had been living with in Muleshoe had taken her to Austin and dropped her off, just left her on the street. Here it was the middle of the Depression, and Malda did not know anyone there and had very little money. She worked three jobs and was paid fifty cents a day, and this got her meals and a room, actually an enclosed porch, from a family there. She eventually went to a business college that led to her getting a job working for an attorney where she learned shorthand. She moved to Dallas later and got the insurance job and lived with relatives. She only had to work one job then.

I got to Dallas by hitchhiking. At that time, most of the Aggies didn't have the price of train fare, or bus fare, so we hitchhiked. In our uniforms, Texans knew who we were, and we could get out on the highway and had no problem getting rides. We had hitchhiking down to a science. So, when I could get away I would go to Dallas to see Malda.

On another occasion my freshman year, I hitchhiked home, a distance of over 500 miles. My mother wrote me that she had a problem with the sharecropper. He hadn't delivered her part of the feed grain bundles he had grown. She needed them to feed the milk cows. I hitchhiked home from A&M and went to his place and told him to start loading those bundles while I stood there and watched. I also told him if he didn't do it, I was going to kick his ass. Well, he did it. My mother said that when I made sergeant in the marines, he said, "Well, Roy always was the meanest kid in the county." But we got the bundles.

I was too young and too small for football. I had been interested in track; I was a pretty good runner. I went down at the time the track team was training, and I quickly discovered that if you weren't there on an athletic scholarship, the coaches were not going to pay any attention to you whatsoever. So, after two or three attempts to train with the team, I saw that that was not going to work. There was a nicely equipped gymnasium on campus. I hung around it, and I started watching the boxers, training and fighting. At that time, we had intercollegiate and intramural boxing. I thought I might like to try that. I started in and discovered that I had a pretty good talent for it. My first boxing match was an intramural match, and I lost it on decision. I learned from that and through my entire boxing career, which carried on into the Marine Corps, I never lost another fight. I boxed in both intramural competitions and intermural fights at A&M. I found that I had been a little conservative. I learned to take advantage of the strength I had developed while handling blocks of ice working for my grandfather and working construction. I was a lot stronger than the average young man. It gave me confidence. Toward the end of my freshman year an upperclassman told me to "assume the position." I told him, "If you want to paddle me, I'll meet you in the gym and beat the everlasting hell out of you." I wasn't bothered much after that.

When the school session was out, I had passed probably half of my courses. I went back, and I went right back to Muleshoe and worked for Sylvan Robinson, the contractor. He and I got along very nicely. I got a pay raise because he realized I was better than a laborer. Through that summer I very carefully saved my money, and with the pay increase I was in much better financial shape the second year than the first. I was also a much better student the second year. I went back to algebra again, and I liked this instructor, and I got an A. In fact I 'aced' the final exam. I also had plane geometry, solid geometry, and trigonometry. There were a couple of other courses that I had failed the first year that I passed the second year.

I had bought two shirts when I started in the second year. As time went along, the elbows of the shirts began to wear out. This $32.50 a month included having our laundry done by the ladies that worked there on campus. They would stitch up the rips in the elbows of the shirts. It was to the point where my elbows were mostly stitches. I finally managed to save enough money to buy three new shirts. While I was having problems with shirt elbows, another student had the soles of his shoes come loose. So, he took pieces of wire and wired the sole back to the upper. Before the year was out the soles were worn out, so every day he put a new piece of cardboard in the bottom of his shoes. This shows how we made out during the Depression. This year I had learned about second hand books, so I managed to get through the second year with an even $400. By the end of the year I was doing a little better financially than I had done before.

I had had such a poor record the first year that I wasn't a corporal. I was just a truck driver and still a private. I was a little better student, but I still had problems with chemistry. I liked chemistry all right, but I just didn't like the instructor. So, he had me go see the dean. The dean was talking to me, and he said, "You know your parents are sending you here to learn." I said, "Dean, you made two mistakes in that statement. First, my parents didn't send me here, I'm here. Second, I think these instructors are paid to teach, so why doesn't he teach?" The dean told me to get out. I'm sure I would have been expelled except the college desperately needed every penny that it could get because it was as about as poor as we were.

At the end of that school year I decided that if I was going to be any success as a student, I was going to have to work out a way that would keep me from having to work while in school. I decided that the best solution would be just to drop out of school for a year. So, I went back to work with the same contractor in Muleshoe, Sylvan Robinson. I was becoming more and more accomplished in all the building trades. I also began to get into the management part of the company. It became real obvious that if I was going to be able to stay with this work, I was going to have to have some transportation. So, I decided to buy a car. In the spring of 1939, for $300 I bought a two-year-old Chevrolet sedan; a very nice car. It had been used by one of the businessmen in Muleshoe, who liked to trade cars almost every year. Now, that solved that problem. But I realized, with having bought the car, I had defeated my ability to meet the necessary finances for going to school. So, I decided the best thing to do would be to stay off one more year. I began to realize that I was going to have adequate money not only for one year but probably for the two years I had remaining. I'd been working steady since school let out in 1938 and had saved a considerable amount of money. I lived in a very thrifty way. I lived at home and was careful to save my money; I did pay my stepfather and mother for board, but it was still economical. I also continued to do my share of the chores, milking the cows, and I still maintained the windmill and that type of thing.

Along about the first part of June [1940] or thereabout, I decided that I'd been working two years, six days a week almost without missing a day. I was a little tired, and I thought, "Well, if I'm going to start back to school, I need to rest up." So, I asked my boss to let me have some time off. I decided if I'm going to take time off, rather than wasting the time, why don't I go down to Lubbock and take a summer course at Texas Tech. So, I did that. I had just turned twenty-one.

I watched the newspapers and the newsreels at the movies, which were the ready news sources then. The newsreels showed the war in Europe that was going on. This was 1940. I became more and more convinced that the United States was going to be drawn into that war.

CHAPTER TWO

The Old Corps: USMC Boot Camp, 1940–1941

Roy Elrod joined the Marine Corps as the world descended into war. War had raged in Europe for a year. In the summer of 1940, shortly before he arrived at the Marine Corps Recruit Depot in San Diego, Germany overran France in only six weeks of blitzkrieg attacks. Hitler immediately followed this success with air attacks on Great Britain intent on defeating the Royal Air Force as a precursor to invasion. In the Pacific, Japan was poised to invade and seize resource rich areas in Southeast Asia to support its vision of an East Asian empire and economic self-sufficiency. It had invaded China in 1937 and established a military presence at various islands in the central and southern Pacific as a defensive perimeter for its "empire." These aggressions put it on the road to war with the U.S. and its allies.

By 1940 the United States, having recognized the danger posed by the belligerent and powerful Japan and Germany, had begun a massive expansion of its military forces. Elrod was part of this. Once signing up for the Marine Corps, he underwent Marine Corps recruit training, better known as boot camp. His boot camp instructors were hard-bitten men, salty veterans of World War I or the "Banana Wars," counterinsurgency operations in the Caribbean in the 1920s and 1930s. They had also served in far-flung and exotic ports such as the Philippines, Guam and China. His instructors were fiercely loyal to the Marine Corps and saw as their sacred duty to make marines worthy of the name out of civilians who knew very little of what the Marine Corps required. Elrod's experience as a student at Texas A&M had prepared him better than most for boot camp, but it was a demanding experience regardless. He came to understand what the Marine Corps stood for and embraced its ethos. It set him on track for a successful Marine Corps career.

While at Tech, I saw an advertisement that the Army Air Corps was taking pilot applications up at Fort Sill, Oklahoma, in September. I decided that I would investigate. So, I gathered up all my paperwork, and when the summer school session was over, I drove up to Lawton, Oklahoma, which was near Fort Sill. After two or three days, I realized that this wasn't something I was really interested in. It was a little more army than I liked. Also, I don't think I was making a very good impression with the people who were doing the interviewing. Most of the boys there had a burning desire to be pilots, but I just didn't have that. I had nothing against flying; it just wasn't something that I was interested in.

So, I just packed up my things and left. I didn't tell them I was dropping out of the program; I just left. As I drove through Amarillo, I saw a sign on the sidewalk: "Marine Corps Recruiting." That intrigued me. I had heard a little bit about marines, but very little. I knew they had something to do with the Banana Wars, and I knew they had something to do with ships. I had heard also something about the marines in China.

Well, I went in and talked to this old sergeant, and he made a real good sales pitch, and I was very impressed. I noticed his uniform. He was really sharp, and you could tell he took great care in its appearance. This was a lot different than the soldiers I had encountered at A&M. He was somebody who believed in what he was advertising and characterized the Marine Corps as an elite organization. He made a good impression. I said, "Well, I'm seriously thinking about that."

He said, "We'll find a place for you."

And I said, "Well, I'll tell you what I'll do. I'm going to join your outfit, but I want three days. I have to go back and quit my job and sell my car."

At the end of the three days, my mother and my sister drove me back to Amarillo, and I reported in to the recruiting sergeant. Since there were no officers there, he couldn't swear me in, but we made out several different kinds of papers. He put them in a folder, gave me a voucher for a train ride and for a hotel room in Oklahoma City, and told me where to report in. So, that afternoon I got on the train that went to Oklahoma City. I reported in and was instructed to come back the next day to be sworn into the Marine Corps. When I appeared the next day, there were four or five other boys about my same age, and most of them appeared to be a little younger. We were all lined up in a row and took the oath. It was September 1940, and I was twenty-one.

The officer gave us our necessary papers. Each one of us had a folder with our papers, and we were given our vouchers for a train ride to San Diego. If you enlisted in the Marine Corps west of the Mississippi, you went to boot camp in San Diego. If it was east of the Mississippi, you went to Parris Island. These vouchers covered our train transportation, an upper bunk in the Pullman car, and our three meals. So, that afternoon— late in the afternoon—we were back on the train. The train went right back through Amarillo and on out to Santa Rosa, New Mexico, and then turned south down through Clovis and Roswell to El Paso and then across the desert of southern New Mexico and Arizona.

We spent a couple of nights on the train, two nights and nearly three days. It was very comfortable. I had not traveled beyond New Mexico, so when we crossed over into Arizona, I was in new country. We changed trains in Los Angeles at about noon. One of the group disappeared. This was during the Depression and lots of young men rode the rails on freight cars. I believe that he had joined the Marine Corps just to get a free ride to California. I've often wondered what happened to him.

The rest of us got on another train from Los Angeles to San Diego. We had almost reached San Diego when the train stopped out in the open countryside. The train sat there for quite some time. I've always been a curious person, so I decided to get off the train and walk back and see what the problem was. When I got to the end of the train, I discovered that there'd been some transient who must have fallen asleep on the railroad track. Anyway, the train had run him over, and by the time the whole train had run over him, he was cut up into several pieces. We were there until the authorities came and picked up the remains of the body.

It was almost dark when we got into the station at San Diego. There was a marine corporal and a bus waiting for us. The corporal had been waiting an hour or two, maybe more, and he was a bit irritated to say the least. He considered it dereliction of duty on our part. He yelled at us to report on time, and he was not interested in any excuses. Right away he began to shout, "Hurry up! Hurry up! Hurry up! Line up! Line up! You're the biggest collection of trash I think I've ever seen!" Things like that. This tirade continued all the way to the base. I thought this was peculiar that he was so upset. I had not heard anything about how the Marine Corps trained or whatever. It was all entirely new.

We arrived at the Marine Corps base at San Diego. First thing was, we were herded into a cinderblock building. There were probably twenty-five or thirty of us in this room. Each one of us had a cot and we spent the night there and ate in the mess hall. We were still wearing civilian clothes.

Early the next morning we were awakened by a marine corporal. He, like the corporal that met us at the train station, seemed irritated and somewhat dissatisfied with us. He told us to strip and put all our clothes in a bag that was going to be sent back to our home address. Two or three of the people didn't have a home address, so they were informed that their bag would be set aside until they left the Marine Corps when it would be returned to them.

We started out on our trek. First was through physical screening, we stripped naked, received several different inoculations, they looked at our mouth and ears and so forth. Still naked, we were hustled into a barbershop area—this was all closed to the public, and got a haircut. This was a regulation recruit haircut, which was a real short cut, but not like the "scalping" they give recruits today, where it's down to the skin. We then went to another building and were issued new clothing, underwear, two sets of khakis, shoes, and a belt; we also got a set of blue coveralls.[1] Next, we were hustled to a place more or less like a post exchange where we were given a two-and-a-half-gallon galvanized bucket and walked past a line of people who dropped in the bucket toilet articles, and items to shine our brass, keep our uniform—just a collection of things. We moved down to a recruit training area that was all tents and assigned to a platoon. There were about thirty people in the platoon. A sergeant and two corporals were our drill instructors [DIs].

Living accommodations were two-man tents with duckboard floors and a folding canvas cot. The walkways were all duckboard—two heavy timbers laid parallel and then short boards placed across them with gaps between the boards. The same kind of thing they used in the bottom of the trenches in World War I. There was a reason for the duckboard. The training area was being placed on sand and muck that was being dredged up out of San Diego harbor.[2] Apparently, President Roosevelt and the navy had decided to make San Diego harbor into a much larger harbor that could handle all types of navy ships. Work was going on pumping this material out of the bay

---

1   The blue coveralls for a work uniform was being phased out at this time; green coveralls had been introduced in June 1940, but evidently recruits were still using the blue ones at San Diego.

2   A large part of the San Diego base was created by converting tidelands to solid ground.

for some time before I got there, so it was relatively dry where the camp was. But they were still in the process of doing that and soil was being pumped up by dredges out in the bay. Where it was dumped was very uneven ground, lots of little hills and valleys. The closer you got to the water, the wetter, muddier, and dirtier the area was. The Marine Corps base and the navy base were right together. We could sometimes hear the navy people training, but we learned very quickly to look down our nose at "swabbies." Marines were obviously much better than they were.

We had a little kerosene stove in the tents. I had started training in the last part of September and we did not finish until sometime in December. So, those little kerosene stoves made the tent quite comfortable. We could put water in the bucket on top of the stove and have warm water. We did have indoor toilet and shower facilities.

When I first arrived in boot camp, there weren't many tents in the area, but the Marine Corps in the fall of 1940 was rapidly expanding. When I joined the Marine Corps, it was not much more than 20,000.[3] Someone said it was smaller than the New York City police force at that time. By the time my three months were up, recruit tents stretched completely out of sight. I expect some of the later ones were in very muddy parts of this area that had just been dredged out of the bay.

There were three of the boys in my platoon who were sons of Hollywood actors or had some association with the movie

---

3   The Marine Corps was indeed expanding rapidly at this time. In mid-1939 there were 19,432 marines and a year later there were 28,345. On 30 November 1941, on the eve of the Pearl Harbor attack, there were 65,881 marines. Henry I. Shaw, Jr., *Opening Moves: Marines Gear Up for War* (Washington: US Marine Corps Historical Center, 1991), p.1.

business. My tent mate was one of them, and they stuck strictly to themselves. I lived in the tent with this kid for thirteen weeks, and we barely spoke to each other. His name was Warner and his father, H.B. Warner, was a movie actor. I remember his father was a tall fellow and usually played some kind of a villain part. These three disappeared near the end. I believed that their parents came and bought them out, which could be done then. I think you paid the Marine Corps the cost of having put him through boot camp. Anyway, they just disappeared.

Our daily uniforms were the baggy blue canvas coveralls that came in two sizes: too large and too small. Our footwear was what they called a fair weather shoe—a brown leather shoe that laced and went above the ankle. We had two pair. One we kept clean for barracks duty, formations and so on, and the other one was our field shoes. We also had a set of the old canvas leggings but rarely wore them as we did almost all our training in the blue coveralls.

We started into training right away, learning the basic formations of squads, basic drill, and the manual of arms. All of this was very simple for me because I had done the same for two years at A&M. Boot camp to me wasn't a struggle. I could perform the old eight-man squad drill from any position in the squad. I knew how to take care of my uniform because we had had to polish our brass, keep our uniforms pressed, and all those things while I was at A&M. All this time I thought it was all peculiar, and strangely comical—although I understood you did not dare laugh or smile—but it was more like I was just observing the action and was not a part of it.

At least one of the drill instructors was with us at all times. They had a rotation that allowed one of them to sleep there at night. They had their own tents. When we had rest breaks, the DIs would talk to us about the history of the Marine Corps, all the marine tradition and lore, and little points of wisdom. I remember old Sergerant [J.A.] Mericantante, who was a sharp marine but apparently had little education. I suspect that he might have been an Italian immigrant. He would say, "Now, while in the Marine Corps, you want to never show your 'igorance.' You must always be as courtesy as possible." One corporal, I thought, was a borderline case. He didn't have the drive and the presence that I had begun to see among the marine NCOs [non-commissioned officers]. The other corporal was a good NCO. One thing they kept stressing to us was teamwork. We were punished for all infractions large or small. For a minor infraction you would get something like scrubbing the deck boards down with a toothbrush. A DI would be standing over us urging on an ever-greater effort. Something was being pounded into your mind at all times.

The DIs carried a little stick that had the projectile and the case of a .30-caliber round on one end—they just cut the cap part off and slipped it over the stick. At the other end they had the brass of a .50-caliber round. The pointed end of the stick was great for encouraging you to line up or move quickly; a punch in the ribs got your attention right away. The end with the .50-caliber brass made a great thing for thumping you across the back or whatever. There were always people that had trouble remembering to step off on the left foot. The favorite cure for that was the DI would strike you sharply across the left shin. They always referred to us as "lad." They'd say, "Now, lad, step off on the one that hurts."

Another punishment was to turn your two-and-a-half-gallon bucket onto your head. This stick then could be used by the DI to hammer on the side of the bucket while you sang the Marine Corps Hymn. And it was never loud enough so he would be whacking on the side of the bucket. If you were caught with your hand in your pocket, you were sent out to the sandy area where they were pumping sludge and sand out of the bay. You filled that pocket with sand and then sewed it up. And you walked around a day or two with that sand in the pocket, and it would rub the skin raw on your leg. After that you remembered to keep your hands out of the pocket.

We found ourselves doing everything together. We went to the head in a group.[4] We took our showers as a group. We washed our clothes as a group. If one person needed a haircut, everybody got a haircut. If one person's shoes needed to be half-soled, everybody's shoes got half-soled. Everything was geared to the team, and we had virtually not a minute to ourselves.

If an infraction involved more than one person, the entire platoon would get extra duty, extra double time—jogging in formation with the rifle around and around the drill area until everyone was good and tired. The whole thing was to impress upon all that each person was a member of a team. If a person dropped their rifle, the DIs would gather up several rifles and put them in the canvas cot and the man would have to sleep, if he could, with all this hardware in the bunk. If one person screwed up, there was a lot of peer pressure put on them to square things up so that they didn't get the rest of us in trouble again. If somebody was having a particular problem, we'd help

---

4   Head was and is Navy/Marine Corps slang for restroom.

them because we knew it was in our best interest. Everyone was expected to make progress at the same time. We began to trade off chores. For example, we had to iron our own uniforms. I never liked to press the shirt, and so I made a deal with another recruit that he would do the shirts and I would do the pants. Teamwork was the key to success.

Our DIs thought the area closer to the water, where it was sloppy and dirty, was a good place for training. They liked to take us down there for squad drill and different types of field training. We practiced infantry maneuvers, "snoop and poop" or fire and maneuver. We'd come out of there covered with mud head to foot. We were immediately put to work washing our uniforms, getting them ready to get dirty again. We had open-air washing areas. One of the things we'd been issued was a little bristle brush called a kai-kai brush. We would spread our coveralls out and scrub them and then rinse them and hang them out to dry. We used the navy system for hanging clothes. They called it "tie-tie." This was a 12-inch piece of white cord with a little metal clip on each end, and you would take a little corner of your clothes and tie it to the clothesline. You were given probably a dozen or so of those. Sailors used them when they washed their uniforms aboard ship. Later I saw how sailors would take a line and tie their clothes to the line with the tie-ties and throw it over the fantail of the ship and let the wake hammer the dirt out. It was very effective.

We had the bolt-action Springfield '03 rifles and the old, long World War I bayonets. We also had the flat, steel helmets from World War I. It was probably the most uncomfortable thing that I ever put on my head, and frankly I thought it gave a very minimal amount of protection. There would almost have to be an explosion directly overhead to do any good, because it just covered the crown of the head.

Reveille was at the break of day. We fell out and exercised before we went to our morning chow. Exercising included jumping jacks, knee bends, running in place, and something called the 16-point movement with the rifle. This involved twisting the rifle in different directions, overhead, out front, and so on. There would be more than one platoon doing these exercises, and it was all led by a DI corporal standing on a high platform. Everyone exercised together with everyone doing the same thing, over and over. Sometimes we would go two or three times through all the exercises.

About the third or fourth week on one Sunday, we didn't have anything in particular to do. We had some free time for the first time since we had been there. Otherwise, the DIs always kept us busy. If there was a pause in the training, the DI would have us write a letter to our families; if someone didn't have a family, they had to write a letter to the DI. But this Sunday was a nice, sunny day. On base there was what was called the "slop chute," where marines could get a beer. We were not allowed in that area at all. We were recruits, not marines yet. I remembered that there was a Coke machine in this little building where we'd been issued our toiletries and supplies in the buckets that first day. I wandered over and got myself a Coca-Cola. They had a machine and you put a nickel in it, and a paper cup plopped down, and Coca-Cola would pour into it. Just as the cup was filled I heard a familiar voice say, "Pour it out, recruit." It was Sergeant Mericantante. He was not too happy that I had left the area. In fact he seemed highly agitated. He hustled me back to our area and sentenced me to do up and on shoulder.

For this, I took the rifle in both hands and pushed it up straight in front of my face and then brought it down behind my head. So, while everyone else was relaxing, I did this back and forth, back and forth, until my arms were so tired I could barely drag it over my head. I never left the area after that.

Incidents like this caused me to realize that I could not just be an observer to what was happening. I began to think about why things happened. These DIs, and actually most of the marines I saw, were very serious about this business of being a marine. It was more than training. It was about making marines, and marines are unique. They expected you to be different if you were going to be one. This caused my attitude to change. For the first time since I had arrived I became a participant rather than an interested onlooker.

When I had been in boot camp probably a month or so, I began to realize that the staff NCOs ran the Marine Corps, and they had a little league among themselves. My mother's first cousin, a marine staff sergeant, was a mess sergeant at the marine base in San Diego. He approached my DI without my knowledge and asked if I could leave base for a visit. So I ended up going to his house for dinner, and that happened two or three times while I was in boot camp. He had been a China Marine. He told me one time that he had managed to spend nine consecutive Christmases in China. When he would be sent back to the states, he would immediately start angling to get back to China because the China Marines lived very well. That was quite a nice break because I saw a different side of the Marine Corps, and he taught me quite a few things to make life simpler as far as what was happening in the boot camp. I didn't stay overnight, but I realized right away if you wanted things done in the Marine Corps, you got the staff NCOs involved—things happened then.

Near the end of boot camp, we had a week at the rifle range, and we had it hammered into our heads from day one that every marine was a rifleman. Your rifle was your greatest friend, and you must refer to it as a rifle. If you referred to it as a gun, you were sentenced to run up and down with the rifle in one hand and holding your crotch in the other yelling, "This is my rifle. This is my gun [referring to your crotch]. My rifle's for killing. My gun is for fun." You did this until you were worn out. They made it very clear that you wanted to do your very best on the rifle range.

Now, the first few days at the rifle range, we learned the range regulations, and you did what they called "snapping in." This would be getting used to the various shooting positions that you got into when you fired for record. At first they were quite painful until your body learned to bend and stretch into these positions. We learned how to aim, how to work the bolt, how to hold the weapon. There was a trick to firing the old '03 rifle. It had a very strong kick. And the cocking lever was a little round cylinder that stuck out the back of the bolt. It had a little button-shaped end, and if you didn't hold your cheek tight against the stock, this cocking lever would come back and cut your cheek right at the bottom of your eye. There were always at least a half dozen recruits going around with a cut under their eye. They also showed us how to blacken our sights on the rifle to make them stand out better and help your aim. We had little carbide lamps that put off smoke for that. We also learned about windage and elevation and that type thing.

Once we began to actually fire the weapon we had to clean them at the end of each day, and for this we used hot soapy water. Keeping this water available was the job of one old marine private. We found out that he was a hopeless alcoholic. He had four hash marks, so he had over 16 years of service, but he was still a buck private. I suppose that the Marine Corps felt that he could accomplish getting hot, soapy water ready for rifle cleaning. If he was put out of the Corps, he would probably starve. The Marine Corps was looking after him. I don't think he was ever really sober; he spent every penny he had on drink. Early one morning we were arriving at the range, and he was standing there, wobbly, holding onto a tree. He had the hot soapy water ready, but he had the fly to his trousers open with his shirttail protruding out, which he grasped as he peed in his pants.

They wanted 100 percent rifle qualification. Minimum to qualify was as a marksman, next up was sharpshooter. If you qualified as a sharpshooter, you got an extra three dollars a month until the next time you went back to the range. Highest was expert. If you fired expert, you got an extra five dollars a month. I had no trouble at all in shooting expert with the rifle. I'd been firing a rifle since I was a very small boy. I enjoyed the range, and that old '03 Springfield was incredibly accurate.

I made it through boot camp without any real difficulty because I was in excellent physical condition from having worked construction for over two years and also having had the time at A&M. I think most important, though, was my attitude adjustment. Once I found out what the Marine Corps expected, I was a pretty decent marine.

At our graduation, we were lined up not knowing what to expect. This very impressive marine officer came walking by, and he had the hardest blue eyes I think I had ever seen. As he came down the row of new marines, he would stop randomly in front of a marine and just reach out with his forefinger and tap him on the chest. He did that to me.[5] Well, it turned out that this was Marine Gunner Henry Pierson "Jim" Crowe.[6]

A marine gunner was the first grade of warrant officer at that time. Crowe, even as a lowly warrant officer, had power enough to come to boot camp to personally select his platoon. Those he picked were going to his platoon, the weapons platoon in the Eighth Marine Regiment. The Eighth Marines had been disbanded at the end of World War I and had been recently reconstituted.[7] Not only was Jim Crowe my platoon leader, he later was my company commander at Guadalcanal and I was attached to his battalion at Tarawa. He had quite a reputation. The generals all referred to him as "Jim" even though his real name was Henry. He was pretty arrogant, but he used to say,

---

5   Elrod opined that he always believed Crowe picked him because he had fired expert on the rifle range and was bigger than the average marine.

6   The rank of "gunner" meant a type of warrant officer. He later became "chief marine gunner." Henry P. Crowe, even at this time, had assumed a notable reputation in the Corps. He had served as an enlisted marine in the Banana Wars—Dominican Republic and Nicaragua in the 1920s and was an excellent marksman and participated in national shooting competitions on behalf of the Marine Corps. He was also a star player on the acclaimed Marine Corps football team of this era. He became a warrant officer, gunner, in 1934. He served three years in China at the American Embassy in Peking. In 1940 he transferred to the Eighth Marine Regiment, which is where Elrod encountered him.

7   The Eighth Marines had been commissioned in 1917 during the World War I expansion of the Marine Corps. The Regiment never deployed to combat but instead was based at Fort Crockett, Texas, to guard oil fields nearby. It was decommissioned after the war, but reactivated in 1920 for service in Haiti to quell the Caco rebellion. Upon successful completion of this mission the Regiment was deactivated in 1925. It was reactivated in 1940 in California as the U.S. military expanded as world events indicated an ever-increasing possibility of war.

"It's not bragging if you can do it." He would salute second lieutenants with his left hand, or with both hands, and if it was a Reserve second lieutenant, he would raise his little finger.[8] But, he didn't really consider second lieutenants as being anything of any great importance.

---

8 Crowe might have learned this while a recruit in boot camp in 1918. In an oral history interview he recounts that as a recruit he was walking and an officer was approaching, knowing he was supposed to salute he got confused and started to salute with his left hand, but quickly corrected and saluted the lieutenant with the right hand. The lieutenant saluted him back with both hands and kept walking, not saying a word. Colonel Henry P. "Jim" Crowe intvw with Ben Frank, 4–5 April 1979, transcript pp. 6–7 (Oral HistColl, History Division, Quantico, VA).

CHAPTER THREE

Eighth Marines: Preparing to Fight

Upon completing boot camp in December 1940, Elrod was assigned to the Eighth Marines, (or the Eighth Marine Regiment; marines simply say, "the Eighth Marines"). It had been reactivated in April 1940 as part of the Second Marine Division. Bases were going up or being improved as an explosion of military construction activity occurred across the country. Elrod trained with the Eighth Marines all of 1941 in Southern California.

While training with the Eighth Marines throughout 1941, war in the Pacific became ever more likely. Open conflict between Germany and Russia freed Japan of a Russian threat. Japan forthwith pounced on Indo-China to secure the natural resources there. This heightened tensions between Japan and the U.S. such that diplomacy offered few options. The Marine Corps continued its rapid growth and marines were deployed in anticipation of war to Iceland and island bases in the Pacific, Wake Island, Midway, Samoa, Palmyra, and the Philippines. Japan recognized that the U.S. was its biggest threat and by attacking Pearl Harbor in December 1941, it hoped to deal a knock-out blow to the U.S. Pacific fleet, or at least stagger it enough to gain time to consolidate *and prepare to defend its newly acquired territories. The Japanese attack on Pearl Harbor and other Pacific bases had dramatic consequences for Roy Elrod and thousands of young American servicemen. They would eventually fight in deadly combat to protect nations and islands in the Pacific threatened by Japan and liberate those that had already fallen to the powerful Japanese military.[1]*

The Eighth Marines were located at Camp Elliott, about ten or twelve miles north of San Diego. There had been an airfield at Miramar, just west of Camp Elliott during World War I, and several times we had company and battalion exercises out in that direction. We found rocks that had been laid out for the streets for the old airfield.[2]

---

1   This chapter relies on Lt. Col. Frank O. Hough, Maj Verle E. Ludwig, and Henry I. Shaw, Jr., *Pearl Harbor to Guadalcanal—History of U.S. Marine Corps Operations in World War II*, vol. 1 (Washington, D.C. Historical Branch, G-3 Division, Headquarters, U.S. Marine Corps, 1958), Henry I. Shaw, Jr., *Opening Moves: Marines Gear Up for War* (Washington: Marine Corps Historical Center, 1991).

2   What Elrod is referring to here is Camp Kearney, which had been an army base during World War I where soldiers were trained and processed for deployment to Europe. It had no airfield associated with it during World War I but after the war an airfield was built called Airtech Field. It supported both civilian and military aircraft. In the early 1930s the navy established a mooring mast at Camp Kearney to handle dirigibles. Then as part of the military expansion prior to World War II, it became an auxiliary airfield with one 3,000-foot runway and two 6,000-foot runways. Training for PBYs (B-24s) occurred at the field during World War II. The Marine Corps leased a portion of the facility in World War II and christened it Marine Corps Air Depot Miramar. Here squadrons were processed prior to deploying to the South Pacific. In 1946 the navy departed Camp Kearney and handed the whole facility over to the marines. The next year, however, the marines departed Miramar and moved into Marine Corps Air Station El Toro in Orange County, at which time Miramar once again fell under navy control as an auxiliary airfield.

When we arrived at Camp Elliot, I joined the regimental Headquarters and Service Company and was assigned to the anti-tank platoon. There were actually two platoons in the company. The other platoon was the Regimental Communication Platoon. The anti-tank platoon was equipped with 37-mm guns. These type guns had been used in World War I against machine gun emplacements.

It was really a very small weapon that weighed 112 pounds and rolled on two bicycle-type tires. These tires could be taken off before it was fired, and it could be set up on a tripod. It could also be fired on the wheels. It had a split trail that absorbed the recoil. We also all had rifles, and the NCOs had pistols.

Camp Elliott was definitely off the beaten path. As I said we were a good ways out of San Diego, and an occasional bus would go back and forth. You never could depend on it. So, if you had a weekend liberty in town, you would hitchhike. My A&M background prepared me for that too.

We lived in tents. Even the regimental headquarters was in tents, two large ones connected together. The company first sergeant had a single tent. We were assigned to two-man tents. The area was very, very muddy. It was late December when I arrived there, and California was having one of the wettest winters on record. We did have electricity, and every tent had a single light bulb hanging down in the middle. We had a kerosene heater for warmth. The deck of the tent and the walks were all duck boards.

When you were off of those areas, the area was muddy. The toilet facilities were a collection of four-hole outhouses. The shower consisted of sheets of plywood turned lengthwise so that only your mid-section was covered, your lower legs and head and shoulders were exposed. The water came out of a single pipe, no-spray nozzle, all cold. One shower was usually all anyone decided to have. What we did instead was heat water in our two-and-a-half-gallon bucket on top of our little stove and then bathe out of the bucket with a cloth.

There were two frame buildings at our camp. One was the mess hall. It was a long, bungalow-style building. It had screens and shutters—wood shutters that could be dropped down over the screen if the wind was blowing or if it was raining. Then there was another very primitive-type wooden structure that had something like a post exchange where we could buy all the necessary toilet articles and living items. Next to it was a "slop chute," a place where we could have a beer after work hours. Beer was five cents a bottle, and it didn't matter what kind it was. I think there were even some Mexican beers, but it was all five cents a bottle.

When we first arrived, we were received by the company first sergeant who welcomed us and told us what a great organization we were joining and so on. He finished up his little speech by saying, "Now, you have just joined the company. I don't want to see you in my tent until you have served at least a year, unless you're sent there on duty. You're dismissed!" That made it clear that we were on probation.

All the staff NCOs and more senior officers were veterans of World War I. The captains and even some senior lieutenants were veterans of the Banana Wars or China or both, as were some of our staff sergeants, sergeants, and corporals. These old marines were well traveled. One of them was Staff Sergeant Dale "Geeber" Martin, who evidently had a girl in every port. His nickname, we were told, meant "pecker" in Chinese.

We didn't do much training activity at first because we were not nearly up to full strength. Our daily activities included cleaning up the camp. We were given instruction on all of the individual duties. It was an extension of what we had learned in boot camp. The food was good, and we got plenty of liberty. At Christmas we were given a seventy-two-hour pass. My tentmate was a farm boy from somewhere in the Midwest, I think Indiana. He and I got along very well. We decided to go to Los Angeles. We got up there and we were walking around in the rain, and I said, "You know, this is stupid. Why don't we buy us a car?" So, the two of us started shopping around, and we found a little two-door Austen. We paid $125 for it. I contributed $15 and he contributed $10 and we planned to make payments. At least we were not on foot in the rain.

When our seventy-two-hour pass was up, we came back down to Camp Elliot. This was right after Christmas. There had been a big windstorm and half the tents were down. Fortunately, our tent was up. There weren't any activities taking place, so we went to the platoon sergeant and got another seventy-two-hour pass and drove back up to Los Angeles. We discovered that we could haul passengers and start earning money to pay for our vehicle. We would charge $2.50 to ride to Los Angeles, up and back. We were up there at the time of the Rose [Bowl] Parade. So, we were able to drive out to the Rose Parade and see that for the first time.

We transported marines into San Diego, too, and we discovered that on the weekend, we could park our car out by the road, and we would get five passengers and charge them twenty-five cents and drive into the YMCA in San Diego. We took turns being the chauffeur. We would haul marines in, and if there was anyone around the YMCA that needed a ride back, for twenty-five cents we would take them back. We were very easily making enough money to make our ten dollars a month car payment and also buy gas for the little car. That worked out very nicely.

A whole lot of our activities consisted of individual strength training, endurance training, and lots of extended hikes over the many hills in the area. We worked and trained with our individual weapons, learning to strip and assemble weapons blindfolded. We couldn't do any live firing there. We also did all the different types of individual and squad drill. There was a good-sized training area right adjacent to the camp. It was quite hilly. Those hills in San Diego had a type of cactus that grew on them and you had to watch for that because it would penetrate our leggings. There were also sinkholes that, with the rain that we were having, if you happened to step in one of those, you'd go halfway up to your knees. When you looked at it, it looked like the rest of the ground but, apparently, underneath the soil there was a layer of clay. On those hillsides, the water would collect and break out in different places.

After the New Year (1941) more marines joined the platoon, and around the end of February carpenters began building wooden barracks. The tent camp was to be torn down, and we were moved to the Marine Corps base in San Diego. This was quite an improvement in our living conditions because we were in nice, permanent barracks with all the facilities. We lived in squad bays. Each squad bay was large enough to take a platoon. All the bunks were double-deckers, and we each had a small wall locker, some shelves, and a footlocker. The corporals had the corner bunks.

When we were there on the base, about the only type of really extended training we got were marches. Crowe had heard that [Erwin] Rommel could move his Afrika Corps forty miles in a day and still fight.[3] So, he decided that we should be able to march fifty miles in a day and be ready to fight. Our conditioning marches became more of a conditioning run than a march. We would fall out early in the morning, stand colors, and then take off in a march/run. One time we went all the way out to La Jolla and back. We took our 37-mm gun, each of the crew took turns pulling it. Crowe was just tough as nails. During one rest break we saw him take off one shoe. His foot was bloody, but he straightened his sock, put his shoe back on, and said, "Let's go!"

We also had to occasionally stand guard duty around the base. I was fortunate in that I only had to stand it one time. I was stationed at post number one in San Diego, which was the entrance to the dock area, right at the foot of Main Street. That was quite interesting because when I arrived there, the sentry that I relieved said, "Now, you've got lots of young women coming in here going to the chaplain's office." He showed me which door to direct them to. None of them ever seemed to come back through the gate. So, I decided there must be some hole in the floor by which the chaplain was dropping these ladies into the bay. Apparently they left from a different way than they entered.

Instead of guard duty Warrant Officer Crowe put me in charge of the regimental recreational facilities. I had baseballs,

---

3   General Erwin Rommel was commander of German forces in North Africa at this time where he was making quite a name for himself in a desert campaign against the British.

gloves, tennis rackets—all sorts of sporting equipment. I was responsible for checking these items out to units or individuals and keeping a record of it all. Every working day I went down to my own little office and managed this little operation. I was left on my own for the most part. I realized that I probably was living a little different than the typical marine private.

Once we moved back on the base at San Diego, we didn't need the car anymore. We had probably paid for a third of it, maybe not quite that much. We'd probably paid three or four months payment. So, we decided we would drive it down to the Austen dealer in San Diego and tell him he could keep it or send it back to the dealer in Los Angeles. He said, "Oh, we could work out special terms." I said, "No, we don't need the car anymore. Here are the keys." So, that was the last that we saw of the vehicle. It had served its purpose.

May 25, 1941
Dearest Mom,
I am glad that you all made it home OK. I sure did enjoy being with all of you, I wish you could have stayed a month.
I took the test for PFC [Private First Class] Thursday and made a 100 on it . . . They will get a rate right now though. They also told me they were going to give me a 6th class specialist rate, that with PFC will make me $44 a month. I guess you all brought me luck. Because I made such a good grade on the exam the Co. commander called me to his office and asked if I would like to try for a commission. I said yes. I will have to have two years in before I will be eligible but he said if my record was kept clean he would recommend me then. I can use

the time to be studying for the entrance exam.

In late Spring my mother, my aunt, and my sister and a girlfriend from Muleshoe came out to San Diego and spent a week. At about the same time I got my first promotion.

Someone decided that we needed some type of a prime mover for our 37-mm guns. The regiment acquired six or eight small caterpillar tractors. So, I was made a sixth-class specialist as a tractor driver. I got an extra three dollars a month for that. So, with my expert rifle qualification and PFC pay, I was making almost as much money as a corporal. Base pay for a private at that time was twenty-one dollars a month. But this gave me a chance to learn to operate caterpillars. We drove them around all over the hills. We learned to back up with one trailer, two trailers, three trailers. We learned to back up around barrels and weave around barrels until we became pretty efficient tractor operators. The tractors were never actually used in a real operation.

In mid-May I was promoted to private first class. This wasn't an automatic thing; it required a written exam. We also had to field strip and assemble every weapon that the platoon had, blindfolded, in a certain length of time. Then we had a hundred verbal questions to answer. The reason these were verbal was that there were still a lot of marines who were functionally illiterate.

About mid-year, one morning we were called down to fall out and various names were called out. The names that were called were told to go up and pack their sea bags. It turned out that those whose names were called were being sent back to the East Coast to join the Sixth Marine Regiment, which was being sent to Iceland to relieve the British troops there.[4] I heard that Crowe used this opportunity to get rid of some marines he thought were not measuring up.

We then began to receive marines again to be built back up to strength. Near the end of summer, apparently Camp Elliot construction was completed, and we moved back out there. This time, we were in nice, wooden barracks, brand-new. They had two-stories. Each floor housed a platoon and had rooms for any of the sergeants that lived onboard.

Back at Camp Elliot now and with the platoon back up to full strength, we began doing platoon and company training exercises, maneuvering all over the hills. A lot of these would involve sleeping out overnight. We were training very hard. There was an area nearby called the M-Range, and there we were able to fire all of our weapons.

Our regimental officers decided to take the regiment on a 180-mile march. We hiked out across the mountains back of San Diego, out to the desert, and back over the mountains, and back around to Camp Elliott. We actually were out thirteen days, but we only marched nine of those. So, we averaged about twenty miles a day. We were beginning to get C rations, but we also had cooks that went ahead of us. We would have breakfast, and then the cooks would go by vehicle and have a hot evening meal ready at the end of the day's march. Sometimes we stopped near a little town back in the hills, and the women would have a dance for us or a social. They would gather up all

---

4   The Sixth Marines were sent to Iceland from San Diego on 31 May 1941. Marines were pulled from the Second and Eighth Marines to bring the Sixth Marines up to full strength.

the local girls. On the weekend, we had a big barbecue. They cooked whole sides of beef, Texas-style. At one point we bathed in a creek, which was the only bath we had on the entire hike. Our route was north out of San Diego, east a number of miles, then back into San Diego by way of El Cajon. We marched down Broadway singing "Raggedy-Ass Marines."[5]

We began to have battalion and regimental-sized exercises. These usually took three, four days. The anti-tank platoon usually acted as the aggressor force or the red force. We had flags with different markings on them to indicate we were a machine gun or we were an artillery gun. We were told by the umpires when to move and where to move to. There was one battalion commander that Crowe didn't particularly care for, and he told me that he would like for me to do something to cause a problem. Well, at Texas A&M, I had been in an artillery unit. I decided to do something to the artillery company that was attached to this battalion. So, in the middle of the night, I slipped into the camp and took the sights off of all four of the guns and put them in a sandbag and brought them back.

When they were having the exercise critique after it was over, the old colonel, [Wilburt S.] "Bigfoot" Brown, was the chief umpire. He came out on the stage winding a big old alarm clock. He said, "I have set this clock to go off in fifteen minutes, and even if I'm in mid-insult, I will have to stop." So, they started in and they came to this one battalion, and the umpires had decided that it had not operated properly against a

---

5 The route out was east to Hodges, then Ramona, Henshaw, and finally Banner, the turnaround point. Returning to San Diego the Eighth went by way of Cuyamaga, Descanso, Dehesa, and Sweetwater.

machine gun. So, the battalion commander was attempting to rebut this and said that he had brought artillery fire on it. I'm sure that Crowe had arranged with Colonel Brown to bring that subject up because Crowe came walking out with the sandbag, and he said, "Well, I do believe that your artillery fire was very inaccurate because here are the sights off of all four of your guns." [Clayton] Barney Vogel, a brigadier general, the Second Brigade commander, was there. He was almost apoplectic and gave this lieutenant colonel a dressing down that he probably remembered for some time. Afterwards, Crowe came to me, and he was so pleased. He said, "I would like to promote you to corporal, but we don't have any warrants. What could I do?" And I said, "Well, I'd like to grow my mustache back." At that time, only sergeants and above could have mustaches or beards—they had to be kept neatly trimmed. So, I was allowed to grow a mustache.[6] People would pass me and look. Sometimes they would turn and walk backward trying to figure out what this PFC was doing. So, I enjoyed that.

In September, when my first year was up, I went to the first sergeant's office and asked for leave. Theoretically, we were allowed thirty days of leave per year, but his limit was fifteen days. So, I got a fifteen-day leave and rode the bus back home to Muleshoe to show off my uniform and my PFC chevrons. Folks were very friendly to a man in uniform, and that included the young ladies, a couple of whom I got to know really well on that long bus trip. In Muleshoe most everyone was interested

---

6 Perhaps Crowe had a soft spot for mustaches. He had one himself that was quite noticeable. It was a handlebar-type, waxed, fiery red, with twirled ends. See Brigadier Edwin H. Simmons, "Remembering the Legendary 'Jim' Crowe," *Fortitudine*, Winter 1991–1992.

in my uniform. I was the first marine ever from Bailey County. People had seen soldiers and sailors but no marines. This visit turned out to be the only leave I had in my first four-and-a-half years of the Marine Corps. I didn't get to see Malda during this visit. We had sort of parted ways after I got in the marines, and I heard that she had gotten married.

Sometime along in the fall of 1941, we were issued .50-caliber air-cooled machine guns. They were in cosmoline[7] but when they were cleaned up and test fired, they would only fire a single shot. By this time, the weapons platoon had grown to be a weapons company. The anti-tank platoon had gone from being a single platoon to four platoons and was denoted a weapons company: the Regimental Weapons Company. My squad leader, a corporal named Verner [E.] Austin, was an armorer, and he and I were authorized to take one of these guns out back of the camp and see if we could make the thing fire like a machine gun. We looked at what was happening, and everything worked perfectly. So, we decided that the recoil spring was not pushing the block back far enough to eject the round that had been fired. We thought that this recoil spring was too strong.

When we took the block apart, we found that there were two concentric coil springs. We took a pair of wire cutter pliers and cut a quarter of a turn off of each spring to see what happened. Well, it seemed to be doing a little better, so we continued to cut off a quarter and try firing again. Pretty soon, we were firing two rounds, then three rounds. We kept track of the number of cuts that we made. Soon, we had the gun firing

---

7   Cosmoline is a rust preventative, a heavy greasy, gelatinous substance applied to weapons while in storage or in shipment.

perfectly. So, the word went out to all the other units to cut so many quarter turns off of each spring and the guns would fire. After that, the guns worked beautifully.

Interestingly, my squad leader, who was a corporal, was married. At that time, you weren't permitted to be married until you were at least a sergeant. If you married, you would be given a "convenience of the government" discharge. He sidestepped that because he had gotten a navy commander's daughter pregnant and married her. So, we called him "Pop Austin." This rule was overlooked in his case. A commander, at that time, drew lots of water.

As far as the enlisted men were concerned, the staff NCOs were the people that ran the Marine Corps. We rarely saw an officer; only at inspections or on some of the larger exercises. We were particularly fortunate, in my unit, to have Platoon Sergeant Geeber Martin, who was not only a great instructor but he was a storehouse of Marine Corps lore. He seemed to be the person that was running things. He was always there and kept a sharp eye on the sergeants and the corporals. Working in the background, though, was Gunnery Sergeant Rickman, who rarely said anything, but you could tell he was all eyes. I expect that he had discussions with the platoon sergeant and probably some of the senior sergeants. We were expanding for the war, and these people made sure that the Marine Corps traditions, history, and character were passed down to younger marines—unchanged.

The regimental commander was a colonel named Larsen, "Heavy" Henry [L.] Larsen. And the three battalion commanders were Lieutenant Colonel Oglesbee, Lieutenant Colonel [Harry B.] Liversedge, and Lieutenant Colonel Frank Hart. Hart was the one that Crowe didn't care for.

We had 81-mm mortars and we had received a new 37-mm gun, this is the one the marines took to war in the Pacific. We had a chance to fire ours a few times before the war started. We could kill anything that the Japanese had. We could penetrate an inch and a half of armor at a thousand yards with armor-piercing shells. We had three types of shells: the armor-piercing, high-explosive, and canister. And those three projectiles were very useful for all of World War II in the Pacific. When we became a company, we had three 37-mm platoons and a machine gun platoon. There were four 37-mm guns in each platoon. The mortars were attached to the battalions.

For liberty during this time, I would go up to Los Angeles. I knew a girl up there, and so I would go out on dates with her. She had gone with me and my tentmate out to the Rose [Bowl] Parade. When we still had our car, she and I rode in the backseat while he drove us out to the parade. On a typical date we would see a movie and eat in some good restaurants. There was one Mexican restaurant in Los Angeles that was very, very good. It was down in the old town of Los Angeles. San Diego is where marines congregated, though. In downtown San Diego, there were probably half a dozen bars. There were at least that many brothels that the navy officers inspected once a week. It was unofficially legal. The fee was two dollars. The first act that was taken after the war started was closing all those brothels.

Liberty usually consisted of a good meal and a few drinks. The beer in town, I think, was ten cents a bottle and mixed drinks for fifteen to twenty-five cents. There was one bar in particular that had real good entertainment. There were some girls there that could mimic the Andrews Sisters, and everybody enjoyed them. The big band sound was the music then. Tommy

Dorsey and two or three others were popular. There was always lots of music. There were also frequent fights between the marines and the sailors. It usually started with an insult, and that was all it took. A fight would break out and lasted until somebody announced the MPs [military police] were coming, and then everybody ran out the back door. That was pretty much the routine. I don't remember any army troops being around. Fights were always with sailors. San Diego was a navy town, and most everything was geared more to the navy. Even the Marine Corps seemed to be closer to the navy at that time.

In late 1941 we had just come back from the field training. We had originally planned to be out on this exercise for two weeks, but we wound up being out for a little over three weeks. But almost the entire month of November, we lived out in pup tents on the range, and we had day and nighttime exercises. We were permitted every two or three days to go by groups back to our barracks to take a bath because we could bathe only out of buckets when we were out on the exercise. It was only about four miles to Camp Elliot; we would just strike out across country and jog into Camp Elliot and jog back.

> *Dec. 1, 1941*
> *Dearest Mother,*
>   *Well I am back from M range, we weren't supposed to come back until Sat. but my section is to go aboard a transport tomorrow. We think that we will only be out a few days or maybe two weeks. We were told the other day that sometime between now and March 1 we were going to the Hawaiian Islands, they didn't say for how long.*
>   *We had a lot of fun out at M range and learned a lot too. We fired our 37s and the 50-caliber ma-*

chine guns too. We had some night problems, etc., also. While we were there 4 of us found some wild beehives and got a lot of wild honey, it was sure good eating.

Our Thanksgiving was the 20th, I went in and had my dinner at the Rendezvous Club in Diego. It was really classy.

The 1st Sgt. told me the other day that he thought I would make corporal before Christmas, I am first on the list now, hope he was right. . . . I am feeling fine, I weigh 187 now and am getting tougher ever day, living out in the open like we have been doing makes you feel good . . . while we were out on the range we had ice a time or two. We heard unofficially the other day that there would be holiday furloughs given out, if there are I will try to come home. Don't count on it yet because we don't know how long they will be or how many will get them. Love, Roy

When the company first sergeant told me that I would probably be promoted to corporal by Christmas time, that I was number one on the list, I was excited. Also, we had received an increase in pay. I don't remember how much, but it was going to be retroactive to the date that Congress authorized it. We heard unofficial rumors that we were going to get Christmas furloughs. I had expressed a desire to get leave and go home for Christmas. I never made it, though. The Japanese changed everybody's plans.

Dec. 7, 1941
Dear folks, Well it is here at last, we have been expecting it for some time now. I guess you all were

listening to the radio today. We are all standing by, all leaves and furloughs have been cancelled, so that ends the chances of coming home for Christmas I guess. All the men here seem to be tickled and are wanting to get into the fight. We all have buddies at every one of the bases that have been attacked.[8]

Monday morning [December 8].

We were called out last night before I could finish [the letter] to stand by our anti-aircraft guns. I am a gunner on one of the crews. There isn't any more I am allowed to write you.

In case we leave here I will get word to you before we leave so don't worry. We are all anxious to get over there. There isn't much excitement here in camp, but I hear that the people in town are pretty excited. Today is payday but we can't even leave the camp so it won't do us much good. We are drawing the back pay from our raise this time. I read in the paper where they have another pay raise proposed in Congress, hope it goes through.

We were all at ease on Sunday morning in the barracks when we heard on the radio that Pearl Harbor had been attacked. This was the only time the barracks was a mess because on Sundays everybody just wandered around in their skivvy drawers and read the paper and did little chores like polishing brass. It was late morning, about noon, when we heard. It wasn't long before the staff NCOs arrived, and they put us in

---

8 Elrod no doubt heard radio reports of Japanese attacks at a number of places besides Pearl Harbor, possibly some were erroneous. Besides a number of locations on Oahu where marines were stationed, the Japanese also attacked Guam, Midway, and the Philippines, all of which had marines present.

field dress, light marching order, had us fall out, and were all issued two bandoliers of rifle or pistol ammunition.

Then the officers began to arrive. Somebody up the line decided that maybe we were getting in too big a hurry, and so all the ammunition was picked up and turned in again.

The radio was broadcasting rumors that ships were seen off the coast of California and that the Japanese had landed in Mexico below Tijuana. This news didn't excite us much. All of us had been looking forward to getting into combat. We all felt like we were extremely well trained and were confident in our abilities to do whatever we were assigned to do. Most of us had been expecting to go to war for some time. We thought it more likely that we would be going to Africa to fight against Rommel's Afrika Korps. Crowe seemed to think that's where our future was.

On that day, word came that we were going to set up on the fence line for Camp Elliot. We moved out onto the hills overlooking Elliot and set up a defense perimeter, dug holes, and we stayed there for two or three days. We were allowed, after the first day, to go by twos down to the barracks to shower and use the toilet facilities.

> *Dec. 17, 1941*
> *Dearest Sister,*
> *I have liberty today, they have arranged it so that one third of us get to come in every third day. Mom, tell the women that I got their box and enjoyed it very much. I would write them if I had time but we are so busy that any spare time we get we want to sleep.*
> *I can't tell you where we are with our guns, but*

it is a place we saw when you were out here. Sister,
you asked about the blackouts, they have had three
here in Diego since the war started. The first one
the people got awfully excited, and they didn't get
the city blacked out very well. The other two were
pretty good because people had time to get prepared
for it. All the civilian traffic is stopped and all cars
move without lights. There isn't anything to it ex-
cept it is just dark. From where I am on my gun I
can see the lights being turned off. Last Thursday
night some unidentified planes were fired on near
the border. I was in hopes that they would come in
range of my gun but they turned back and we never
did see them up here.

Don't worry about me any, if we do get action,
and I hope we will, I know my work and think
I can take care of myself. Our General promised
the Regiment that we would get to see some action.
That is what all of us have been wanting.

We got our dog tags the other day. They have
our name, service number, blood type (mine is A)
and the date we were vaccinated for blood poison
[tetanus]. There are two of them about the size of a
half dollar and hang around your neck.

P.S. I weigh 193 now, I am not getting fat either.

One night, we were awakened and told to get aboard trucks.
We climbed in the trucks and took off. We had no idea where
we were going. They had started the blackout, and I was sure
that this driver was going to wreck the truck driving with no
lights in the dark. After dark, civilian vehicles, unless it was an
emergency, were supposed to be off the streets and roads.

We drove through San Diego and out to Point Loma, and then on out to Fort Rosecrans. We had been issued some water-cooled .50-caliber machine guns. They had apparently been on a ship because they were on iron pedestal mounts. We were to set-up area defense to protect the air base at Coronado Island and also to protect the entrance to San Diego harbor. San Diego at this time had city-wide blackouts. From Point Loma we were high enough that we could watch the city blacking out.

We were bivouacked in an empty ammunition bunker, sleeping on a concrete floor. Each marine had a shelter half, a poncho, and two blankets. It was cold and it was rainy. We stood watch on the gun, two hours on four hours off, twenty-four/seven. I was a senior private first class, so I was the gunner on my watch. We never were really warm and never really dry. We began to really need sleep. I only got a total of twelve hours sleep in the first two or three days. We were all pretty miserable, continually cold, often wet, and always hungry. We heard there were enemy planes flying around Tijuana. I hoped that they would fly where I could take some shots at them with that machine gun. I doubt that we would have been that effective against an enemy aircraft. We could probably have fired just enough rounds from our machine guns to let an attacking plane know where we were.

Apparently, up the chain of command someone realized that I had some construction experience. So they moved our unit away from this defense area that we had on Point Loma, and I was put in charge of a group of marines at a bulk fuel post. They were building wooden crates to hold two five-gallon cans of gasoline. My job was to make sure the marines that were nailing these together understood how to do it and that they didn't leave any "shiners" in the crates. These protruded in and rubbed against the side of the cans and cause leaks. We slept at this bulk fuel place and from time to time food was brought by. It was hot chow too; they brought it to us in insulated cans. Actually, I wouldn't say they were hot meals—they were warm meals. We again were living totally with just our shelter half, our poncho, and two blankets. We did this for several days. Then we got the word that we were moving out.

> *Jan 14, 1942*
> *Somewhere at Sea*
> *Dearest Mother,*
> *I don't have any idea when you will get this letter, but don't know when I will get a chance to write another either.*
> *I am feeling fine and having a lot of fun. You realize that we are unable to say where we are or anything of that nature. All I will say is that it is hot here. . . .*
> *Mom don't worry about me when you don't hear from me, because I have no idea at all when I will get to write. I have some good news for you. The Capt. told me that I have made corporal and will get my warrant very soon. So, when you write I will be corporal. . . . I love you all, Roy*

One day my platoon sergeant came by and said, "The Marine Corps has commandeered three matching steamships, and we're going to be sailing out." We had no idea where we were going. I later found out that we were going to Samoa. No one in the regiment knew much, if anything, about Samoa. The intelligence officer was told to get into civilian clothes and go to the library and check out books on Samoa, without attracting attention, so he could give us briefings. My platoon sergeant also told me, "You're going to be in charge of loading the number one hull, the *Lurline*."

The other two ships were the *Matsonia* and the *Monterey*. Our regiment, the Eighth Marines, was going to be the nucleus of the Second Marine Brigade. Larsen had been promoted to brigadier and was put in command. This was the first combat-organized group on the West Coast. It had its portion of engineers, medical people, communicators, artillery, and transportation, so it was organized to operate independently. Each one of these ships could carry a battalion with its attached reinforcements and other support and service units.

I had several marines working in the hull, and we loaded ammunition. The ammunition was sling-loaded and swung down to us in the hold. This kept us moving at a rapid clip. The nets swung in as fast as we could stack the ammunition. No one told me how to do this, and there didn't seem to be any organization in the way the loads arrived. Whatever was in the truck that came in from the supply place is what was loaded aboard. We loaded everything from 175-millimeter artillery shells, to rifle and pistol ammunition, to grenades. The 175- and the 155-millimeter shells came with two or three projectiles banded together. There was no powder for these, only the projectile. We were able to stack this stuff pretty well. Once in a while, one of the crates would be broken, and what I did was use the loose boards to wedge between some of the larger shells, to tighten things up and cushion them. We worked twelve-hour shifts, and it took about three days to load the ship. I don't know how efficient our loading was, but at least the ship didn't blow up.

In the meantime, there were civilian crews welding machine gun mounts on the deck and one five-inch gun on the bow. They also set up iron tubs around the guns. When it came time to sail, some of these civilian welders had not finished, but the ship sailed anyway. They enjoyed a free ride to wherever we were going.

We were restricted to the port area, and there was a perimeter set up around it with our marines on guard to keep unauthorized people out and to keep us in. My girlfriend from Los Angeles came down to see me, and the platoon sergeant gave me a note that would let me get off the dock but not to go into town. We said our goodbyes, and I went back to work and she returned to Los Angeles.

Before we sailed the company commander called me into his office and told me I had made corporal, and just before we sailed the platoon sergeant came by and said, "Oh, by the way, your warrant for corporal came through. You're promoted to corporal." (They didn't have the rank of lance corporal in those days.) I went from PFC to corporal. So with that I was in charge of a 37-millimeter gun, one of the new guns, and the gun crew of seven other marines. We had had a chance to fire this gun only a few times. We had received them just a few days before Pearl Harbor. It was brand-new and we were really proud of it. The gun weighed 910 pounds and had a split trail.[9]

---

9   Elrod is referring to the M3A1 37-mm antitank gun. It was based on the German *Panzer Abwehr Kanone* (PAK)-36, and developed by the U.S. Army in the late 1930s. It replaced the previous 37-mm, the French-made Puteaux gun (mentioned by Elrod earlier) used in World War I. The M3 was adopted to be

The ships were incredibly crowded; in fact my unit slept on the open deck. We had canvas cots right next to the superstructure, and we had a canvas overhead. When we got to sea, we discovered that the canvas tarp really didn't help much because with the ship underway or with any breeze, any rain or spray came straight in.

I decided that we could set our gun up on the deck and rig it in a way that it could provide extra armament for the ship. They were very worried about Japanese submarines, and our ships zigzagged almost the minute they left San Diego. I talked to some of the ship's officers and got their approval. I found three heavy pieces of timber, and I chained them down to the ship in a U-shape so that the trail of the gun would recoil against these pieces of timber. There were some skeptics about just how well this would work. After we had been at sea for a few days, I convinced somebody to give us a chance to try this out. So, our escort destroyer was designated to go by and throw some wooden vegetable crates over the side. They were out 600 to 1,000 yards. We fired the gun and hit those crates with our second shot. People then decided that this might be a good idea. I figured we had at least a gambler's chance of being able to hit the periscope on a submarine. I also knew that the weapon was powerful enough that if the submarine showed itself that we could punch a hole in the hull.

---

able to destroy newer tanks. At the time of its production it could destroy any tank being produced in the world. By the time the U.S. entered World War II it was outmatched by current tanks, especially those in the European Theater. Japanese tanks, however, were lighter and more vulnerable and therefore the M3A1 was effective against them. See Henry I. Shaw, Jr. *First Offensive: The Marine Campaign for Guadalcanal* (Washington: Marine Corps Historical Center, 1992), p. 23.

The civilian crew was still on and operating the ship. We ate in the regular ship's dining room. The first two or three days we ate in shifts because there were more of us than the dining room would seat. These first days the waiters were dressed in their tuxedos with the towel on their shoulder or over their arm, as if we were regular civilian customers on a cruise to the Far East. After we'd been at sea two or three days, they were in their undershirts and unshaven, and it was a whole new ball-game. The food remained the same, though. It was excellent.

We hadn't been at sea more than three or four days when we began to get out of the cold, wet weather that we were having there in southern California. We still had no idea where we were going, but the skies began to clear. It was sunny and warm, and this made life much more comfortable. It wasn't so bad sleeping on the deck. I had two men on watch all the time. The schedule was two hours on, four hours off.

We had been at sea maybe four or five days, and other navy vessels joined up on our ships. One of them was the carrier USS *Yorktown* [CV 5] and several destroyers and cruisers.[10] The *Yorktown* would fly planes off in the early morning, and they would make a circuit around to check for Japanese ships and then do the same thing in the evening just before dark, flying air patrols. The first time we saw flight operations, planes were taking off. They were not using a catapult, and the first plane started rolling forward, and it reached the end of the flight deck and waddled over into the water. The carrier was

---

10   This was the *Yorktown*'s first wartime mission, escorting the Second Brigade to Samoa. It had arrived in San Diego only a week earlier (30 December) from Atlantic duty.

being followed by a destroyer to pick up any survivors. So, then the number two plane followed. The same thing happened. And the number three came, and he got down within six or eight feet of the water and then began to climb. Everybody on the ship cheered. I was thinking that these pilots had little, if any, training flying off of carriers.

The old marines aboard the ship with us put us through the "Crossing the Line" ceremony when we crossed the equator. It was an all-day process. They poured stuff on you, and other things to sort of humiliate you. It was nothing serious, just skylarking. The oldest sailor on the ship, they dressed him up, and he was "King Neptune." He had a big belly all greased up, and we had to kiss his belly and then we were shellbacks.[11]

After we had been at sea for about ten days we were told we were going to Samoa. Nobody knew much about it.

---

11   Elrod is referring to the U.S. Navy's traditional Crossing the Line ceremony in which individuals who had never crossed the equator went through an initiation upon crossing it for the first time if aboard a U.S. Navy ship. Its origins reach back into distant time when sailors were quite superstitious and hoped to appease the gods of the sea, Neptune, etc. It was carried forward into the modern era, although few believed in Neptune. The ceremony in World War II days, before the U.S. military cracked down on hazing, could be quite arduous, and included some pretty rough hazing. This does not seem to be the case with Elrod's initiation. After the ceremony the initiates, called "pollywogs," became "shellbacks." It is unusual that this occurred aboard a civilian passenger liner and included a large number of non-sailors but the tradition applies to all "mariners," and as Elrod attests, it was the old sea-going and China Marines who instigated the ceremony.

CHAPTER FOUR

Exotic Samoa: Defending the Southern Lifeline

After the Japanese attack on Pearl Harbor, the Allies were justifiably concerned about the Japanese threat to Australia and New Zealand. The Japanese were at their zenith and seemed unbeatable. The same day that they attacked Pearl Harbor, they also attacked the Philippines, beginning a campaign that would lead to the conquest of the Philippine Islands. They also began a push eastward through the Pacific that would reach the Gilbert Islands only 2,400 miles from Hawaii. These attacks revealed Japan's ability to deliver a powerful punch deep into what had been considered safe territory. As the previous chapter indicates, California and Mexico seemed in peril. The line of communication between Hawaii and Australia was essential to keep Australia, an important ally, from falling into Japanese hands. The U.S. determined to defend this line by manning islands that lay along the line of communication. One group of islands, the Samoans, seemed to be especially vulnerable. The main island of Tutuila, or American Samoa, was defended by the marines of the Seventh Defense Battalion, a force of less than 500 that had arrived in early 1941. The attack on Pearl Harbor spurred the U.S. to action. The Second Marine Brigade, of which the Eighth Marines comprised the main element, was rushed to Samoa, having been given only two weeks to organize for combat, load out, and sail. Corporal Elrod was a member of the regiment's weapons company. The Second Brigade arrived at Tutuila on 9 January 1942. About nine months later, Elrod, now a second lieutenant, and the Eighth Marines departed Samoa, headed to Guadalcanal and their first combat. The feared Japanese invasion of Samoa had never occurred. The marines were ready to defend Samoa nevertheless. While there the marines and native Samoans came to appreciate one another and lived amicably. The marines trained and became inured to the tropics, factors that benefited them at Guadalcanal where the climate was miserable and the combat was fierce.

We were briefed on the little people knew about Samoa at the time, but it was very sketchy. Samoa is about 2,500 miles southwest of Hawaii. Pago Pago harbor was a very deep and very large and well-protected harbor. The entrance was quite narrow. The harbor was the crater of some ancient volcano that had formed at least part of the Samoan chain.

The Samoan chain consists of a number of islands: Tutuila, which is American soil, and Upolu, which was referred to as Western Samoa and was under the protection of New Zealand. Then there was Savaii, which was still further to the west. But the Samoans said it was so steep and so rugged that it was virtually uninhabited. Those were the only three significant islands in the chain.

American Samoa, or Tutuila, had a ridge down its center. The whole island was about 25 to 30 miles long and somewhere around three to five miles wide at the widest. The north side of the island is very precipitous. There were only two small bays. One was Pago Pago, and the other was Fagasa Bay, but both had to be resupplied by boat. The central mountains were steep and rugged. There were a few trails—foot trails—that went along at various elevations that the natives used.

We arrived at American Samoa after about fifteen days of sailing. Our brigade was there to defend Samoa, so they spread the units out along the southern side of the island because that's where the road was. The road actually ran from one end to the other. This road was mostly covered with broken coral and was an all-weather road, but rough, just a jeep trail. There was no road on the north side. Small detachments of marines were placed at Fagasa Bay, on the north side, but they had to be supplied by boat, and the troops had to be taken there by boat. There was a very narrow and precipitous foot trail to it from the south side. I talked to some marines that crossed it, and in some places you had to climb sheer cliffs. It was quite a process.

I had been warned ahead of time to be ready to land as soon as we got there. So, my squad took its gun and with a Jeep pulled it into a position on the other side of Pago Pago Bay. We took up a position at the southeastern entrance. There was a rifle company in that same general area. I just assumed we were attached to them, and we ate in their mess. I had a speaking acquaintance with the officers and the battalion commander.

He had his headquarters there, but they didn't bother me. They left me on my own.

With us having come out of California in the middle of the winter, the heat and the humidity were very oppressive. I had a hard time adjusting to it. There were literally swarms of flies and mosquitoes and ants. We dug into a hillside and made a little flat area for the gun. We also received a water-cooled .50-caliber machine gun on a pedestal. We cleared out a fairly wide area to set up our gun and the .50-caliber. For protection on the front, we made a heavy wall of sandbags. We discovered that this wasn't going to work because the jute from the sandbag in that humid, warm climate, after two or three weeks, just rotted away and the sand dribbled out. So, we worked night and day improving our position and putting logs up, and we filled the gaps between them with sand. We then had a pretty significant position. The only time we had any action was one night a Japanese submarine fired four or five rounds over the island from the north. The rounds went over the mountain and hit on the other side. It was probably a three-inch gun—it wasn't very big—whatever the deck gun was on the submarine. The only thing they succeeded in hitting was Shimusake's bush store. They were the only Japanese on the island, and we thought that was very appropriate. Everybody got a big kick out of that.

I had plenty of ammunition for both the 37-mm and the .50-caliber, so we would get the Samoans to take an oil barrel or something out in the surf for us to target practice on. I was left strictly alone. Nobody was telling me what to do, and we did quite a bit of live firing. I was satisfied that we could have made a significant effect on anyone that tried to come in the harbor because that 37 would penetrate over an inch of steel at a thousand yards.

The island had been administered and run by the navy, and they considered American Samoa their territory. Their head-quarters was at a little village at Pago Pago. They had a navy admiral there. They had a five-inch gun someplace, and occa-sionally they would shoot it. The navy had set up a little group of Samoans as a sort of a pseudo-military thing that they called the Fita Fita Guard. They had formations for change of com-mand and other things. Their uniform was a lava-lava wrapped around their waist and a white T-shirt and a strange looking little round cap.[1] Their ranks were shown by black borders on the bottom of the lava-lavas.

We had a fale—this was their native-type house—and it was large enough for my whole squad to stay in. We stayed there for several weeks, and then the company commander, Captain Crowe, came and moved us because either the navy or the artillery had set up heavier guns to cover that area. They moved me to a place called Coconut Point, which was a little point that was on the western side of Tungasah Bay, and there was a pretty nice little beach there. Here was one of the few places on American Samoa that was flat enough and with the right kind of soil for cultivating coconut trees. Lever Brothers owned it. We set up at the end of that point. We lived in a py-ramidal tent, and the other gun from the section was placed on the opposite side of the bay. We ate there with an engineer or transport company that was farther back on Coconut Point.

---

1   The lava-lava is a traditional Samoan garment. It is a sarong-like skirt that wraps around the lower body.

The section sergeant lived in the same tent with me. We made an arrangement to communicate with the other squad once or twice a day at a given time by semaphore.[2] So, I learned to send and receive semaphore and that was interesting.

While we were there, the Seabees[3] and marine engineers started building a landing field; it was being built in a little shallow bay. Even at high tide, it was no more than eight or ten feet deep. They were digging up coral from an area back in the island and actually filling out into the bay.

One day, an American civilian who was working there came over to me and said, "I've been having real problems with finding Samoans to drive my big Euclid crawl back trucks hauling this coral." He said, "I just had one, who was making his first backup to dump, and he panicked and jumped out of the truck and the truck, went right over the incline into the drink." I told him we can do that in our off time.

Some of my marines began to do this, and I think they were being paid a dollar a day, which is the same thing they were paying the Samoans. I'm sure that he had them on the payroll with a Samoan name, but the marines were able to pick up a little extra money.

I found the Samoans to be quite interesting. They were Polynesian and a very handsome people. They had dark hair, their skin was a little dark, but not black. Their hair was straight, and the young girls were really nice-looking. The natives lived

---

2   Semaphore is a way of communication using signal flags and a common way of communication between ships.

3   The Seabees—slang for U.S. Navy construction battalions (CBs—thus Seabees) were specific U.S. Navy units dedicated to construction activities ashore. They were great friends of the marines as they improved conditions ashore often while the enemy was still close and fighting.

and dressed pretty much as they always had. The men and the women only wore the lava-lava, and they were bare from the waist up. This caused some excitement amongst the marines initially, but it really didn't take long for us to get used to see-ing bare-chested women. Most of the natives could speak some English; some were quite fluent and some spoke very little, if any, English. The navy had had schools there. I think they were taught sort of a mixture of English and Samoan. They all went barefoot, and they could walk over sharp coral. Actually, if we walked on that in our field shoes, we had to be careful or it'd cut through the shoes. So their feet must have been like iron. Of course, they went barefoot from day one.

There were a few little corrugated metal shacks that they lived in, but most of them still lived in the traditional Samoan fale. There were little bush stores where they could buy a few canned items. Canned salmon was one of their favorite things. The Samoan diet consisted of taro, breadfruit, coconut, and a lot of fish. The Samoans made all different kinds of things from the breadfruit, the coconut, and the taro. It was a starch-rich diet. The only protein they really got was from the fish, but their food was more or less tasteless. The marine cooks tried to use breadfruit and taro, but they cooked it up and served it in the mess. It would keep you alive but it was tasteless. Some of the taro roots were two feet, even 30 inches long. They were dug up by Samoan women with a sharp, pointed stick. One time I was watching some of them dig taro and these men were sitting back under a coconut tree. I asked them, "You know, the women are out there digging, why don't you help them?" And one said, "Well, digging taro is very hard work. Samoan man is too busy for this work." So, he wasn't going to do women's work.

We worked out an arrangement with some of the Samoan women to do our laundry. For 50 cents, they would do our laundry for a week. They'd wash it and iron it, and the iron they used was fired by coconut shell charcoal. The women would sit down cross-legged on a mat and iron the clothes. They came back looking very nice.

We were sleeping on folded canvas cots and mattresses that we had brought from the States. At night you would perspire quite freely. In fact, we were perspiring most all the time. It rained almost every day around three or four o'clock in the afternoon. When we first got there, we would put our ponchos on. Well, you'd just get soaking wet with sweat, and then you would smell. It wasn't long until we discovered that a better way was to put whatever you didn't want to get wet on top of your head and put your cover on top of it. You got wet, but when the sun came out, you got dry and drying from the rain wasn't nearly as smelly as drying from sweat.

Our mattress pads got very smelly and because there was no good way to clean them, after a week or so we just started doing like the Samoans, sleeping on a canvas mat. It was much more comfortable and we got a little relief. We could just put it out, wash it off, and dry it in the sun, and they would be ready to go again. We put it on our cots, but the Samoans put the mats right down on the coral floor. Instead of a pillow, they used a wooden block that was about eight inches long, about three inches wide, curved slightly, and polished to a very smooth surface, and they put that under their neck, and, amazingly enough, it made a very comfortable pillow. Most of us at one time or another used one of these.

The mosquitoes were very annoying, and we all had mosquito nets. In the daytime, we'd roll up our mosquito net, and then at night you'd want to be sure and shake it out because there were always mosquitos inside. Green lizards, called geckos, were in our fale, and they would catch these mosquitoes. We established a working relationship with the lizard. All the insects were a real problem—flies, ants, and mosquitoes., The heat and humidity would soften the chocolate in the candy bars that we had until it was just a gooey mess. Those ants could find them no matter where you put it. I even tried hanging a sock from one of the beams in the fale and put it in there, and the ants found it. Once they got in it, it was too hard to get them out. They were trapped in the chocolate. For a while we tried to pick them out, but after we'd been there a week or two, we thought, "Well, fine," and just ate the ants with the chocolate. We discovered that ants had a slightly acidic taste, which wasn't all that bad.

We ate a lot of coconuts. The coconuts that you see in the U.S., they're referred to as copra. They didn't use those as much as they did the ones they called the nu, which was really a green nut that was still on the tree. The milk from the nu was very refreshing. It made an excellent thirst quencher and had some food value, too. When the coconuts fell off the tree, they had a very heavy husk around them. The Samoans had a sharpened stake stuck in the ground. They would bang these coconuts against the pointed end of that stake and pierce that husk and rip it off in pieces. We discovered that the old World War I pick, called a pick-mattock, that about half of us marines had—the other half had a shovel entrenching tool—you could push the blade of the pick mattock into the ground and put your foot on the handle and use the pick side to pierce the husk of the coconut.

There was a community water outlet nearby, and the Samoans bathed there, right out in the open. They kept their lava-lavas on and never really exposed themselves. When the ladies were bathing, we'd train our binoculars on them, but we never saw anything, except what was above the waist. They went around that way all the time anyway. The toilet facilities in these villages either were little outhouses built on stilts over the water, but in many cases they would go down and have their bowel movements at low tide. So the whole village would be down there—men, women, and children all at the same time. After we'd been there a while, we picked up the Samoan culture and went right down with them. When the tide would go out, it would clean everything up. So, it worked out real well.

When we arrived there were a few married marine officers and a few NCOs there with their families. The families were living in two pyramidal tents fastened together. They were there to train Samoan young men as Samoan marines, who were to provide protection for their island.[4] The agreement was that they would never be taken off the island for any other purpose. Their uniform was different from the Fita Fita Guard. They wore a khaki lava-lava that really, I think, was made from a canvas sleeve for holding a marines' bed roll. Their uniform was the

---

4   These marines were part of the Seventh Defense Battalion, which had arrived in Samoa 15 March 1941 to train Samoan men to assist in the defense of the islands and established the First Samoan Battalion, a native marine reserve unit. Charles L. Updegraph, Jr., *U.S. Marine Corps Special Units of World War II* (Washington, D.C.: History and Museums Division, Headquarters, U.S. Marine Corps, 1972), p. 64.

lava-lava, nothing above, and they wore a cloth cap, a marine fore and aft cap with a marine emblem on it. They had their rank, stripes, sown on the lower hem of their lava lava. They were trained with the [Springfield] '03 rifle and light machine guns. The marine officers and NCOs that had been with them were absorbed into our unit and their families left on the same ships that brought us in.

When we were there for the first few months, it was strictly defense. There was a continual effort to improve the quality of our positions. Units established caches of supplies up on the ridge in a convenient place to store things, food, ammunition, and so forth. The plan was we would defend the beaches as long as we could, and then we would fall back to the interior and fight as guerillas.

We did quite a bit of marching around because that was the way to stay in condition, and we used the footpaths that were in the hills. We had morning calisthenics. I looked after my squad, and occasionally Captain Crowe would come by. I saw him no more than once a week. I was left very much on my own. He had been promoted to captain and given command of the weapons company. We went directly from warrant officer to captain. He never was a lieutenant.[5]

Life there fell into a routine that was very repetitive. There were times we would have what they called a smoker, and boxing matches were the main attraction. We'd leave two men on the gun and go to the smoker. I was still doing quite a bit of box-

---

5 Crowe had been commissioned a Marine Gunner (a warrant officer rank) in September 1934. He was promoted to Chief Marine Gunner in April 1941. He embarked with the Eighth Marines for Samoa in January 1942, and the following month was promoted from chief gunner to captain. https://www.usmcu. edu/?q=node/1624

ing then, and I fought in these smokers. One of the company officers years later told my wife that he'd made a lot of money betting on me in the fights. As I mentioned earlier, when I was first learning to fight at Texas A&M, I did not win my first fight. I never lost after that.

We continually practiced our gun drill. We always had plenty of training ammunition, which had a continuous tracer so that you could follow the line of the flight and this was excellent for training gunners. The gunner and the loader in my squad were both very good. Exceptionally good. It was amazing—the 37-mm gun was as accurate as a rifle.

The first supply ship did not come in until we had been there for 90 days. Our food was ample, but it began to be monotonous. The cooks had gallon cans of food, and they prepared it, but it got to taste like the same thing. As we moved toward the end of that 90-day period, we were using more and more of the taro and breadfruit.

A lot of times if we had some relationship with some Samoan lady we'd get to eat with the family. There was a lot of that going on, dating Samoan girls, and there were some serious romances. I had one boy who was determined to marry this Samoan girl. I knew that wasn't going to work. As a squad leader I tried to manage my marines the best I could, especially if it had anything to do with his marine duties. I told him, "We have to keep our mind on what we are here for. We can't do that." I don't know whether he went back after the war or if he even survived the war. I believe there were one or two weddings. The native morals were much more relaxed. For example, each village had their virgin, but to qualify as the village virgin she had to not have had a male child.

About the third month that we were there, I was called in one day by Captain Crowe. He wanted my squad and another squad to go to Western Samoa. There were no marines on Western Samoa (Upolu). It was a New Zealand-controlled island, and it was some 90 miles farther west of American Samoa.

We went over on a seagoing minesweeper named the *Turkey* [AM-13]. This boat was captained by a crusty old navy chief, and he was extremely proud of the boat, and he ran it with an iron hand. He told us that he was the only American vessel to get out of Pearl Harbor under its own power while the attack was going on. He was quite proud that he had saved the *Turkey* without a scratch. We had our guns and ammunition and a stock of food on the fantail of the tugboat. We had a swollen sea that day, and waves would often break over the fantail, and we'd be in water almost up to our knees. He was towing an LCM, a landing craft-mechanical. Apparently, it was needed in Apia Harbor. Three different times the tow rope parted. After the third time, we were probably 15 or 20 miles from Western Samoa, and the chief put two of his crew on the LCM to drive it under its own power.

When we arrived at Western Samoa, we found it much more westernized than American Samoa. There was a lot more land there that was suitable for Lever Brothers' coconut plantations. More people lived in corrugated metal buildings, and the town of Apia was large enough to actually be called a town. The harbor was more of a lagoon than a harbor, and ships could not come all the way in. You had to unload your ship's cargo onto barges.

No one knew we were coming or had any idea what we were supposed to do. We only had vague notions ourselves. Each of our squads had a 37-mm gun. Sergeant George [F.] Fincke came with us. Just about everyone on the island was a native. There were probably a dozen New Zealand military people, and they appeared to serve as police. There were other New Zealanders who were government officials.[6]

At first, they put us at a place called the racecourse, and there were some horses there. They said we could use the horses. For a day or two we rode these horses around like West Texas cowboys and then decided that—I don't know if I made the decision or the sergeant did— this wasn't something we needed to be doing. We turned the horses in.

My squad was ordered to set up on a beach on the south side of the island. The other squad stayed on the beach that covered the entrance to Apia Harbor. Fincke stayed with them. Some Seabees and other engineering troops had moved in, and they were building a landing strip in the vicinity of the other squad's position.

I moved my squad in to a little village called Lalaili on a very nice beach and there was a small stream nearby.[7] It was almost directly across the island from Apia. We moved into a vacant native fale. On this side it was more primitive; none of the homes were metal. I kept two men on the gun 24/7, and I told the local chief I would like a stalk of bananas to be kept hanging at our fale.

We had taken some food over with us, but it wasn't long before that was exhausted. All that was left were some C ra-

---

6 There were actually 157 New Zealand military guarding both Upolu and Savii. Hough, Ludwig, and Shaw, p. 89.

7 Elrod, with his wife, had visited this island on an around the world tour in 1973. He commented in his interview that, "When I visited the spot in 1973 there was no sign that it had ever existed."

tions, pineapple juice, and a few things like that. We had nothing to cook with, so we had to eat the food just as it came out of the can. When we had exhausted that food, we used our own money to buy tins of food from one of the Lever Brothers bush stores.

We exchanged our dollars for New Zealand pounds and shillings and so forth. Before we ran out of money, we ate in a Chinese restaurant in Apia that made the best fried rice that I have ever put in my mouth. There was also another restaurant run by a woman who was a half-caste. Her mother, a Samoan, had been married to a New Zealand trader. Her name was Aggie Grey and we ate in her restaurant a couple of times.[8] From the village we could see the house where Robert Louis Stevenson had lived. He went there when he had tuberculosis and had died and was buried there. This house was being taken care of by the natives and the New Zealanders. It wasn't open though, so I only saw it from the outside.

Once I moved around to the south shore, I didn't leave my gun area very often. I felt that either the gunner or I should be there with the marines who manned the gun. When we ran out of money, I decided that we couldn't afford to starve. So I went into the bush store and signed for food in the name of the United States of America, Corporal Roy Elrod.

---

8   Aggie Grey was actually very well known, not only on Western Samoa, but throughout the South Pacific. She founded and operated not only a restaurant but also a hotel and resort. She was born in 1897 and died in 1988. Elrod visited this site in 1973 and made the following comments about Aggie Grey in his 2012 interview: "On my visit in 1973 we stayed two nights in a motel run by her daughter, also named Aggie Grey. Also we ate in the restaurant. The daughter told me she was nine when we came in World War II and she recalled the marines riding ponies [see above]."

I also went to the New Zealanders and said we needed some kind of a vehicle so that we could make patrols twice a day along the road that went across the south side of the island. We were given a little truck, no cab. It was not a very attractive vehicle, but it would run. Again, I signed for that in the name of the United States, Corporal Roy Elrod.

With that we would make a patrol sending the driver and another marine out right after dawn, about 12 or 15 miles up the road toward the west. Then we'd make another patrol in the late afternoon. We had an opportunity, again, to do quite a lot of practice firing. I inspected my marines every day. Marines had to keep their clothes clean and shave every day. We did calisthenics every day. We ran a tight ship. With the rigorous exercise, we kept in good shape except we just weren't eating very well. My breakfast consisted of sliced bananas with a little canned milk. It wasn't very tasty, but it kept me alive.

Every day the young people of the village, along about four o'clock in the afternoon, would walk about 50 yards up this little stream. There was a pool of nice, clear, cool water that was about waist-deep, and they would bathe there. So we decided that that's what we should do. We would wrap a towel around ourselves and go up and bathe. They never did take their lava-lava off. They would just wash underneath them. They said, "That was Samoan custom." And I said, "Well, American custom is we bathe naked." The girls giggled for a day or two. After that, they would wash our backs, and nobody was concerned about it. So we really lived in a native way.

I made friends with the chief of the village. He had a daughter that was probably 18-years old, and I sort of courted her a little. Every once in a while, the chief and his wife would have me come over and eat a typical Samoan meal with them in the evening. It would be fish and different things made out of coconut, bananas, and taro. It was tasteless. It was a very monotonous diet, but they were a very hardy people.

We had been there a few months and one morning I got word that there was a group of ships coming in. I went around to Apia, and I reached the landing beach about the time a marine colonel came ashore. I saluted and said, "Sir, I turn over the command of the island." He said, "Who the hell are you?"[9] They had no idea we were there. I said, "Well, we've held onto this place until you got here. Can you get us on a ship back to American soil?" By this time he was worried that he should know something but didn't. He said that he could do that. I went back around to where my squad was.

A day or two later a motorcycle came up with a sidecar that had a marine captain sitting in it. He had a case of beer on his lap. It turned out it was Bruno [A.] Hochmuth,[10] who

---

9   This was apparently elements of the Seventh Defense Battalion, which arrived 28 March on Upolu, commanded by Lt. Col. Lester A. Dessez. Gordon L. Rottman, World War II Pacific Island Guide (Westport: Greenwood Press, 2002), p. 89. Apparently Elrod and the group he was with were the earliest marines to arrive on Upolu and had been pushed forward to defend Upolu as best they could until more marines could arrive. The marines were tremendously worried about the security of Upolu after the Brigade intelligence officer, Lt. Col. William L. Bales visited the island and reported back to General Larsen: "In its present unprotected state, Western Samoa is a hazard of first magnitude for the defense of American Samoa. The conclusion is unescapable that if we don't occupy it the Japanese will and there may not be a great deal of time left." On 3 May, a much larger force, the Third Marine Brigade arrived to defend Upolu. Hough, Ludwig, Shaw, pp. 89–90.

10   Hochmuth, a native of Houston, Texas, served as an officer with the Seventh Defense Battalion. In the Vietnam War when he commanded the Third Marine Division, he was killed when the helicopter in which he was a passenger exploded in midflight. This made him the senior-most officer killed in the Vietnam War.

I'd known at Texas A&M. He was a senior my freshman year. He eventually became a two-star general and was the senior American casualty of the Vietnam War. He remembered me, and Texas A&M people, Aggies, we stick together, very much like marines. We all drank some beer, including my marines. I wanted to put on a demonstration for him, so we tied three oil barrels together, and I told two Samoan men to take their pau pau and pull these drums out to sea about a thousand yards. I told them, "When you see me drop my hat, you turn loose and come to the shore because we're going to start shooting." So they got it out there, and I dropped my hat. When they saw that they started for the shore. You would have thought that there was a motor on that pau pau. The paddle blades were flashing. These three barrels were bouncing up and down in the waves. We were using training ammunition, and my gunner fired that first shot, and it went over the barrels. Then the second shot hit the barrels and smoke came pouring out. Hochmuth was very impressed.

The next day, word came that the ships would be going back shortly and for us to come around the island to Apia where the ships were. When we got aboard the ship, nothing was happening. This cargo ship was manned by a civilian, merchant marine crew. I went up and asked the first lieutenant on the ship what the problem was. The barge to unload on was alongside. He told me, "Well, this is a civilian crew, and their union won't permit them to work on Saturdays."

I said, "Well, I'm not captain of this ship, but if I was they'd have an opportunity to swim back to the Golden Gate." I looked over at the mast, and there were three levers at the base of the mast that operated the boom. It seemed simple enough, so I said, "My men can operate this. We'll run the two winches and the boom and we'll unload the damned ship."

So we did. We used the ship's cranes and a Caterpillar tractor that was also loaded on the ship's deck, to get everything out, including two old World War I "Long-Tom" 155-mm howitzers that were tied down mid-ship. In a little over a day we had a standard sized liberty ship unloaded. We sailed back to American Samoa. When I got back, I was told I had been promoted to sergeant while I was gone. Later, I got a letter of appreciation for unloading that ship, too. It had gone through the chain of command, and all the necessary officers had signed it.

When I got back to American Samoa, now being a sergeant, I was in charge of two guns. We were sent over to Fagasa Harbor. This was on the north side of the island, and this was my first trip there. The only way to reach the bay by land was via a steep, single file, switch back foot trail. We carried our packs and individual weapons. Everything else was taken around the island by boat. Within a few weeks the engineers had built a tractor road.[11] We stayed there only a short time; our two guns covered the harbor well—if the Japanese were to try a landing.

Around mid-year, another marine regiment arrived to relieve us.[12] We were probably one of the best-trained regiments, but we had now, for several months, been in a strictly defensive position. For the first time since we had arrived in Samoa, the companies and the battalions of the Eighth Marines were

---

11   Elrod commented: "When I visited the island in 1973 I was able to drive my rental car to the bay. The village of Fagasa no longer existed."

12   This would have been the Third Marine Brigade, which contained the Seventh Marine Regiment. It arrived in May 1942.

brought together. We started training for offensive operations instead of training for defense. The Samoan people called us the old marines, and they called the recent arrivals the new marines. By now, the Samoans had developed a little appreciation for money. They charged the new marines a dollar for doing their weekly laundry, while we were still paying only 50 cents.

We got the new utility uniform while in Samoa: herringbone. It included the utility cap. Before we had worn the pith helmet, a useless piece of gear covered with a thin fabric over pressed paper. It disintegrated in wet weather. We much preferred the campaign hats, what DIs wear now. We had worn them previously. These were a great piece of gear. They kept the sun off, and they kept the rain from dripping down the neck of your poncho. We hated to see them go away, replaced by the pith helmet.

When the Regimental Weapons Company was brought together, Captain Crowe picked a spot out on Coconut Point near where I had had my gun before. It was a nice area, clear with coconut trees scattered around. There were tents there, too, already set up. Crowe liked it. We were isolated, and he had the horsepower to get our own galley out there. He didn't want us to be with the, as he said, "regular marines." He made us believe we were better than they were, that we were special. He didn't want us to get contaminated with some of the habits that he didn't approve of.

He had a mess sergeant named [Elijah J.] Bell. Bell had a long, drooping, red mustache and part of the time he was a staff sergeant, while part of the time he was a sergeant. This depended on what Crowe thought of the meals that were served. It was a game they played.

June 20, 1942
Dearest Mother,
Things are working out fine for me. I am going
to officers' training class now. Unless something un-
expected happens, I should be finished by the time I
write again. I have worked a long time for this and
I don't intend to stop until I have my commission.

We hadn't been there but just a week or two, and Crowe called me in one day and said they'd come out with a thing called a field commission. "How would you like to be a second lieutenant?" And I said, "Well, Skipper, I guess it's really no worse than being a sergeant." He said, "I'm going to recommend you." They recommended some 120 of us to be promoted. Of course, they weren't going to send us to OCS [officers candidate school], so they made a plan to screen us. They loaded us on some trucks and took us to Mormon Valley. It was actually more like a canyon, a pretty rough area.

This screening process took about three weeks. The first part was to set up our tents and form a tent camp. We cleared out brush, and they wanted the camp camouflaged with camouflage nets over the tents. There was a staff sergeant named Spoon, who was a communicator. We worked together to weave pieces of dyed canvas—to simulate leaves and foliage—into the nets then we attached a wire to each corner of the net. I got an idea of how we could get these camouflage nets over our tent before we put the tent up [and] we put the tents underneath. This was big enough to cover probably 20 or 30 feet square, and each tent had its own net. A little box and strip building for a galley or mess hall was also set up.[13]

We did night compass marches, we did grenade throwing, and we fired weapons. The whole thing was just to give the people that were on the committee, who were going to make the recommendations, a chance to observe us and see who was officer material.

One test was at night, and the goal was to creep into the mess area without being detected by the enlisted men that served on the committee. I was one of the few people who got in without being caught. I deliberately waited until way deep into the night when they would be tired and not quite as alert as they had been earlier in the evening.

I realized later that I showed leadership by my guiding the people in getting the net up and other things. I wasn't conscious of me leading at the time. But everything I've ever been involved with, I want to put my oar in the water. When the final time came for a decision, out of the 120, some 90 were promoted. Half were made warrant officers, and half made second lieutenants. I was promoted to second lieutenant. Most everybody went back to a different battalion than the one they came from. I didn't; I went back to the same platoon that I had been in, the Second platoon of Regimental Weapons Company. So, I was discharged as an enlisted man and commissioned as an officer. My date of rank for lieutenant was the second of May, 1942. I was not able to actually pin on my officer insignia until July. In those days, when you were promoted, it was almost always

---

13 A box and strip building was made out of 1" x 12" boards side by side vertically with a 1" x 4" board nailed over the seams.

backdated. Then we got back pay, so along with the promotion came a good chunk of money. It was a very good deal.

> *August 5, 1942*
> *Dearest Mother,*
> No, I haven't lost my pen or broken my arm! The reason that I didn't write while I was in school was that I wanted to find out about my commission. I am now a 2nd Lt. My commission dates back to May 2. We had to work hard in school but it was worth it. My real work is just now starting though. . . . My pay is now $186 per month. Tell everyone hello. All my love. Roy
> P.S.—that was too bad about Malda and her husband.

> *August 29, 1942*
> *Hello Boy,*
> Your letter came several days ago but I have been a little slow getting it answered. We are pretty busy down here these days.
> No Carl, that wasn't my picture, those were soldiers not marines. Mom sent it out to me and asked about it. This commission is something that I have wanted for a long time. There has been a lot of hard work but it is worth it. The job of getting up out of the ranks is a pretty big one. My work has just started though. Now I will have to work and study all the more. The pay is pretty good, I make $186 now, if I was married it would be $265.
> Looking back the old U.S. seems like a pretty good place. Enjoy it while you are still there. If you come up for the draft see about enlisting in the Marine Corps Reserve before you are taken. Stay

out now but if the draft is about to get you don't for-
get the marines, we manage to struggle along with-
out the U.S.O., hostesses and butlers and still get the
job done. Your pal, Roy

So I went back to the same platoon that I had been a three-striped sergeant in, but now as the platoon commander. The former platoon commander who had joined us a month or two before was gone when I got back. I never knew what happened to him. I remember being very unimpressed with him anyway. There were two guns of my platoon at Fagasa Bay, where the former platoon commander had been. The other two guns were still at their position over by Coconut Point where the airfield was being built. After a week or two, I received word that we no longer needed the guns at Coconut Point because the airfield had pretty much blocked off the entrance to that beach. They wanted to move those two guns back over to the southeastern point of entrance into Pago Pago Harbor. This was the same place I had been as a newly arrived squad leader. I decided that since I knew that area, I would go there, and I would leave my platoon sergeant at Fagasa Bay. That was the situation that we worked out. Later both sections of my platoon were consolidated back at Coconut Point. I had my whole platoon there.

My old platoon sergeant [Raymond M.] Clarke, who had been my boss before, was now my number two. He gave me no trouble. Clarke was a big help. One time, I had my platoon out there at Coconut Point doing some close-order drill. I didn't like the way one of the marines was acting, and I started to use the same procedure I would have as a sergeant. I was going to grab him by the stacking swivel and straighten him out.[14] But Sergeant Clarke said, "Sir, I believe the lieutenant should let me handle this." I said, "Sergeant Clark, you're absolutely right." He was very, very helpful. I couldn't have had a better relationship. None of my former peers gave me any trouble. I think partially this was because they had seen me fight in those smokers.

My platoon had about thirty-six men. I had four squads plus the runners, the drivers, just the usual overhead. Each squad was assigned to a 37-mm gun, so we had four guns. With three platoons in the weapons company, that gave the regiment twelve 37-mm guns. My platoon also had two .50-caliber machine guns, one for each section of two guns. Each squad also had a .30-caliber machine gun.

When I came back from the officers screening course, Crowe called me up and said, "Now, you're going to be faced with all kinds of things. It's up to you to decide whether you do it or not." That was about all he said. He had his tent where he could keep a sharp eye on everything that happened in the company. My practice was that the first face that my platoon saw at reveille was mine, and the last face they saw before they went to bed was mine. I suppose he approved of that.

He had made it very plain to me that he didn't really consider second lieutenants as officers. They were just sort of trainees. He wanted to make sure that I didn't get carried away with myself. As a sergeant I had had a Jeep, but Crowe made it clear that as a second lieutenant, I did not get a Jeep. General Larsen

---

14 A stacking swivel was the metal band assembly near the muzzle of a rifle. Marines used this term to describe getting someone's attention by grabbing them by the throat or collar.

had set up a policy that once or twice a week he would have one or two of the newly promoted people come and have dinner with him in his mess. His headquarters was about five miles from where our company was. When my invitation came, I had my light pack, my weapon, my steel helmet and so forth, and I started walking out of the camp. Crowe called me over and said, "Where you going?"

I said, "Well, I've been invited to the general's for dinner."

"Go and get a Jeep," he said.

So, I took a Jeep. He didn't want me to walk. I guess he felt like he had made his point and actually, I didn't think much about that. I really was motivated to make my platoon as good as it could possibly be.

Behind my back I was referred to as a "hard ass." I was fair, and I established with the men the understanding that if they were right, I was in their corner. If they were wrong, I'd take them down. My leadership principles were: I never told them, I showed them; I didn't send them, I took them. I expected everyone to do his share of the work. On one march going over the mountains, one of my marines, a short-legged fellow, abnormally short legs, kept falling behind. I told the man behind him, if he keeps falling back more than five paces, kick him in the butt and tell him to move the fuck out. He told me later that was a turning point for him. He realized that I expected him to be on the par with other marines, that he was equal. That was the first time anyone had treated him so. No one ever told me how to be an officer. I had seen plenty of officers, and in my mind I knew what a good lieutenant was and what a bad lieutenant was. I tried to emulate the good ones, pick up the good habits.

Jim Crowe was a role model for me. I had watched a lot of what he did, and I copied it. It's hard for people to realize the stature that he had in the Marine Corps then. One day Brigadier General Larsen came into the camp with his sedan and driver. I happened to be nearby, and he called Crowe, "Jim, come over. I've got a two-star general coming to visit, and I don't have a thing to feed him." Crowe yelled out, "Bell! Bring the general one of those hams. No, bring the general two of those hams!" These were canned hams. General Larsen was shaking Crowe's hand and said, "Oh, thank you, Jim. I knew you could take care of me." During this period ships came in, and they had enough beer on board that each man got two cans of beer and each officer got a case. Once Crowe was talking to this one company commander and asked him about beer for the troops. The other company commander said, "Well, you know, there just isn't enough to go around, so some of my people only got one can." Crowe said, "You know, that's amazing. Most of my people got three. Some of them got four cans." Crowe had deflected their beer ration to his company. He loved to rub other company commanders' noses in it. This was called 'cumshaw' in those days; it meant obtaining something through unofficial means.[15]

---

15   According to Miriam Webster's dictionary this term originated with British sailors who had visited Chinese ports "during the First Opium War of 1839–42. 'Cumshaw' is from a word that means 'grateful thanks' in the dialect of Xiamen, a port in southeast China. Apparently, sailors heard it from the beggars who hung around the ports, and mistook it as the word for a handout. Since then, U.S. sailors have given 'cumshaw' its own unique application, for something obtained through unofficial means (whether deviously or simply ingeniously)."

The Navy really thought they owned Samoa. They had a little navy officer's club out in the harbor called Goat Island.[16] Since I was now an officer, I thought I would visit. It was only maybe 50 or 75 yards out and there was a wooden walkway out to it. They made it very plain that marine officers weren't welcome. I wandered out there and ordered a beer. Well, I got the beer all right, but I got lots of hard looks, and they made sure that nobody spoke to me or even acknowledged that I was present.

We had time there to train for a month or two. It was very difficult to train in large units. A time or two I would be attached to a battalion with my platoon, and we'd make a march out to the end of the island, which was about halfway around the island, because our main camps were pretty close to Pago Pago Harbor. We'd walk from one end of the island to the other, sometimes at night. It was difficult to do any useful offensive training. But during our time there we gradually adjusted to moving in the jungle and to tolerating the heat and the insects and so forth. We probably went into Guadalcanal better prepared than any other group of troops that ever went there because we had been in Samoa for eight or nine months. We were acclimated, and we understood the jungle.

Sometime in late summer we heard that we would be going to Guadalcanal where the First [Marine] Division had been fighting. We had been hearing about Guadalcanal and were quite interested, of course. A liaison officer and two or three senior NCOs from the First Division came to Samoa, and they

16   Elrod related that Goat Island was gone when he visited Tutuila in 1973. Where it used to lie in Pago Pago harbor is now Sadie's Hotel.

briefed us on what we were going to be getting into. The NCOs briefed the senior NCOs of the regiment and the officer briefed all the officers; we knew we were headed for a tough situation, but we were looking forward to getting into combat. In October we were loaded on a ship and sailed for Guadalcanal.

Guadalcanal

Guadalcanal Perimeter
1 November 1942

CHAPTER FIVE

Guadalcanal: We Were Living Like Animals

The Battle of Guadalcanal fought August 1942 to February 1943 was pivotal for Allied success in the Pacific. It was the first offensive action taken by the U.S. against either Japan or Germany. It was imperative that the U.S. seize the airfield being built by the Japanese on Guadalcanal. It was much too close to a critical ally, Australia. Success there not only relieved pressure on Australia but also gave the Allies a toehold in a strategically important region. It served as a springboard that began the roll back of Japanese presence in the South Pacific.[1]

The First Marine Division landed on Guadalcanal on 7 August 1942. The Eighth Marines landed three months later in early November to reinforce the First Division. In

---

1 Contextual material for this chapter comes from Lt. Col. Frank O. Hough, Maj. Verle E. Ludwig, Henry I. Shaw, *Pearl Harbor to Guadalcanal-History of U.S. Marine Corps Operations in World War II*, vol. 1 (Washington: HistBr, G-3 Div, HQMC, undtd); Henry I Shaw, Jr., First Offensive: The Marine Campaign for Guadalcanal, (Washington, D.C.: Marine Corps Historical Center, 1992) and Richard B. Frank, Guadalcanal (New York: Penguin Books, 1992).

between a desperate battle had been waged. Many believed that the battle was a lost cause and that another Wake Island, when the small marine garrison had to surrender to the Japanese, was in the making. When the Eighth Marines came ashore, the battle still raged, and historians have called November, "critical November," as the Japanese also brought reinforcements to the island to deal once and for all with the tenacious Americans.[2] The Japanese renewed their attacks with vigor and determination on the perimeter that guarded the all-important Henderson airfield. The Allies were determined to hold on and they eventually cleared Guadalcanal of the Japanese.

Once ashore on Guadalcanal Second Lieutenant Elrod's platoon of 37-mm guns was enthusiastically welcomed by the marine infantry units. The marine infantrymen did not envy the 37-mm gunners. They were at the front, but unlike infantrymen who could fire from a dug in position, they had to expose themselves while loading and firing the gun. Their only protection was the ¼-inch thick steel plate shield on the gun. The Japanese very much wanted to eliminate the 37-mms. Like a flamethrower or machine gun, it packed a powerful punch.

Despite the hard fighting, the most enduring challenge of Guadalcanal was the sub-tropic conditions and the dearth of supplies. The marines who had been there from the beginning suffered the worst. Living conditions had improved only slightly when the Eighth Marines came ashore. Like the early-arriving marines, Elrod and his marines experienced short rations, sickness, and living, as he said "like animals." When the Eighth Marines departed Guadalcanal

2   Hough, Ludwig, and Shaw, p. 357.

in February 1943, the tide had turned, and victory was assured, but they were a much worn combat unit.

I went aboard a troop transport with one of the infantry battalions, probably the Second Battalion.[3] The brigade was essentially disbanded because when we arrived at Guadalcanal, we were attached to the First Division. It took about a week or ten days at sea to transit to Guadalcanal. There were no practice landings or anything of that sort. We headed straight for Guadalcanal. During the voyage to Guadalcanal other navy ships, including an aircraft carrier, appeared and covered us. This transport I was on was so crowded about all we could do was exercise and clean weapons. I reviewed my men on tactics and procedures that we planned to use.

A day or two before we were due to arrive, I received word that they wanted our 37-mms to be ready to disembark as soon as the anchor was dropped. We were ready and my unit was one of the first ones off the ship. My memory is that my platoon was unloaded on October 30. Four LCVPs [landing craft, vehicle and personnel] were waiting when the anchor dropped on the ship.[4]

I later learned that the ships that brought us in also left before they were totally unloaded. But the navy admirals at that particular time were very nervous. All they needed to do was get a rumor that Japanese ships were coming and they would pull anchor and set sail. We hadn't brought many supplies from

---

3 Elrod and his platoon sailed aboard the USS *Barnett* (AP 11) to Guadalcanal.

4 The Eighth Marines began landing 3 November.

Samoa because, frankly, Samoa wasn't oversupplied to begin with. We had to leave some for the marines remaining and defending Samoa. So, we were short on supplies from the beginning at Guadalcanal. This seemed to be the norm. We noticed the poor condition of the marines that were there. They were ragged, exhausted, and thin. They had really taken a beating.[5]

We were met at the shoreline by a marine guide and taken inland probably half a mile. The area where we dug in that night was another Lever Brothers coconut plantation, very neatly kept. I was told to dig in there and wait until morning and we would be moved up to the front lines. Everybody was tired and a little excited. We dug just little shallow holes. In the middle of the night the Japanese plane widely known as 'Washing Machine Charlie' came in and dropped a few bombs.[6] He was aiming at the airfield; that was their main target. Fortunately, they missed it as often as they hit it. We did not know that our first night there. When those bombs started to drop, it didn't take me long to get out my entrenching tool and start improving that hole; I could hear the other marines, and they had their shovels and picks going. After that, nobody ever had to tell us to dig in. We dug proper holes from that time on.

The next morning my platoon was taken up and we joined one of the units on the front line of the perimeter defense.

---

5   The marines had been hard pressed for supplies from the beginning. The U.S. Navy was quite reluctant to get its fleet in a vulnerable position with a powerful Japanese navy that lurked in Solomon Island waters.

6   This was a single aircraft that flew over almost nightly and dropped a couple of bombs. It did little damage except to harass the marines, deprive them of sleep, and jangle their nerves. It seemed to be a common tactic the Japanese used and is mentioned by marines in other campaigns.

After that I don't remember seeing any of the rest of the Regimental Weapons Company. I heard that once we [the Eighth Marines] arrived, it was the first time that there were enough marines to make a solid perimeter defense around the airfield. The entire operation at Guadalcanal was for the protection and operation of that airfield.

The marine infantrymen really welcomed our arrival, and we moved right into position with them. We used canister a lot, and with that it was not practical to be behind our infantry because they would have been in great danger. Canister was basically a large shotgun shell.[7] The canister, besides offering good protection, stripped away foliage and brush and created better fields of fire. This was another reason we were popular with the marine riflemen. When the Japanese attacked the perimeter these canister rounds were quite effective; they never penetrated our lines in any force. We dug positions for the guns about 16 or 18 inches deep so that we could load them easily, and everybody could move around to load and fire it, with at least some protection. These positions were dug in such a way

---

7　Elrod is saying that canister would not be effective fired over friendly troops to the front. It was only effective when fired directly at enemy troops. In an interview with Major General James L. Day, by Benis M. Frank, 24 Oct 1989, transcript (Oral HistColl, History Division, Quantico, VA), Day, who also served as a 37-mm platoon commander, elaborates on the effectiveness of canister: "Yes, the canister was a weapon that you almost cannot believe. As I recall there were 144 [actually 122] pellets in that thing and they were about .38-caliber size or larger and it just completely created a swathe wherever you fired it. The idea was to be able to, to have the chance to fire it. The Japanese were such great infiltrators that, unless you had a barrier in front of you like a river or an open spot, they were right across, and they did not attack with a lot of screaming—in some cases they did—but most of the time they infiltrated right up to well within grenade range before they got up, and then it was just a matter of if they got up within thirty-five yards of you, if you had a round in the chamber and that is what they kept in those 37-mm, to get that first round off, and then you could load it so fast that you could get other rounds off. But being able to zero in on them before they were on top of you was a big problem."

to allow us to swing the trails right and left—we could then reposition the gun's muzzle right or left if we had targets that were further than the gun would actually traverse.

I realized though that even dug in my gunners and crews were still exposed to enemy fire. In fighting along the perimeter, enemy troops often got within rifle and even hand grenade range. The Japanese grenades were not that reliable. On one occasion myself and one of my marines ran down a Japanese soldier. He was hiding behind a tree and as we approached he tossed a grenade that landed right at the feet of this marine. It exploded but did very little harm, and disintegrated into fragments like sand, and it just sort of burned his legs. We called them "sand grenades." But at times it was close quarters fighting. The Japanese saw that our guns were something that caused a lot of trouble for them, and would come after them. If my gunners were going to be able to fight their guns the way they should, they needed to feel secure, they needed more protection beyond what that little shield offered. We had the .50-caliber machine guns, but in some locations it was difficult to find a good place to set them up. I requested, through the chain of command, four Browning automatic rifles [BARs]. They were lighter, could be picked up and carried by a marine, and were good for close in fighting.

I was told none were available. I wasn't satisfied with that answer. So I took two marines and we "wandered" along the line, and if we saw one against a tree or laying around, we "liberated" it, cumshaw. Captain Crowe was very impressed by that. I had learned from him. He thought officers should do what they needed to do to take care of their marines. I designated certain marines that I believed could be counted on to man these recently acquired BARs and protect the crews. This became their sole duty in combat: to protect the gun crew while they fired the gun. This worked out well.[8]

The action was sporadic, and there were times when it was really just monotonous. Sometimes you were under fire all day and part of the night. Then there would be days when there were just occasional shots. The Japanese never attempted to attack from all directions. When we first arrived up through the middle of December what the division command did was to move my platoon of 37-mm guns and the others, I suppose, to points on the perimeter where they thought the Japanese might attack, or the danger points. I didn't know who decided or how they decided where we should go. We moved so often, I never really got to know the people we were assigned to. We would move to one place, dig in, and sometimes the attack came that was predicted and sometimes it didn't. We didn't stay long in any one place, only a few days or a week. The Japanese kept probing first one area and then the other. I served in just about every part of the perimeter line except the eastern part. I never

---

8   Elrod was right to be concerned for his marines. In the Day interview, MajGen Day related, "No one wanted to be in the 37-mm platoon . . . the gunner's head and shoulders and everything were exposed and of course, the first time they fired, I saw that happen on Guam, where we fired a canister round and I think it killed six or eight Japanese—then you were targeted because it is just like a machine gun or anything else, once you blast then they know if they are going to have a counterattack that they are going to try to take out that type of weapon. I think that is why most people kind of looked forward to being with the rifle platoon. Because then you were down low and you could protect your hole and do a pretty good job of it. Whereas with that 37-mm, although it was a very formidable weapon, it could knock out anything the Japanese had in the way of tanks, it was an exposure type of a weapon and no one looked toward being there with any mild enthusiasm."

did go there. And even though the airfield was what we were primarily there to defend, I never once actually saw the airfield or General [Archibald A.] Vandergrift's headquarters.[9]

On Guadalcanal, the low ground was where the jungle was. Most of the ridges were barren at the top. If you were going to defend the ridge, you really tried to defend it from a military crest, and you could drop back down behind there to do your other activities, like eating rations or resting. Once, when we were with Colonel [Clifton B.] Cates' unit [First Marines], I saw that the best position for one of my guns was a little hill near the center of my position.[10] My marines were weak and sick at this time, and I didn't think they had the strength to get a gun up on top. It was pretty steep. We decided to use a Jeep to get it up there. One of my marines, a wild corporal, [Kenneth C.] Langness, had proven he could handle a Jeep very well. So we put tire chains on the wheels, put it in four-wheel-drive, and tied a couple of cases of ammunition to the front bumper to hold the front. I had a marine on each side of the Jeep holding a rope attached to the front end to keep it from raising up and flipping over. The corporal backed up and went

---

9   General Archibald A. Vandegrift was the First Marine Division commanding general. He later became Commandant of the Marine Corps. For his leadership of the First Marine Division at Guadalcanal he was awarded the Medal of Honor.

10   Clifton Cates was a prominent marine leader. He retired as a four-star general and was Commandant, 1948–1952. As a young lieutenant he fought with the Sixth Marine Regiment in France in World War I. In addition to commanding the First Marines at Guadalcanal, he later in World War II also commanded the Fourth Marine Division in the Marshalls Campaign, Tinian, and Iwo Jima. He is one of the few officers of any service who commanded a platoon, a company, a battalion, a regiment, and a division under fire. He won nearly thirty decorations including the Navy Cross for his World War I action.

roaring up this hill, throwing dirt in all directions. He got the gun to the top. Colonel Cates came by and was a little amazed. He asked the corporal, "How in the world did you get that gun up there?" Langness replied, "Well, I pulled it up with a Jeep. The lieutenant said to do that. We do what the lieutenant says." Colonel Cates laughed and walked away. Later I was able to put Langness in for an aviation commission, and he got it. He went to flight school and became a Corsair pilot.[11]

Nighttime was a spooky time along the perimeter. It could be the blackest black and the jungle made strange noises with the numerous critters that populated the jungle, big spiders, crabs, and what not. There was always in the back of our minds the knowledge that the Japanese liked nothing better than to sneak into a foxhole and cut a marine's throat. There would be shouting back and forth, mutual insults passed with the Japanese. Of course, their English was very poor. Some might have spoken good English, but all of them had problems with Ls and Rs. For passwords we would try to get a word that had letters that would be difficult for them to repeat. We always had a password and a countersign. I told my men to not fire unless they were certain it was a real threat. To do so gave away our position, and it caused the other marines to awake and go on alert, thus depriving them of sleep.

I had one marine that had a tendency to take shots at night, and I kept after him. He swore he could hear the Japanese out there doing their death chant. I said, "I know you don't speak

---

11 Kenneth C. Langness did indeed become an officer, but evidently before he went to flight school, he commanded an infantry platoon in F Company, Second Battalion, Eighth Marines. He was wounded leading his platoon at Tarawa. He lived to be ninety-years-old and died in Morristown, Arizona, in 2012.

Japanese. How in the world would you know if you heard something like a death chant?" I told him, "I'm going to have to break you of this firing at night." We had strung up wire in front and tied in it empty brass shell casings so they would jangle if someone walked into it. We also had tripwires laid out with C ration cans tied in. I ordered him: "You get out in front of the wire and dig yourself a hole. That's where you're going to spend the night." I sent him out there with only his mess kit knife and a legging lace. I wouldn't let him have his weapon. In front of him I had this corporal that would carry out my instructions to the absolute word. He kept his head shaved and I called him Curley, but his real name was Ward. Speaking in front of the trigger-happy marine, I said, "Curley, if he gets out of the hole tonight shoot him." When the marine left, I said, "Curley, make sure that nothing happens to him." The night passed without him firing, and he never fired again at night.

I soon discovered that worse than the Japanese were the living conditions on Guadalcanal. We were living really like animals. If it rained, we got wet. If the sun came out, we got dry. If you were close to a river and you could keep from being exposed to sniper fire, we would take a bath in the river. Of course, we watched for alligators and crocodiles. If there was no river, we didn't bathe. We would be desperate to be clean, though, so if it started raining, and we were clear of snipers, we'd strip, and soap up. If it stopped raining before you got rinsed off, then you just had a layer of soap on you until the next time it rained.

Living on the front line, we had no tents. There was nothing in front of us but the Japanese. We lived in holes, but we dug our holes so when it rained, the water would run to one side. That way we could take the helmet cover off and with our helmets bail the water out. That kept us from having to actually sleep in the water. That didn't keep the rain from falling on you. Sometimes we tried to rig a shelter half over the hole but there was no real way to stay dry.

Occasionally, when we would have one of the fold-up stretchers around, I would open one up and sleep on it and this would keep my body an inch or so above the ground. We all wanted to have as light a load as possible, and so I had a half-blanket. I slept on that and we would usually cover ourselves with a poncho or something to ward off as much rain as possible. We quit trying to stay dry. If you had something that you wanted to keep dry, you'd keep it under your helmet on top of your head. Marines put letters or pictures or the people who smoked would put their cigarettes there. I never smoked.

It didn't take long for my marines to get sick. I developed a case of malaria after only about a week, that along with dysentery and diarrhea. I remember one night I sat on this box over a slit trench streaming with diarrhea, shaking with malaria, and throwing up. With these sicknesses it made it difficult to keep things in your stomach. At the same time, Japanese mortar rounds were landing behind me, and as I sat there in the pouring rain and with mosquitoes biting me, I said to myself, "I wonder why they can't get one of those rounds in here where it will do some good?" That was the low point.

But everyone was sick, everybody had malaria, and diarrhea was very common. It just amazed me though the endurance that the marines showed. As time went by, and as marines were evacuated because of disease or combat wounds, the word went out that unless you had a fever over 104, you weren't allowed to go to sick bay. The corpsman would have to do what he could to medicate you, but you were not leaving.

So the longer we stayed, the more the men suffered. It wasn't just sickness. We were ridden with jungle rot and skin infections. We had to be very careful with any kind of skin abrasion or cut because with the sweat and body oils, the mud and the dirt, and the dripping humidity, you had an excellent chance of getting an infection if you were not very careful. I got fungus in my ears. I found that 100 percent pure alcohol would reduce the fungus, so one of the old chief pharmacist's mates gave me a little bottle that would fit right in one of the ammo pouches on my belt. If my ear started itching, I would put a few drops of alcohol in it.

We received a new drug called atabrine, and it was supposed to help prevent malaria. It had a strange side reaction, though. It turned the skin yellow, and the whites of the eyes would turn canary yellow. The scuttlebutt [rumors] began that this was going to destroy male virility. I told my marines, "Look, there isn't a woman within 2,000 miles of here and I wouldn't bet the stump ranch that any of us are going to get back there anyway. Take the damned pill!"

I had the section sergeants, the corpsman, platoon sergeant—and I did it myself—follow along to make sure each man took his atabrine. I am not sure how well it worked. Even though we had lots of losses to malaria, it probably would have been much worse without the atabrine. All I can say is at least enough of us survived to finish the campaign.

Foot problems were rampant. With the leather field shoes we had, and the amount of humidity and mud and rain, our feet were rarely dry. I had my men take their shoes off and massage their feet, turn their socks wrong side out and put them on the other foot. I don't know whether that helped or not, but I felt that it was some kind of a change.

Food was always in short supply. We were truly on starvation rations. Everyone was losing weight. I dropped down to about 165 pounds from over 190. Many times we had nothing but a little captured Japanese rice, but it kept us alive. The canvas bags that the rice was in had rotted and the first couple of inches of rice were hardened. Once we broke through that the rice was good. Often we were not where we could cook the rice, and we discovered that you couldn't store it, even in our mess gear. It didn't take any time at all before it went sour. We learned to keep it in socks because then it could breathe. So we carried rice in socks, and it was good for two or three days.

We had plenty of ammunition, though. We never lacked for 37-mm rounds. Although it seemed we were always short of hand grenades. We had to conserve them. Also, mortar ammunition, it was in short supply.

I saw it as one of my main jobs as a lieutenant to know my marines. One of them, I noticed, never shaved. He did not need to; he had no beard. This raised my suspicion. One day I asked him, "How old are you?"

"Oh, I'm 17, lieutenant."

I said, "Damnit, I'm not going to do anything to you. Tell me the truth—how old are you?"

"I will be 15 my next birthday."

I did not bother him about it. He was probably the best Browning automatic rifleman that I ever saw. He could play a tune with it. I said, "How did you get into the Marine Corps?"

He said, "I stole my brother's birth certificate."

So here he was, a 15-year old boy, but really a good marine. He was not the only one, there were numerous underage marines, and I often wondered if those who came in under false names ever got their records straight. Many, I surmise, never did. But this marine, by the time we were on Saipan, about eighteen months later, he had grown a few inches, was over six feet tall and weighed about 175 pounds.

While the sickness took many marines, we also had many killed and wounded. I don't think any of my marines ever suffered casualties from the Japanese naval shelling or their air attacks. Most of our casualties were from Japanese mortar rounds or rifle bullets. Mostly rifle bullets because I think they were having supply problems probably even worse than ours. One of my marines got hit by a sniper round, it hit right near the crotch, in his groin. The round had ripped a gaping hole in him. The flesh was torn back and bubbly yellow fat was evident. A main artery was severed, and every time his heart beat, blood spurted three or four feet in the air. He was mostly worried about his 'plumbing' though. I told him, "It's in good condition. You've just got a hell of a hole in your thigh." I had the corpsman ride with him back to the aid station for fear that the tourniquet would slip off because we were using a rubber tube tourniquet. And when it got blood soaked it would slip. After that, I acquired a strap bandage tourniquet and carried that in my belt for the rest of the war.

Another time, an infantry platoon leader and friend—we had gone through the Samoa officer screening program together—had his platoon join mine on the left. He went out on patrol, and he was shot in the right thigh. He came back in, and I was there when the corpsman cut his pants open. Fortunately, the bullet had passed through his thigh, and there was a leather string hanging out of his leg. I said, "Ski, what the heck is that?"

"Oh, that's the string on my locker key. I don't want to lose my locker key."

I said, "Look, you can take a hammer and knock the lock off."

"No, I want that key."

So the corpsman worked around and managed to pull it out. The bullet had hit the key, and the key was actually folded back around the bullet and had been shot into his thigh. So he went away with a nice souvenir. But his key was no good for his locker after that.

The people that were around the airfield probably endured more fire than anyone because they were at the bull's eye you might say. There was a naval battle in early November.[12] I happened to be fairly close to the coastline at that time, close enough that we could see out to sea from our position. In the dark you could see the gun flashes and even watch the Japanese 16-inch shells sailing overhead, a big red tracer streaking over with a rumbling sound like a passing freight train. Luckily, they were going over our heads.

Every once in a while we would see an explosion of a ship, and everyone would cheer and clap. We assumed that those were Japanese ships. It was very surprising the next morning

---

12 Elrod might be describing the naval battle that began on 13 November off Savo Island. This battle, although a success for the U.S., was costly. Of the thirteen American ships engaged, only one escaped without damage. Six American ships were sunk. The Japanese navy was covering a convoy of transports carrying reinforcements, the Thirty-Eighth Division. Despite losses in the naval fight and punishing air attacks the next day, the Japanese managed to land 10,000 troops. These were the last Japanese reinforcements to reach Guadalcanal.

when we looked out and saw some of our cruisers with gun turrets hanging over the side or missing a part of its superstructure.

Along the perimeter we maintained an aggressive defense, and that meant lots of patrolling. We would try to find out where the Japanese might be massing for another attack. They used the trails in the interior of the island to move from one area to the next. By checking these trails we could see signs of Japanese troop movement, there would be tracks or abandoned gear and equipment. These indicated troop movement and direction they were heading.

Although we were a 37-mm gun crew, we were regarded as infantry and we went on patrols. Of course, we left our 37-mms in their positions and carried infantry weapons on these patrols. As a lieutenant I was expected to lead patrols, and I led several with the various battalions I happened to be positioned with. I remember once when I was attached to Colonel Cates' First Marines he told me, "You know, I realize that I'm assigning you to more patrols than the average. The reason I'm doing that is because you get the information, and you bring your marines back."

The maps that we had were made up from aerial photographs or mosaics put together. They really were not very good partly because when the photos were made clouds had covered some of the terrain. Nine times out of ten, the area where you were operating would be a blank labeled: "cloudy area." So when we patrolled an area, we walked it to find out what was really there in addition to finding out something about the Japanese. When I was at Texas A&M, I learned to use surveying instruments—a plane table, an alidade—and actually did map making. I didn't have any of those instruments at Guadalcanal, but

I could use what I called my seaman's eye to discern landforms, and I estimated heights in order to get the contour lines in. If we patrolled in one of those clouded over areas, which was often, I sketched in the landforms.

Our patrols were various types, and you had an assigned mission for each patrol. I was never sent out to engage the enemy. You were either sent out to look at a specific area or to find a particular thing. Sometimes we would go out for just a few hours, other times longer. The longest one I made was three days. And they were different sizes. Sometimes, there would only be two or three men. Others were larger. A two-squad patrol [about twenty-five men] was the largest one that I ever led. That was on that three-day patrol.

The technique we used when we were going out was to find a spot where the Japanese had little, if anyone, present. We sneaked out in that area, and got deep enough behind them to be able to move inland behind their lines. We never came back in through the route that we went out. I always made sure to get in touch with the commander of the unit where I would be reentering the lines. I didn't want my patrol to get shot up by our own marines.

If we were going to be out overnight, we would pick a good defensive position and dig in and as soon as it was real dark, we would move to our real position and set up there. I never spent the night at the place where we were when the sun went down.

On patrol I insisted that my marines not drink or use water out of a stream. You had no idea where the stream came from. If you could find a little seeping spring—if it wasn't seeping very fast—you could take an entrenching tool, make a little hole there, and fill canteens. We always put a couple of Halzone tablets in our water just in case. It didn't taste particularly good, but I don't remember any of us ever getting sick from the water.

You had to be very quiet, no talking, no noise, and move very stealthily. On several patrols I actually saw Japanese. Sometimes we heard them, and sometimes we smelled them, or any combination of these. I was expected to observe the enemy, but not be seen. There were occasions where patrols were ambushed. That never happened to me. I think maybe that was luck. Who knows?

> *Dec 6, 1942*
> *Dearest Mother,*
> *I found another envelope so I will write again today. Everything is going ok here. I am losing a little weight but am feeling fine. We only eat two meals a day here so you can tell the folks back home that they aren't the only ones who ration things. . . . Mom I am enclosing a 50 yen note (Keep it for me). It is one of the few souvenirs I have picked up. The Jap who was carrying it is now in the same condition as the good Indian. Most of my souvenirs are in my head though. . . . Well no more for this time, love to all of you, Roy.*

It was just a matter of continual movement, continual hunger. People were ragged. I don't think there was ever a time where the marines on Guadalcanal were adequately supplied. When the First Division first landed, the navy pulled out with a lot of the supplies. It never got any better. Morale was pretty good. Oh, people bitched about food. When you became really hungry, food became ever present in your mind. This was one of the few times when you would hear marines talking about food rather than women.

> *December 28, 1942*
> *Dearest Mother,*
> *Well Santa Claus came alright. Yesterday I got two packages, one from you, Claude & Grandmom, and one from Unkie & Grandmother. You still know what I like, my little knife had worn out so was glad to get another. The toilet kit is what I have been needing, I don't carry many toilet articles, they were always getting scattered all through my pack. It will fit nicely. We live on just what we can carry on our backs. I am carrying four knives now, the two you sent, a scout knife and a 10 inch stabbing knife I made out of a bayonet. Unkie sent an assortment of candy, this stationery and a couple of magazines, Grandmother sent one of those little service Testaments.*
> *My Christmas could have been a lot worse but I don't want to spend many more like it. I am feeling fine Mom & getting along O.K. don't worry about me. I have been very fortunate with my boys as far as casualties are concerned, I hope my judgment & luck will not fail me.*
> *We had a good Christmas dinner it was our evening meal. As I have already told you we eat only two meals per day. It consisted of turkey, English peas, mashed potatoes & gravy, cranberry sauce, olives, fig pudding, nuts and chocolate. There was plenty too and everyone got all he wanted to eat.*
> *It is plenty hot here now as you know this is our summer, & there are more flies than you could*

ever imagine. The mosquitos are big but don't bother much.

Give my love to all the folks. There isn't anything more to write, I only know what I am doing & can't write about that so there isn't much news I can give. Everyone at home knows more about what is happening than we do. All my love, Roy

We did have a Christmas dinner on Guadalcanal, on the bank of the Matanikau River. We were right up in the front lines. That was the first real meal that we had had since we had landed. We had turkey and all the trimmings—the works, a regular Christmas dinner. They brought it up in heated and insulated containers and they just dipped it out into our mess gear, it was a little bit on the cool side, but we would've eaten it raw.

Jan 4, 1942
Dear Mom,
The fruit cake and candy came yesterday, they were sure good. A little tasty chow sure comes in handy out here. Everything is going well, and I am feeling fine. My boys have been very fortunate as far as casualties is concerned. . . . At 12:05 day after tomorrow I will have been out of the States for a year. It has been a very eventful one too. During that whole year I haven't slept in a real bed or sat in a chair more than a dozen times. It has really not been too bad though, it is surprising how you can get accustomed to something. The thing that is the worst for me to get used to is the two meals a day. You can understand that.

Sometimes marines or sailors from the back area would come up to the line looking for souvenirs. Japanese teeth with gold crowns on them were good articles of exchange. We could trade teeth and an occasional flag to either Seabees or aviators for things that were hard to get otherwise. The Seabees were professional scroungers. They had a knack for acquiring hard to find goods—liquor, lumber—things that were considered real luxuries, like food.

We became very impressed by the Seabees at their ability to fix or make things. Many of them were older men. They had been full-time construction workers before the war. They knew exactly how to build whatever we needed built. We had great appreciation for the navy doctors, the corpsmen, and chaplains, too. They considered themselves marines. They were far more marine than they were navy. Once in a while there would be religious services, and the chaplains would circulate around and talk to marines.

We had an attitude about the Japanese that began when we were briefed by the First Marine Division liaison officer that had visited when we were on Samoa. We became convinced that the Japanese were a merciless foe, and we went there with the idea of killing them all. We maintained that attitude for the entire war. We had a deep, undying hatred of anything Japanese, and there was no mercy shown. There were a few Japanese that had been captured, but I think these were ones that had gotten through the frontline areas and were caught by people in the rear. I remember once when we were moving from one position to another we went by a burial ground, and there was a big red-haired corporal there with three or four Japanese prisoners who were digging graves. One of the Jap soldiers laughed about something, and this big corporal went over and took him by the throat and strangled him. I could've stopped him, but I thought justice was being served, so I didn't interfere.

In December when the Regimental Weapons Company had come together, the Eighth Marines were the right-hand unit on the western perimeter, and my platoon actually tied into the sea. This was at the mouth of Matanikau; the perimeter was not pushed out to the Matanikau until after the Eighth Marines arrived. I think by this time each regiment had its battalions in a cohesive area. Before it had just been a matter of trying to build up strength wherever the Japanese happened to be attacking.[13]

My platoon of guns was at the mouth of Matanikau because there was a sandbar that built up at the mouth where the river current met the sea waves. The tides moved back and forth, and it dropped sand in there. Even at high tide, the water across the sandbar probably wasn't more than knee-deep. It was the only place on the Matanikau that tanks could cross. So we were there to keep Japanese tanks from crossing.

Apparently, a unit of 37-mm guns of the Fifth Marines had been there before I moved into position, and a number of tanks had attempted to cross. They had killed all of the tanks, probably with assistance from artillery. Four of the blasted out tanks still sat there in the river's mouth.[14]

---

13 The Matanikau was key for defense of the perimeter as it was a natural barrier. First Marine Division units had tangled with Japanese troops, which were in force on its western banks since late September.

14 While the Fifth Marines were there immediately prior to the arrival of the Eighth Marines along the Matanikau, the tanks were probably hulks from the 23 October battle during which Marines of 3d Battalion, 1st Marines, firing 37-mm guns stymied a nine-tank attack at the mouth of the Matanikau.

We hadn't been there long before I discovered that at night Japanese snipers came out and got inside the tanks, and they'd shoot at us. The only armor-piercing ammunition I used at Guadalcanal was to kill snipers inside those tanks. We took casualties from time to time from those snipers. It became a daily morning requirement to shoot rounds into those tank carcasses. This went on for several days, maybe a couple of weeks. I finally prevailed upon the marine engineers to blow the tanks up. And they did a beautiful job. When one of them exploded, a large piece of an engine hatch cover landed right by one of my gun positions. It probably weighed 50 pounds. It would have killed somebody if it hit him. But it didn't.

We kept a real sharp eye, watching out to sea. One day one of my marines came running up. He said, "Lieutenant, there's something out there." I trained my glasses and looked out and saw something. It looked like someone swimming. I had a marine, a Cajun, who was probably one of the best warriors I ever knew. I called him "Little Beaver." There was a comic strip in the newspapers in the States at that time, and it had a little Indian whose name was Beaver. I nicknamed him after that, his real name was [Leroy McM.] Burgess. He could throw an ax at a tree and stick the blade in the tree every time. He said, "Lieutenant, I'll go out and see what's happening." He stripped down to his skivvy drawers, took the belt out of his pants, strapped a knife on, and swam out.

It was probably 200 or 300 yards out to where this man was swimming. It was a marine, and Burgess brought him in. I questioned this marine and found out that he had gone out on the south side of the perimeter with a patrol. They were ambushed, and he was the only survivor. He survived, he said, by running inland and then circling deep behind the Japanese lines, around to the west, until he got to the sea. And he knew if he could swim long enough he would eventually get back to our perimeter. He had barely made it. He had been in the water three or four hours when we found him. He was absolutely exhausted. He had shed his shoes, his shirt, and everything except his pants. I quizzed him, "Why didn't you take your pants off?" Well, he was rather sheepish, and he finally said he didn't want to have the fish bite off anything he didn't want to lose.

We stayed in that position until sometime around the first of the year. This was not long after the army division moved into Guadalcanal. General Vandegrift had turned over command of the island to the army general, and the First Marine Division had departed.[15]

I got familiar with two army regiments that had earlier arrived, the 164th and the 182nd. The 164th was a North Dakota National Guard unit.[16] They were real fighters. The marines made them auxiliary marines. They seemed to be able to talk the same language. Their regimental commander was the town barber, and they were a very un-military organization, but they could fight. They were mostly Scandinavians, farm boys, country boys. They were good. The 182nd [Infantry Regiment] was entirely different.[17]

---

15 The First Marine Division was relieved on 9 December 1942 by the U.S. Army Americal Division, or Twenty-Third Infantry Division under the command of Major General Alexander M. Patch. The Eighth Marines remained engaged in Guadalcanal, however, until February 1943.

16 The 164th Infantry arrived on Guadalcanal on 13 October 1942.

17 The 182nd Infantry arrived on Guadalcanal on 12 November 1942.

It was decided by higher authority that we now had enough strength there that we could, for the first time, go on a real offensive. The 182nd moved through the area from the beach inland across the only road that went to the west. They passed through where my platoon was. They lasted about two hours, and here they started stringing back. One walked out into the water in front of one of my gun crews. He threw his hands up and fell in the water. One of my marines started to go get him, and I said, "Let the son of a bitch drown."

Well, he got up and came on in, and it wasn't too long before another soldier walked by. I don't think he knew I was an officer. He pitched his M-1 rifle, one of the new Garands—we were still using the '03 Springfields—and two bandoliers of ammunition over to me and said, "Here, Marine, you'll need this more than I will."[18]

They decided that the marine units would do what the army troops had failed to do. We attacked across the Matanikau and on to the west and got as far as Point Cruz. That was very thick jungle. All along the flat areas, along the coast, there were no coconut trees. The coconut trees only grew where the Lever Brothers plantations were. Coconuts had been one of our food

---

18   The M-1 Garand was an extremely effective and popular rifle. Although the semi-automatic M-1 Garand became the standard service rifle for the U.S. Army in 1936, it was not until late 1941 that all army units had them. The marines did not yet have them, simply because of a lack of supply at that point in the war. This included the later arriving Eighth Marines. The marines prided themselves on their marksmanship and making every shot count. They believed that the bolt action Springfield was more accurate and conserved ammunition. But stories of marines stealing Army Garands at Guadalcanal might reveal how many marines really felt. See Shaw's First Offensive, p. 33.

supplies. With no coconuts we were really hard pressed for anything to eat.

There was a fourth platoon in the Regimental Weapons Company that was equipped with two 75-mm pack howitzers. They were on my right side and they set up out on Point Cruz itself. We moved up and broke through that first Japanese line. We dug in there and stayed in that position until the middle of January.

We began to hear that the Eighth Marines would soon be departing Guadalcanal. Before we did, it was decided that we would help with an attack on the next and final Japanese line.[19] When the day came for the attack, 15 January, we attacked just like infantry; we didn't take our 37-mm guns with us. When we started the attack, my runner and I led out with a couple of scouts on each side. The rest of my platoon was to follow behind. We had probably fifty or sixty yards to cross to where the Japanese were actually dug in. As we approached their positions, a Japanese machine gun opened up. When it opened up—and I wasn't aware at the time—one of the bullets apparently cut my pistol holster loose from my belt. I did have the M-1 rifle that the army soldier had pitched to me a few weeks earlier. We pressed on toward the machine gun position, and I got right up to it. When I dropped to the deck, I was close enough that I could reach with my right hand the barrel of the machine gun. It was a Nambu. It was actually like a submachine gun, but it fired a belt of ammo. I just reached over with my hand and caught

19   This refers to a XIV Corps-wide offensive against the Japanese that began on 10 January. The Eighth Marines joined the attack on 13 January, driving toward the west. The Eighth Marines remained in this fight until 17 January. Hough, Ludwig, and Shaw, pp. 566–567.

the barrel and pulled it out of the hole. I don't think the gunner expected that because he didn't try to hold onto the gun. The barrel was hot, and I burned my hand a little bit.

My runner was just to my left, and by this time we could see they had a log cover on top of this emplacement. I could see the entrance that was around in front on the side of where the runner was. I signaled for him to make a little noise. As he did, I crawled over the top and lifted up two of the logs. They were only three or four inches in diameter, and there was about six or eight inches of dirt on top of them.

When I raised the logs I saw inside their dugout. There was a little platform right under where I raised it up. One of the Japanese was lying on his stomach with his rifle and bayonet up pointed to the entrance. I could see the gunner just to his left, who was still in front at the firing position. They were on full alert. They'd heard the noise my runner was making. I was holding the M-1 in my right hand like a pistol, and the two logs with my left hand. When I lifted the logs, the Japanese soldier who was right under me turned his head around. He didn't get his weapon around. As he turned his head, I put a round in his forehead; the muzzle of the rifle was no more than four or five inches from his head. I immediately then put two rounds in the gunner's head because he was beginning to swing around in the hole. That took care of that machine gun position. It was a good thing I had the Garand rifle. I would not have been able to shoot that rapidly with just one hand; the bolt action '03 Springfield required two hands to operate. The second Jap most likely would have killed me.

We went probably another fifty yards or so and dug in for the night. We had cleared the defensive line that was alongside the road. It was obvious that even though we had broken through along the road, the unit to our left had not seized the hill that overlooked the road. There were machine guns and mortars up there. We could not move down that road with those there. The next day, 16 January, the battalion decided to attack the ridge and clear it of Japanese.

Crowe volunteered my platoon to the battalion commander to support the attack. We had to gather up cooks, drivers, runners, and clerks to bring it up to the strength of a regular platoon. I marched with my platoon over to this company area on my left. It was about forty-five minutes or so before it was time for the attack.

When I got there I found the company commander, a captain, with two of his lieutenants. They were in a hole playing cribbage. I said, "Captain, I've come over to reinforce you for the attack." He mumbled something about they weren't sure they were going to be able to take off at H-hour. That told me right away why they had failed to take the ridge in front of them in the first place. When they made that comment, I unsnapped the flap on my pistol—incidentally I had gone back over the route of our attack on the first day and found my pistol and gotten another holster—but I didn't actually draw it. I said, "If you bastards won't fight, stay the hell out of my sight." The only thing that kept me from shooting all three of them was that I was afraid it would delay the attack and cause a problem. I was determined we were going to go to the top of that hill.

I got hold of the company first sergeant and told him that we were going to go at the time of H-hour. It was just a few minutes away. I said, "Tell your people that every mother's son of them is going up that hill. Have your heavy machine guns fire about twenty paces in front of us and walk your 60-mm mortars over the top of the ridge. Get me two of your best people to work with my platoon sergeant to see that anybody that needs encouragement gets it."

We took off and we had to go down through the valley. We moved up the ridge where the Japanese were. We knocked out some positions on the way up, and then we cleaned up the top of the ridge. After the attack I sent my platoon back to the company area, and my runner and I took a direct route back to company headquarters. I wanted to report in to Captain Crowe. It was about a half-mile back and we soon found ourselves in head high kunai grass. I began to get a little nervous. I thought, "What if all the Japanese had not been cleared out yet?" I got even more worried when we came across the bodies of five or six army troops, probably from the 182nd, just lying next to each other. We made it back safely to the company area. The battalion commander and Captain Crowe were there. There was a first lieutenant there with the battalion commander; he was sort of like an aide. The battalion commander reached over and took off one of this first lieutenant's collar bars and one of his shoulder bars and pinned them on me. I was immediately promoted to first lieutenant, back dated to the first of January. I was also awarded the Silver Star.

I was pleased, but I didn't really understand the connotations of the whole thing. The captain of that company that did not attack and his lieutenants were gone; where they went or what happened, I do not know. Apparently, they were relieved. I never saw them after that. I believe that the captain was responsible. I expected the two lieutenants would have done something more, but they followed their skipper's lead.

At Quantico fourteen years later, we were invited to a party a colonel was having in his quarters aboard base down from Harry Lee Hall. That street is where a lot of colonels lived, and we called it "Whiskey Gulch" in those days. When I went in, well, here this captain was, but he was no longer a captain. He was a lieutenant colonel. I was a major. When he saw me, he went out through the kitchen and left. Somebody else had to take his wife home that night. I realized that I had taken a chance by taking over his company, but the battalion commander said that we had saved his reputation.

> *Jan 20, 1943*
> *Dearest Mom,*
>   *Things have been happening so that in the last few days it has been impossible to write. I am fine and getting along O.K.. These boys of mine have certainly given a good account of themselves out here. I wouldn't trade them for any bunch of men I have ever seen. Mom, I say boys I guess because so many of them are so young but they are men every one of them. It is really a sight to see the way they go after the Japs.*
>   *It has been raining all afternoon. We have become so accustomed to it that no one ever pays any attention, of course you can't ignore the mud. I bet it was never as deep in France as it is here.*

After that attack on those two days, the army unit passed through us. From that time on, they were pushing up. They didn't push very hard. I think they probably could have wiped out the entire Japanese force if they had used a little more aggression. We were pulled back and told to prepare to leave the island. When we got back to where the army base camps were, for the first time we got decent meals. The first sergeant and I got in the Jeep and went over to the army's storage area and found a tent that had uniforms in it. There was this army corporal there and the first sergeant told him, "Corporal, you go out and talk to our driver while the lieutenant and I transact our business." What we did was get two sets of uniforms—shirt, pants, underwear, socks—for each one of my men. Some of our marines were in rags, but when we left the island, we were wearing army field uniforms.

We had probably ten days or so that we were waiting for the ships to come in. One of my men came up and said, "Lieutenant, my family comes from a long line of moonshiners up in the Alleghany Mountains. I've found one of these Japanese wooden tubs and some cornmeal and yeast and so forth, and I can make us up a very nice batch of mash." And I said, "Well, that sounds like a very first-class idea."

Well, after four or five days, when the ships that were going to take us from there arrived, it was still brewing and not quite finished. So we decided rather than to waste this, we would sample it. Everybody dipped their canteen cups in, and it was still bubbly and working, but obviously there were quite a bit of alcohol in it. By the time these soldiers that were on the ship began to come through, here were these skinny marines staggering around. And you could tell by the looks on their faces: "What on earth have we gotten into?"

One of my best marines, the Cajun boy that I called 'Little Beaver,' was lying down on the ground and he was mumbling, "Don't let me miss the ship. Don't let me miss the ship." We loaded up and the ships stopped at Efate, and there was an officer's club there. The officers got off the ship, and for the first time we went in and had some drinks. It was then that we felt like we were really in civilization; everything in the club was clean and nice.

> *Feb. 14, 1943—At Sea*
> *Dearest Mother,*
> *For the last few days there hasn't been a chance for me to write. I don't know yet whether we will be allowed to write about our next station or not, but I will say that everyone is looking forward to it with pleasure. The boys have done some good work and the last 13 ½ months haven't been any too easy.*
> *The other day in a news broadcast it was mentioned that some Senator wants MacArthur to run for Pres. in 1944. I really hope that the people at home have more sense than to make a mistake like that. I doubt very seriously that there are very many, if any, men who can take Roosevelt's place during the war. Certainly MacArthur isn't one of them.*
> *We have all been discouraged by the showing that the Army has made, except for a few units it has been very poor, this statement isn't inspired by professional jealousy either. The Navy has certainly done, and is doing, a wonderful job though. You will never hear a Marine who was in this area say anything against the Navy. The Air Corps is doing a good job too.*

We didn't have much regard for [General Douglas] MacArthur, we called him "Dug-out Doug." We thought highly of the navy. Yes, we were pissed off that they did not bring in the supplies, pulling out early before supplies could be unloaded, but the carrier air force and the navy people with us, the chaplains, Seabees, and corpsmen, we considered very beneficial and as I mentioned earlier, almost like marines. We developed a great appreciation for our aviators, both marine and navy. We didn't see a lot of army aviators, but we appreciated them all. We called it the Cactus Air Force, and actually we believed that they had saved our butt. They attacked the Japanese ships that were bringing in reinforcements and actually did a lot more to the Japanese Navy than our own surface navy did. We watched dogfights. There was never a doubt amongst us that our pilots were better than the Japanese.

It wasn't until we were aboard ship that we were told we were headed for either Australia or New Zealand. Then shortly after it was settled that we were going to New Zealand. For the first time, everyone was paid. We had five or six months of pay, and so gambling games started all over the ship.

On one of the ships, I found out later that as people won, the games got fewer and fewer. In other words, people were losing all their money and could no longer play. This one marine wound up winning practically all the money that was on the ship. He threw away everything in his pack in order to hold the money. When we got to New Zealand, he went to one of the smaller hotels and rented an entire floor and gave the hotel owner that pack full of money and told him, "I'll have identification cards for all the people in my company. I want you to keep that floor available for them and keep beer available until we leave or the money runs out." So, a good guy who had several thousand dollars. His company then had a great place to hang out, drink beer, and take their girlfriends.

Roy Holland Elrod—boot camp, September, 1940.

Boot camp platoon, Elrod is first on the left, second row from the top.

Elrod collection

Eighth Marines on 180 mile, Southern California, April 1941.

Elrod collection

Marines pulling the older variant of the 37-mm antitank gun at M-Range, Camp Elliott, California, 1940–1941.

ELROD COLLECTION

Colonel Henry P. "Jim" Crowe, later in his career. Note the remarkable, by Marine Corps standards, mustache.

OFFICIAL USMC PHOTO

M3A1 37-mm anti-tank gun.

Marines help themselves to Japanese food stores at Guadalcanal.

Elrod with war correspondents at Guadalcanal Matanikau River position observing blasted Japanese tanks along the beach. Elrod is far right.

ELROD COLLECTION.

Elrod's position—on ridge to far right at the Matanikau on Guadalcanal during January 1943 fighting.

ELROD COLLECTION

Marines attack up the road—area near the Matanikau, up which Elrod's platoon fought in January 1943.

Japanese propaganda taken from a Japanese body, Guadalcanal.
Evidently this Japanese soldier had fought against the Australians, as
that is who the propaganda is aimed at.

First Lieutenant Roy Elrod, Wellington, New Zealand, 1943.

Major General Julian C. Smith, USMC, commanding general Second Marine Division at Tarawa.

OFFICIAL USMC PHOTO

Elrod (left) with businessman Charlie Prevost and best friend Captain Blair Nelson in New Zealand.

Some of Elrod's Marines in training at Wairoo, New Zealand.

ELROD COLLECTION

Elrod (center) with friends Melvin Seltzer (left) and unidentified Marine officer (right) at Wairoo, New Zealand.

Second Lieutenant Harvel Moore in New Zealand. He had been an enlisted man in Elrod's platoon at Gluadalcanal and Elrod recommended him for commission. Killed third day at Tarawa.

Elrod collection

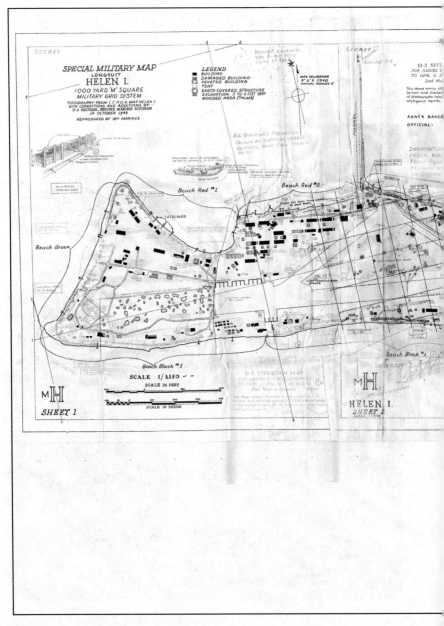

Tarawa map that Elrod carried during the battle. It has his own markings he made as he attended pre-invasion briefings.

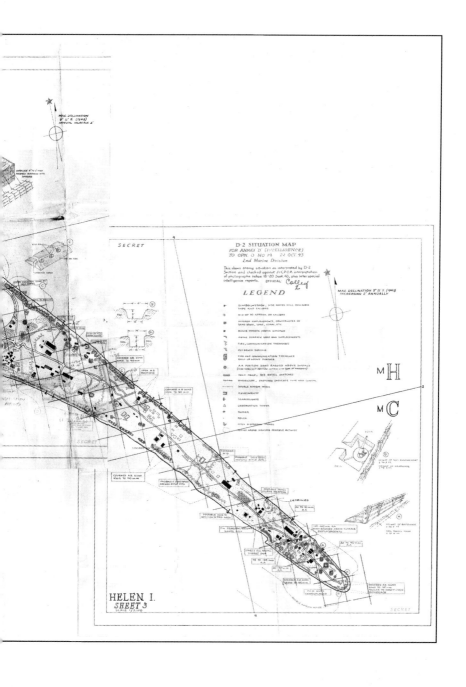

Major Henry P. Crowe on the telephone at his "command post" at Tarawa.

First Lieutenant Alexander Bonnyman Jr. Medal of Honor recipient at Tarawa.

Official USMC photo

Bombproof attack, Tarawa.

Marines overlook battlefield, 37-mm antitank gun in the foreground.
Official USMC photo

WITH MARINES ON TARAWA—Lt. Cecil Brown, 27, of Tallassee, Ala., holding his rifle (left, above), and Lt. Roy H. Elrod, 24, of Mulshire, Tex. (right), are among U. S. Marines gathered on a pier on Tarawa Island in the Gilbert group of the South Pacific after the victorious battle in which they captured the island Nov. 20. At Tarawa, the Marines are said to have suffered the largest casualties in their history. (Associated Press photo.)

Newspaper clipping of Elrod (right) and fellow Marine officer Lieutenant Cecil Brown. Elrod warned his mother in a letter home about this picture. He said it "won't be very good looking as my face was pretty dirty."

ELROD COLLECTION

Elrod (left) and Seltzer on liberty, Hawaii, 1944.

Pre-invasion bombardment at Charan Kanoa, Saipan.

OFFICIAL US NAVY PHOTO, #80-G-238357 NATIONAL ARCHIVE

US Marine 75-mm halftrack in the attack at Saipan.

OFFICIAL USMC PHOTO

Japanese reinforced cave at Saipan.

OFFICIAL USMC PHOTO #83566

Garapan, Saipan, being shelled by marine artillery.
OFFICIAL US NAVY PHOTO, #USMC 84911, NATIONAL ARCHIVES.

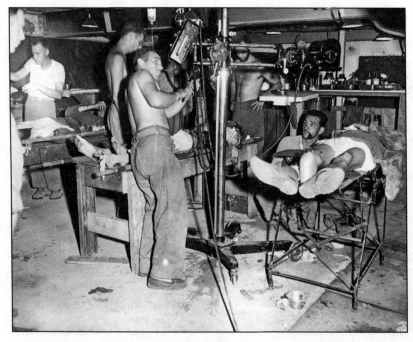

Saipan field hospital.

Captain Roy Elrod (right) receives his Silver Star for action at Guadalcanal from the US Navy commander of the U.S. Navy hospital, San Diego, California, 1945.

ELROD COLLECTION

Malda Chandler, 1944, as a flight instructor, Ft. Stockton, Texas.
Married Roy Elrod, December 1945.

ELROD COLLECTION

Roy H. Elrod shortly before his death in December 2016.

PHOTO COURTESY OF STEVE HANSEN

CHAPTER SIX

New Zealand: Paradise Found

The Eighth Marines were relieved by army units and began a withdrawal from Guadalcanal on 31 January. They sailed to a rest and recovery camp near Wellington, New Zealand. It was a premier location, paradise-like, for the marines who had endured Guadalcanal and indeed a primitive environment in Samoa before Guadalcanal. As Elrod noted in a letter, he had not slept in a bed or even sat in a chair but a few times in the 13½ months since leaving San Diego. Elrod and the Regimental Weapons Company sailed aboard the USS Crescent City (APA 40) and arrived at New Zealand on 6 February. These marines had suffered not only from combat but also from the extremely unhealthy condition.[1]

Before we left Guadalcanal, I, along with two of my marines, went up to the battle area by the Matanikau. We took four empty sandbags and picked up four Japanese skulls and eight thighbones. On the way to New Zealand,

---

1 This chapter relies on Henry I. Shaw, Jr., Bernard C. Nalty and Edwin T. Turnbladh, *History of U.S. Marine Corps Operations in World War II, Vol. 3, Central Pacific Drive* (Washington, D.C.: Historical Branch, G-3 Division, Headquarters, U.S. Marine Corps, 1966).

I got permission from the captain of the ship to go down in the hull any time I chose so that we could maintain our guns and vehicles. We tied a skull and crossbones on the radiator of each Jeep. I knew we were going to Wellington, and I knew there would be a parade through the town. I felt arriving there with skull and crossbones on the front of our Jeeps would set the proper tone. I felt like a warrior and wanted to show that we were a different kind of group. When we reached our camp on New Zealand, we removed the bones. We threw the thighbones into the garbage but the regimental staff wanted the skulls. They sawed them off above the eyeholes and used the brain pans as ash trays in the regimental mess.

> *Feb 26, 1943*
> *Dearest Mom,*
> *Well I have reached my destination safely. We have been here several days now. I sure am glad to see a little civilization for a change. I don't know yet if I am allowed to say where we are, but it is one of our rest areas. The boys needed it too, this campaign hasn't been an easy one. The people are sure friendly here, especially the women, most of the men have been gone for a long time. I enjoy seeing healthy clean little kids again too. We are getting our first milk and fresh vegetables for over a year too, I am gaining back my lost weight about a pound a day.*

There was a parade at Wellington, and more. Our ship arrived mid-afternoon, and a delegation of three women came to the ship and announced that they were having parties dockside, and they wanted the marines to come to the parties. I went off the ship and went to one. The mothers seemed to want to hook their daughters up with marines. The Fifth Marines had gone through there while they changed the loads on the ships before they went to Guadalcanal, so they had seen some marines.[2] I met a girl at this party, and apparently the young ladies were as interested in intimacy as the marines were. She lived not far away. She said she was actually a caregiver and housekeeper for an older couple. So, when we got to her house, she said they're probably still up. They had their car parked in a shed-like garage because of the shortage of gasoline. We went in the car and we were intimate. The girl went in the house and I walked back to the ship. I felt like this was going to be a great place to be.

After Guadalcanal, the New Zealanders had the notion that we had saved them from the Japanese. They felt very vulnerable as the only thing between them and the Japanese was some water. A girl I dated there for a good while had been provided cyanide pills by her mother to take if the Japanese were to invade. She incidentally was a corporal in the New Zealand Auxiliary Force and served as a driver for a New Zealand brigadier general. All their young men had been gone for several years, fighting Rommel over in the desert. There were just old men, wounded veterans and young boys, barely 17 years old, who were training to go as replacements. Young men were in very short supply. Well, the next day we unloaded, and we made the parade.

---

2   The Fifth Marines and other parts of the First Division had come through New Zealand for only about a month, June-July, prior to their invasion of Guadalcanal which occurred in August 1942.

Afterwards we drove out to a place called Paekakariki, which was about twenty miles northwest of Wellington. They had a camp set up for us there. There were tents that probably had been left there by the Fifth Marines before they went to Guadalcanal. I teamed up with another lieutenant in my company, Melvin Seltzer, and we lived in a little pre-fab hut that they [the New Zealanders] had made for their own troops. They were barely big enough for two cots, some two-foot lockers, and we had a little kerosene stove. Crowe was up to his usual speed. It wasn't long before he had gotten a couple of small, crude buildings for mess halls, one for the sergeants and officers and one for the troops. He also got a little four-room house for the officers to live in. We had only been in New Zealand for a month or so when he was promoted to major and was given command of the Second Battalion of the Eighth Marines.

During that period of time, they sorted out the worst cases of malaria and sent them back to the States—malaria, dengue, and the other things. All of us were in very bad physical condition. We did virtually nothing except try to get well during those first two to three months. Everyone was eating like wolves. We were literally recovering from starvation. My normal breakfast was five fried eggs; either bacon, ham, or sausage; toast; and two or three glasses of fresh milk. We had a corporal whose father had been a green grocer in New York City. Major [George D.] Rich, [company commander who had taken over after Crowe was promoted and became a battalion commander], said, "Why don't the officers and the sergeants all contribute a little bit of money every payday to this private, soon to be corporal, [John M.] Othites, and let him drive around over the countryside and buy up little extra goodies from the different farmers." He was second generation Greek and was a very good bargainer. Our company was drinking over fifty gallons of milk a day. During that period of time, the Second Division averaged about 1,200 men a day in the hospital. Most of these were malaria cases.[3] They discovered also that some marines had picked up filariasis or elephantiasis. The legs, the arms, and the scrotum would swell. The worst cases were sent back to Crater Lake, Oregon.

This was the first time the Second Division had been together since it was first authorized. We had the Second Marines, the Sixth Marines, the Eighth Marines, and the Tenth, which was the artillery battalion. We didn't do much training [initially], just enough to keep discipline. Then we began to receive replacements because we had been at 50 percent strength or less. As soon as we had gotten most of our replacements, we started in the normal training cycle. During those first few months my old platoon sergeant, Raymond Clarke, was promoted. He had been promoted to gunnery sergeant, and then he was made warrant officer. I got a new platoon sergeant who had arrived in the company in San Diego shortly after I did, Staff Sergeant Louis [H.] Ramsey. He had joined the regiment in San Diego shortly before the war. We had General Julian [C.] Smith assigned as the division commander. He was a two-star general. He commandeered one floor of the Windsor Hotel for division headquarters; he and the division staff and the enlisted that were assigned to the division headquarters all lived in that hotel. General Smith was always out and around. You would see him two or three times a week. He did his real

---

3   The Second Marine Division was truly wracked with illness. It arrived at Wellington with 12,500 diagnosed cases of malaria.

best for the men; He was well liked. Everybody familiar with him called him "Uncle Julian." Not to his face of course. He was a small man, very meek in appearance, but he had a will of iron.

> *March 11, 1943*
> *Dearest Mom,*
> *Several of your letters have reached me in the last few days, so I will whip out an answer.[4] We aren't working now but are getting liberty and rest. The people are very friendly here, especially the women.[5] They aren't quite all up to the same par with American women though. I am going with one girl who is about 5'7", 125 [pounds], very black hair and almost blue eyes, also a pretty figure. She's*

---

4   Roy had received a body of letters from home written on the occasion of his twenty-fourth birthday, 23 June 1943.

5   Roy notes the friendliness of the New Zealand women. This was a result, as he says, of the dearth of young New Zealand men who had been sent off to fight. "Suddenly, in strolled the Americans: all smiles, perfect teeth, and looking like Clark Gable. Their uniforms were smart and well-tailored (at least by comparison with the New Zealanders'"baggies'). They had money (about £5-$400—a week in pay, about twice what New Zealand soldiers were paid and similar to the average wage for civilian New Zealanders, who had to cover their living costs), and they were looking for fun. Their lucky date could expect taxi rides, meals out, exciting new tastes such as ice-cream sodas or cocktails with Manhattan names, evenings spent dancing wildly to bands or snuggling up at the movies, and a gift of nylons to clinch the deal. There might even be trips away to see the tourist sights. And next day there would be a thank-you bouquet of flowers or a box of chocolates. The Americans brought excitement and glamour.... They also brought good manners. New Zealand women were used to men who paid little attention to female needs. In pre-war New Zealand, society had been highly segregated by gender. Many men felt easier in the company of the boys from the scrum or their mates in the bar. The visitors, however, had a charm that flattered. They doffed their hats, were openly appreciative of good looks, and were concerned about a woman's comfort. Their talk had an optimism and easy confidence that was attractive. How pleasant was that phrase which flowed from their lips, 'Thank you, Ma'am.' It was not surprising that many Kiwi girls found themselves falling in love." http://www.nzhistory.net.nz/war/us-forces-in-new-zealand/yankee-boys-kiwi-girls

about the prettiest one I have seen here.

Myself and 3 other officers have rented a furnished house in town, so we are catching up on a lot of the comforts and things we had missed out on. The place here reminds me a lot of Diego (I mean the country) not the town.

Mom regardless of what the papers and radio say we Marines didn't leave the Islands until Feb and everything was about finished. I don't know what they have been telling you back there, but everyone who writes me says they expect us back soon. You can expect the Marines back about 6 months to a year after the war is over. Except for a few individual cases. We are veteran troops and are needed badly out here.

Everyone was living well in New Zealand. There were three of us that had decided because of the scarcity of hotels and so on that we needed to get a house in town when we were on liberty. I had started dating this girl, Joy. She said that her mom would be willing to rent their house. They had some other place to live and probably needed the money. So we rented this house in Wellington at 263 Coots Street. It had three bedrooms, a bath, a kitchen, a living room, dining room; it was very, very comfortable. We made a deal with the lady next door to clean the house for us. Now we had a nice place to take our ladies, to party, whatever. My girl's mom was always most appreciative of American items I could obtain for them that were in short supply in New Zealand. Things like fruit juices, American cigarettes, and, interestingly, toilet paper. The New Zealand toilet paper was not high quality, so when I came to visit I would bring a couple of rolls of toilet paper.

One of the officers I shared this house with was Captain [Gordon] Blair Nelson,[6] the other was Captain Bob Oddy.[7] I was a first lieutenant. Marines tended to give one another nicknames. I called Nelson "Blair the Neltz," and Oddy "Robert the Odd." My nickname was "Roy the Rod" (a take-off on Elrod or El Rod). We paid for the rent three ways. It wasn't a whole lot as I recall. Nelson could play the piano. He was quite a wheeler and dealer. He went to music stores to rent a piano but was not having any success until he told a sob story to this one music store owner. The store owner let him rent his daughter's piano during the time we were there. So we had a piano. And then, somehow, he also made connections with a New Zealander named Charlie Prevost, who said that he was a wool comptroller for New Zealand. He had two cars: a big, old four-door sedan Packard and a small car. Their gasoline ration was severe, probably five or six gallons a month, so he couldn't drive the Packard. The deal we made with him was that we would keep him supplied with gasoline for the small car, and

6 Nelson survived the war. Elrod said that he had elephantitis and was evacuated to Crater Lake, Oregon, before the Eighth Marines shipped out for Tarawa. He married a Canadian girl and eventually moved to Saskatchewan, and worked in broadcasting with the Canadian Broadcasting Company; he was inducted into the Canadian Broadcasting Hall of Fame. Married to Mary Murphy for sixty-two years, he raised a large family of six children, and was a civic leader in Saskatoon. He and Elrod kept in touch, mainly exchanging Christmas cards until he died in 2012 at the age of ninety-four.

7 Oddy married a New Zealand girl after the war and remained in the Marine Corps. During the Tarawa battle he was the executive officer of Lawrence Hays' First Battalion, Eighth Marines. He served as an infantry officer in Korea and Vietnam and retired as a colonel in 1966 after twenty-six years active duty. He died in January 2016 at the age of ninety-seven.

we would use the Packard. Now we not only had a house, we had transportation.

> *August 2, 1943*
> *Dearest Mom,*
> *The reason this letter is delayed is that I have been away for a week with a deer hunting party. Two officers and myself took a group of the men up in the hills to hunt. We killed several deer and a lot of wild hogs. The venison sure tasted good. The hunt was a lot of fun for a change.*
> *This weekend I went to a wedding and last week one of our company officers was married. In fact quite a large number of the boys are.*[8]

The sheep ranchers wanted the marines to come and hunt deer and wild pigs. Everything that the New Zealanders had in the way of ammunition was going to their troops in North Africa, so these people hadn't been able to shoot the game. I made several trips, sometimes as long as three or four days, out to these various ranches and shot deer or pigs. We had gotten a new regimental commander, [Colonel Elmer E. Hall]. I thought it would be nice to get on the good side of him, so I gave him about a 90-pound little wild sow that I killed. He was tickled to death about that.

When we began training, we started out with just the very basic training. The place at "Piecock," short for Paekakariki, was a New Zealand national park. So there was plenty of room for us to have weapons training there. Staff Sergeant Ramsey and

---

8   Nearly 600 Marines of the Second Marine Division took New Zealand wives during their stay. Col. Joseph H. Alexander, *Utmost Savagery* (Annapolis: Naval Institute Press, 1995), p. 88.

I wanted to find some way to train our crews to shoot the 37s accurately because I had very few of the old-timers left. All my squad leaders and some of the gunners were left, but about fifty percent of my platoon were replacements.

We discovered that we could strip an '03 rifle down to just the barrel and the works and take the block out of the breach of the 37, bore a hole in an empty 37-mm shell casing, put the barrel of the .30-caliber in there, and then wedge it into the breach of the gun with wedges. That way we could fire single shots of 30-caliber ammunition right down the center of the bore of the 37. I rigged up three posts several feet apart, and then I got a small diameter rope and ran ropes and pulleys so I could have a moving target going parallel to the front and one at about a 45-degree angle. This was right there at the edge of our camp, but there was a hill behind to block the rounds. We were able to train the marines in all our squads to track and follow these moving targets. We also trained in a desert area northwest of Wellington where we had ample space to fire every weapon we had. We were able to fire our four 37s. Out here we could tie a Jeep to a sled and pull a target along at various speeds to represent tanks. We actually were able to train very, very well.

The 37-mm could traverse in elevation and direction as well. The gunner had two controls. The right hand controlled the elevation, and the left hand controlled the traverse. There was always more control in the traverse. The gunner had to become ambidextrous. In his right hand palm he controlled the elevation, and it also had a button that would fire the weapon. He could just push with the palm of his hand and continue to track.

The loader was just to his right. In loading the loader would hit the extraction lever to kick out the casing. He'd do that with his right hand. The number two man would lay a new round in his left hand, slam that in the breech, and close the block with his right hand. This required lots of training to develop the accuracy so that round would slam right in and close. We got to where we could fire eight to ten rounds per minute just as smooth as anything. All the while, the gunner's still tracking the target. If the target moved beyond the limits of track, there was one man assigned to each trail spade. If the gunner told them to move left or right, they could pick the trail up and drop them. And the spades on the end of the trail would dig into the ground and that would stop the recoil. The gun was so powerful that [when] every round [fired], the rubber tires would cause it to bounce. So it took lots of training. We did that for hours at a time. I rotated the entire squad through this training.

I kept the best shots as the regular gunners. Everyone knew what his regular position was, but he could perform the other positions, too. We had a corporal squad leader for each gun. Usually the gunner was a PFC [private first class], but there may have been a few exceptions to that. The corporal squad leaders supervised the whole operation, passing on directions. I had two sergeants who were section leaders, two guns in each section: first section, second section. Then I had a platoon sergeant. It was a pretty good, well-organized arrangement. I had four guns and there were three platoons of 37-mms, twelve guns in each weapons company, so each battalion had a platoon of 37s. The Regimental Weapons [Company] was almost battalion-size. We were far larger than the average company and were independent of all the infantry battalions. The commanding officer of the weapons company reported directly to the regimental commander.

The battalion landing teams had different attachments of various and sundry people that made them a well-rounded unit. Besides a weapons unit, like the 37-mms, it had medical people, engineers, motor transport people, and so forth. In theory they could operate independently. My platoon, Second platoon of the Weapons Company, was attached to Crowe's battalion, Second Battalion, Eighth Marines. Later in the year [1943], we had division exercises up in the desert area on New Zealand. That went on for about two weeks. This was up at Wairoa.

> *Sept 2, 1943*
> *Dearest Mom,*
> *Your letter of Aug 13 came yesterday. There were three Muleshoe papers too, none of the maga-zines have come yet but guess they will before long. Mom, did you get the flowers I cabled you for your birthday?*
> *Everything is fine here. We are working hard and are ready for any job they want us for. Most all the old men are ready to get going again.*

My veteran marines sensed that it was not going to be long until the next "show," and they were anxious to get started. About this time, in late September, Crowe came to me and said they were having a division commander's meeting about the next operation, and he wanted me to go with him. I'm a first lieutenant and he took me, not one of his company commanders, not the battalion executive officer. He took me. This was at the division headquarters building, a very nice building, at McKay's Crossing. I'm the only person in the room below the rank of major, General Smith and [David M.] Shoup,[9] who was the plans and operations officer, he was a lieutenant colonel, was there. They had a sand table set up and discussed the next operation. This sand table model was Betio Island. Of course, we didn't know that. We had no idea where or what area we were going. Division [commanders] knew, but they didn't tell anyone else, not even the regimental or the battalion commanders. They talked about the island itself. I was all ears and very, very quiet. I was in the back, but I was listening to everything. They talked about the problems of a reef. There had been all kinds of attempts to find out more about it, from old traders and others that had been up in the area—New Zealanders or Australians. There was some strong question about the tides. There was only a small window of time in late November that this operation could take place. It had to take place before the first of the year because Admiral [Chester W.] Nimitz was going to have to turn a lot of these ships back to the Atlantic.[10]

I went back and started thinking about this. Of course, we had fording kits for our Jeeps, which let the Jeep go through about three feet of water. With the size of the island and so forth, I realized we were not going to be able to land these Jeeps. I felt there was a very strong possibility that we weren't going to be able to land the boats because of the reef. Our 37s had to go in to the LCVP [landing craft, vehicle and personnel], the Higgins boat. It had a ramp on the front. I thought about this

---

9   David M. Shoup would become Marine Commandant, 1960–1963.

10   The Second Marine Division had been given the mission of assaulting and securing Betio in August 1943 when Vice Admiral Raymond A. Spruance, commanding the Central Pacific Force or Fifth Fleet, visited Major General Julian Smith at Wellington. Shaw, Nalty, Turnbladh, p. 37.

and realized that the only way we're going to get these guns ashore was to pull them in with men. So I had rope slings made that dropped over a man's shoulder with a hook on the end. Ramsey and I looked over the guns, tried all kinds of arrangements, and finally found a system where most of the squad could be hooked to the gun. For practice we started pulling these around in camp. Really, two men could pull it on smooth, even ground, but I knew it was going to take everybody's effort if we were going go in through the water over the reef.

For some reason, no one seemed to pay any attention to what my platoon was doing. Everybody thought I was a little strange anyway; I was always doing some weird thing like that. Nobody got excited about this, having my guys pull the guns around, just another crazy thing Elrod is doing. I believed that we had solved the problem of how to get the guns ashore. Then I began to think about ammunition: "What is the water going to do to the shells?" I got a five-gallon bucket, filled it with water, threw a couple handfuls of salt in it, and then I took two armor piercing rounds, two high-explosive rounds, and two canister rounds, stripped them out of the cardboard case, and dropped them in this bucket of water and left it overnight. The next day, the platoon sergeant and I took one of the gun squads out and fired into this hill outside of camp. We fired all six rounds without a single failure, so I decided that the rounds were waterproof.

With that information I was able to make arrangements for a 100 rounds per gun to be tied on the guns. The guns themselves weighed 910 lbs., and the weight of the ammunition would add probably another 150 or 160 pounds. Then I got poncho-shaped canvas containers that you could throw over your head and over the top of the pack, and you could put four rounds in the front and four rounds in the back. I got one of these for each man, that way I was able to take close to 150 rounds per gun ashore. They were loaded like donkeys. With their packs, weapons, and equipment, and pulling their part of the gun, I think they were carrying close to 200 pounds. Knowing that we were going to have to load these off the ship into the LCVPs, we made little rope slings that would allow us to guide the gun to the boat because I figured the surf would be pitching the boat up and down. In the meantime, all our troops in the division received the M-1 rifle, the Garand. That was a big improvement over the old '03. We were still wearing the old WWI helmets while we were training in New Zealand, but by the time we left New Zealand everyone had the modern helmets.

Of course, the time we were in New Zealand was their late fall and winter, and it just began to be spring when we left. The weather there was pretty harsh, cold and rainy. I said something to one of the New Zealand shopkeepers about the rain. He said, "Oh, I wouldn't say it was rainy here, I would say it was changeable." And I said, "Yea. It changes from a drizzle to a downpour." There were some other interesting things about New Zealand, like that the bars all operated on limited hours. The last one I think ended around six or seven o'clock at night, and they called it the six o'clock swill because they would try to drink as much as possible before the bar closed—both the marines and the natives. We discovered that the amount of liquor was pretty limited, but we found that you could always find someone around one of these bars that was willing to sell a bottle on the side for more than normal cost. They didn't call them bootleggers as they were known in the U.S. They called them a "sly grogger." Grog was what the rum was called that they served on the British ships, so the sly grogger. We all had our own little sly grogger.[11] Another little interesting thing about New Zealand: I always liked a chocolate malt. They had what they called milk bars; we'd call them soda fountains. I went in this one milk bar and told the people there that I'm going to make something, and whenever I come in, this is what I want you to give me. Well, I made a chocolate malt, and they decided that one shilling would be a fair price. After that when I came in they'd make me one. Once the owner said, "You Yanks are always wanting chocolate. Why don't you use more raspberry?" I said, "Because we like chocolate better than raspberry."

When we were preparing to leave New Zealand, the division had a week or ten-day exercise up to the north of Wellington at Wairoa. We practiced both assault and withdrawal. The chiefs of staff referred to the Second Marine Division as being trained amphibious troops, which was just a figment of somebody's imagination. We did get a chance to actually load into ships' boats a time or two, but there were so few ships that it was primarily at the battalion level. We had at least lowered our weapons and our troops into the LCVPs and LVTs.

The division made very extensive, detailed plans for a practice landing up at Hawke's Bay, on the eastern shore of the north island. Even to the point of hiring entertainers, who were going to put on entertainment for the troops. This was actually a ruse, meant to deceive the Japs about our destination and

---

11   The alcohol purchased from sly-groggers could be pretty raunchy. One New Zealand history site described it as "vinegary wine." http://www.nzhistory.net.nz/war/us-forces-in-new-zealand/yankee-boys-kiwi-girls

schedule. How many people this fooled, I don't really know.[12] Anyway it was a very elaborate arrangement to screen our departure, which included a planned dance when we returned.

New Zealand was beginning to have fairly strong stirrings of liberalism, and when it came time to load our ship, the dockworkers at Wellington decided this would be a great time to strike for better working conditions and higher pay. Everyone had very seriously misjudged General Julian Smith. He called in a company commander of one of the infantry companies and instructed him to have his troops load weapons and affix bayonets. They went to the dock and drove every New Zealander off the dock and set-up a perimeter. During the entire time of loading, there was not a New Zealander allowed to be on the dock. We loaded our own ships. Fortunately, I didn't actually have to use my marines on the working parties. It was primarily the infantry battalions that did the loading, so we lucked out on that. I do remember it was raining the whole time we were loading. There were cardboard boxes and things scattered around on the wharfs. The cardboard melted. The cans of food were rolling around. It was pretty much a mess. Here are these troops that have never worked at this kind of detail before, how did they manage to load the ship? I've often wondered what would happen today if our military went into a place and drove off the dockworkers at the point of a bayonet.

We sailed out, heading south like we were going to Hawke's Bay until the ships got out of sight of land. Then suddenly

---

12 Elrod doubted that it fooled a lot of people because his New Zealand girl-friend cried upon his departure for Hawkes Bay even though the official word was that they would be returning to Wellington. The division had also made arrangements for a dance to be held upon their return and sent out invitations.

there was a turn, and then we headed back to the north. We had a practice landing in the New Hebrides. This was not really a very good place to have a practice landing, but at least it gave the troops a chance to come off the ships into the LVTs and so forth. They had set up a line of tape about fifty yards inland from the beach, and we weren't allowed to cross beyond that point. We did land in surf there, not a reef, but just a condition such that the LCVPs weren't able to go right up to the shore. We didn't get off on dry land. We got off in water about knee-deep. These islands had been under French control, but with the political conditions in France at that time, these people that were in the administration of the islands were not really sure if we were friendly or if they were supposed to be friendly with us or not. That was why it was such a limited distance that we could go ashore. Now these amphibian tractors, even the LVT-2s [the new version of the LVT, called the Water Buffalo] did not have a rear ramp, so you had to climb over the side. It was however a little bit faster, a little bit bigger. We didn't have the new LVTs. They were on their way; they had been loaded on LSTs in California. There was huge concern about whether they would actually arrive in time for the Tarawa battle, because I think the top speed of the LST was ten or twelve knots. You know a 4,000 mile haul. So, there was a lot of breath holding.

During this practice landing, I don't know what actually took place, but the commanding officer of the Second Marine Regiment was relieved.[13] The colonel's name was [William M.] Marshall. General Smith appointed Shoup, who was a lieuten-

---

13   There are a couple of different views on why Marshall was relieved; some say he got ill, others say he had a nervous breakdown. See Alexander, pp. 93–94.

ant colonel, to be the regimental commander because he was familiar with the plan. He was immediately promoted to colonel.

On board the ships, here I was attached to a battalion, and really the only person I knew in the battalion was Major Crowe, the battalion commander. I was on a speaking acquaintance with some of the other officers, but I was among strangers. The first lieutenant that had the engineer platoon that was attached to Crowe's landing team was Alexander Bonnyman. He and I became good friends aboard the ship. He and I had not met before, but since both of us were sort of outsiders, we talked often, and it turned out that he had been a prospector and mine operator in northern New Mexico and southwestern Colorado—areas that I had been over. So that gave us a lot in common. I learned an awful lot about prospecting because he not only looked for several metals but also turquoise and anything of value. He was one of the last real, old-time prospectors. He was some eight or ten years older than I was. He was a little old to be a lieutenant, but apparently after he had come into the Marine Corps as an enlisted man, he was promoted to an officer. We became good friends.[14]

---

14   Alexander Bonnyman, Jr., born in 1910, was from Tennessee, where his father was president of a large coal company. Bonnyman attended Princeton University and was a "first string" football player there. He left Princeton in 1930 without graduating. He attended U.S. Army Air Corps pre-flight training in 1932 but was discharged after a few months without becoming a pilot. He went to work for his father and by 1938 had his own copper mine near Santa Fe, New Mexico. He enlisted in the Marine Corps in 1942 as a private. He served with the Sixth Marines in the Guadalcanal battle and received a field commission in February 1943. He was promoted to first lieutenant in September 1943, and assigned as the executive officer of 2/8's shore party when Elrod met him immediately prior to Tarawa. http://www.mcu.usmc.mil/historydivision/Pages/Who's%20Who/A-C/Bonnyman_A.aspx

At Sea
Nov 16, 1943
Dearest Mom,
    Don't worry about the Christmas box, there really isn't much that I need. All I can send you and the family is my love. You draw on my account and buy things for everyone. Whatever you think best. Pick the nicest one for yourself. It was good to hear that crops were good back home. The Horsleys are good people to have on the place.[15] Have they been living in our house?
    It is plenty hot, all the officers are sitting around in the wardroom with their shirts off. Of course it is worse at night than in the day time because we have to close all the ports for blackout.

We were aboard ship [the USS *Heywood* (APA 6)] for quite a long time. I don't remember the exact days, but it was probably two or three weeks because it was quite a long distance to travel.[16] As soon as we had come back aboard ships from the practice landing, the word was passed to brief the troops on where we were going. That's when they brought out the sand tables with the models and so forth. For the first time, company commanders and platoon leaders and senior NCOs were able to see what we were going to be faced with.

---

15   This Horsley family farmed the Elrod's farm while they were in California, and remained in Muleshoe after the war. A son, Lee Horsley, was born in Muleshoe in 1955 to the family and became a noted actor.

16   The Second Marine Division sailed from New Zealand on 1 November 1943. Alexander, p. 89. The distance to Tarawa was about 3,000 miles with the New Hebrides where the practice landings occurred, about half way.

They briefed us on the concept of the whole operation. Still, no one actually knew about the name Tarawa or Betio. As far as we knew, we were going to land on an island or an atoll somewhere—an island code-named "Helen." For the first time people were given word about the reef situation. There were continued briefings, practice moving boat teams up to their loading, debarkation stations, and so forth. We didn't move our weapons up there, but we moved back and forward so everyone knew where their station was and more or less the order in which they would be landing. It was on that trip when this message was intercepted from the Japanese admiral on Tarawa that he had sent back to Tokyo, saying that he had the island so well defended that a million men couldn't take it in a hundred years. And that was announced to the troops.

We primarily spent our time cleaning weapons and just trying to exist. The living conditions were pretty bad. The galleys weren't able to handle all the troops to eat at the same time so different groups were eating throughout the whole day. The food aboard the ship was reasonably good. Surprisingly, the marines got along pretty well with the sailors. I don't remember encountering any real bad weather. It may have rained a time or two, but the weather was a considerable improvement the farther we went because it had been raw and cold in New Zealand. Most of the marines tried to find someplace to sleep on the deck. In the troop spaces it was absolutely miserable. There was no air circulation, no air conditioning—only small little ports to the outside. I visited my troops, and I tried to keep their spirits up, encourage them. In their berthing area it was hot, and it stunk of body odor. The heads reeked. Everyone was running around in their skivvies. The men were sleeping on little metal bunks that were attached to a pole on one side and held by a little chain out to the outer edge, so they could be pulled up and make a little more room for troops to move around. But the bunks were five high. I remember a real broad shouldered man in there, and he had to swing out of the bunk and hold on to the upper bunk and turn over. Otherwise he would rub his shoulders on the man above him. I tried to get my men on deck whenever there was a chance to get some exercise. We did all kinds of running in place and jumping exercises. I remember the ship we were on had a continual list. It would list to starboard for a while, and suddenly it would tremble and shake and roll over and list to port. I don't remember the ship ever sailing with the deck being flat. It was just an old ship that had been converted into a transport.[17] It was pretty primitive, it was old, and it was a long sail. I don't remember how long, but it was just long. This was partly because we had gone out of our way to find a place for the practice landing down in the New Hebrides. When we finally arrived off the coast of the [Tarawa] atoll it was still dark. We could hear the naval gunfire preparations and see the flashes.

---

17 The USS *Heywood* was indeed old. She had been built in 1919 as a freighter named *Steadfast*. She was rebuilt and renovated in about 1930 and converted to a passenger-freighter named *City of Baltimore*. She was acquired by the navy in October 1940 and converted into a troop transport. http://www.history.navy. mil/photos/sh-usn/usnsh-h/ap12.htm

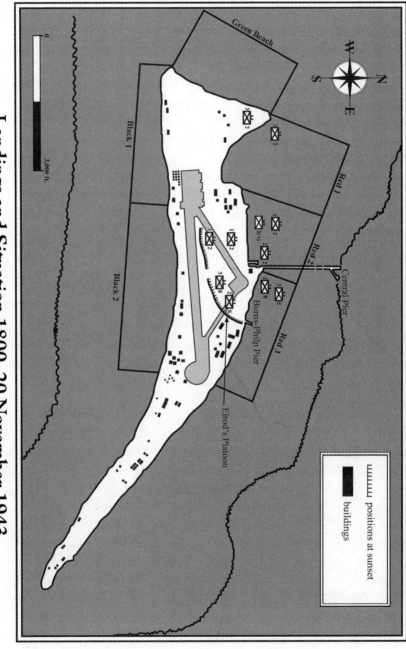

Landings and Situation 1800, 20 November 1943

CHAPTER SEVEN

Tarawa:
Hell Realized

*The battle for Betio, Tarawa Atoll in the Gilbert Islands
is one of the Marine Corps' iconic battles.[1] It was an
early and especially harsh test of Marine Corps amphibious doctrine that they developed between World War I
and II. Tarawa was a small island, a narrow flat strip of
sand about three miles long and 600 yards at its widest.
The Japanese had taken possession of the Gilberts on 10
December 1941, having occupied it in its eastward thrust
across the Pacific commensurate with the Pearl Harbor attack. It served as part of the outer ring of defense for the
Japanese empire. The U.S. wanted Betio because it had an
airfield from which aircraft could range Japanese positions*

---

1   This chapter relies on Henry I. Shaw, Jr., Bernard C. Nalty, and Edwin T.
Turnbladh, *Central Pacific Drive—History of U.S. Marine Corps Operations in World
War II*, vol. 3 (Washington: Historical Branch, G-3 Division, Headquarters, U.S.
Marine Corps, 1966); Col. Joseph H. Alexander, *Utmost Savagery* (Annapolis:
Naval Institute Press, 1995); Capt. James R. Stockman, *The Battle for Tarawa*
(Washington: Historical Section, Headquarters, U.S. Marine Corps, 1947);
Robert Sherrod, *Tarawa: The Story of Battle* (New York: Duell, Sloan & Pearce,
Inc., 1944); Eric Hammel and John E. Lane, *Bloody Tarawa* (Pacifica: Pacifica
Press, 1998); Lt. Gen. Julian C. Smith, "Tarawa," *United States Naval Institute
Proceedings*, November 1953.

in the Marshall Islands. Victory at Tarawa however had bigger significance. Admiral Chester A. Nimitz said, "The capture of Tarawa knocked down the door to the Japanese defenses in the Central Pacific." When the marines assaulted Tarawa about 3,000 tough Japanese soldiers, rikusentai, the elite of Japanese combat troops awaited them.[2] The Japanese were confident that they could throw the Marines back into the sea. Their defenses seemed impregnable, underground pill boxes, machine gun nests, and iron-enforced concrete bunkers. Coast defense artillery could hit the marines' assault craft at a good distance. Bands of interlocking machine gun and mortar fire ripped assault formations as they waded ashore. The marines had a long wade in to shore. A reef banded the island about 600–800 yards out from shore and it kept the landing craft, Higgins boats carrying marines, from getting their load of troops to the beach. Only the new amphibious assault vehicles (AAVs—other names included "amtracs" [amphibious tractors] and LVTs [landing vehicle, tracked]) that could crawl over the reef deposited their loads directly on the beach. The marines only had enough of these for the first three waves. The marines in the Higgins boats had to wade ashore through the lagoon of knee- to- chest- high surf, all the while exposed to Japanese fire. The severe test of Tarawa provided plenty of lessons learned for later amphibious assaults. Most importantly it proved that a defended beach could be conquered, a concept that many believed at the time was impossible. But it took

---

2   In addition to these combat troops, there were 2200 supporting personnel and construction workers, many of whom were Korean laborers. Sometimes the *Rikusentai* are called Japanese marines, though this is not an official designation. Nevertheless, their mission was very marine-like. They were a light infantry force and served as a Special Landing Force for the Japanese navy to seize and occupy small Pacific islands. Many of the *rikusentai* at Tarawa were veterans of earlier combat episodes. Alexander, p. 22–25.

the guts and determination of marines to bear it out. The Marine Corps suffered slightly more than 3,400 casualties. One-third were killed in action in the three-day battle. There were seventeen Japanese soldiers who survived.

It was one of the Corps' bloodiest battles, vicious close quarter combat. Unit cohesion broke down, and individual marines or small groups took it upon themselves to press forward. There was no retreat for either side, no way off the islands. The only way off was in victory or in death.

We had reveille at about four o'clock, but we had been up and dressed before the wake-up call.[3] We were about six miles off the entrance of the atoll. We had been briefed about the approach. We went off into our boats. We knew what order we were going to be landing. They would say, "Boat team number [so and so], up to your debarkation station." Knowing how we were going to have to unload or load into the landing craft, LCVPs, I had devised rope slings for my 37-mm guns. The slings fitted under each tire, and these had a rope that extended up to a central hook on the ship's hoist and allowed the gun to be lowered into the boat. Another long rope hung down into the boat from the gun, and the troops who had gone into the boat first could use this rope to guide it in. The gun would come over the side, and we were able to make the loading easy. That was my own idea, I don't know what the other 37-mm gun platoons did.[4]

---

3   Loading of troops commenced at 0425, USS *Heywood* Action Report, November 29, 1943, U.S. Marine Corps History Division, Archives, Quantico, VA, hereafter USS *Heywood* Action Report.

4   The LVTs (landing vehicle tracked, amphibious tractors [amtracs]) that carried troops and equipment ashore had no ramp; everything and everyone went over the side. The 37-mm were much too heavy to heave over the side. At least one

Each gun crew was in its own boat. The way I set this up, I was in the number one boat, which would be on the right. I had a section sergeant on the number two boat, another section sergeant on the number three boat, and then my platoon sergeant, Staff Sergeant Louis Ramsey, on the number four boat. So, I had a sergeant in each boat except mine, with the corporal squad [one gun and its crew] leaders and the gun. I did not load our Jeeps, the prime movers for the guns. There was room in the Higgins boats for them, but I didn't think they could get over the seawall or through the surf. The water was too deep, the fording kits—special kits put on a Jeep's engine to allow it to operate in water—would not have worked in water over about 30 inches or three feet in depth. Because of that I never intended to use my Jeeps, and I did not have them loaded.

I had an advantage that others did not have because I had heard that briefing back in New Zealand and had a good idea of the conditions. As I mentioned earlier, I had decided that the only way we were going to get our guns ashore was to pull them ourselves, and we had made rope slings for every member of the gun squad. I had also made special preparation to carry as much ammunition as possible. I felt that I had done every thing conceivable to get us ashore successfully.

---

battalion had difficulty loading the 37-mms into the LCVPs, or Higgins boats. The USS *Sheridan* (APA 51) reported that it had "difficulties" because of "faulty planning for the boating of LCVPs, 37mms, jeeps, and cats…" Then there was the problem of the reef for the gun crews that made the assault in LCVPs, the dearth of 37-mms involved in the action indicates that the reef probably inhibited most crews from getting their guns ashore. Report on LONGSUIT Operation, USS *Sheridan* (APA 51), U.S. Marine Corps History Division, Archives, Gray Research Center, Quantico, VA. Other 37-mm gun platoons might have had trouble loading their guns. Report on LONGSUITS Operation, USS *Sheridan*, U.S. Marine Corps History Division, Archives, Quantico, VA.

I do not know of any other 37-mm guns that made it ashore. I did not see any others in action at Tarawa.[5] I had heard that Bob Sherrod wrote that on the second or third day he saw two Jeeps pulling 37s down the pier. Knowing what the conditions of the pier was, I don't believe that's the case. The pier after the first day was covered up with boxes of food, crates of ammunition, and other supplies.[6] There's no way in the world a Jeep could have gone down that pier. I never saw another 37-mm in action during the battle, and I have always believed my guns were the only ones to make it ashore.

During the loading transports shifted location because the navy had become convinced there was a submarine near. Anyway, the transports went out to sea and left some troops floating around in the Higgins boats. I don't know if this is what happened to me, but I know that we floated around in a Higgins boat for a long time.[7] We joined up with other units

5   The 37- mm guns of the different battalions played a minor, if any role at all in the operations of the other battalions. The Second Battalion, Second Marines reported: "The 37-mm gun crews were used as infantry and the breech blocks of the guns were removed and hidden. Two guns however were set up in the triangle and we lost five men out of six men. It was reported that these guns fired on some targets." A marine, Dexter E. Greer, from this battalion's 37-mm platoon wrote in 2008 that when the ramp went down on his landing craft, "the gun tumbled out and sank in about twelve feet of water. That was the last we saw of our 37-mm gun." (Author's files Quantico, VA). The commander of the Third Battalion, Second Marines suggested after the battle that the 37-mm guns should be "left behind." The commander of the First Battalion, Sixth Marines reported that he did not "employ my 37-mms at all." See Tarawa After Action Reports, U.S. Marine Corps History Division, Archives, Gray Research Center, Quantico, VA.

6   Robert Sherrod, *Tarawa: The Story of a Battle* (New York: Duell, Sloan and Pearce, 1944), p. 101.

7   The wave that Elrod's platoon was in, the fourth wave, loaded at 0705, and almost two hours later at 0853 it left for the line of departure; the *Heywood* reported that this wave landed on the beach at 0920. Action Report, USS *Heywood*.

that were going to land in the fourth wave on Red Beach 3.[8] Sometime that morning is the first time we were told the first three waves were going to be in the amphibian tractors, and the fourth wave and others after was to be in boats. I had been briefed on how to position my boats, and the boat officers used flags to signal the coxswains when to move here and there to position their boats. The young naval officers, JGs [lieutenant junior grade] and ensigns that were the boat officers, did a magnificent job of getting into the right place.[9] They were in small motor boats that could maneuver around to signal the boats. The scheme of forming up and so on had been very well done.

There were two destroyers, the USS *Ringgold* [DD 500] and another [the USS *Dashiell*, DD 659], that actually went into the lagoon.[10] Everyone was impressed with the amount of gunfire that was being delivered by the navy ships on the islands. The Japs had four and five inch guns on Tarawa. The big, eight-inch guns had been knocked out by the time we were

---

8   There were three designated landing beaches along the northern side of the island. These were Red 1 for Third Battaion, Second Marines (3/2), Red 2 for Second Battalion, Second Marines (2/2) and Red 3 for Second Battalion, Eighth Marines (2/8). The order of landing was 3/2 to land first, followed by 2/8 and 2/2 at about five minute intervals. See Smith, p. 1172. Green beach on the western side of the island was a contingency beach and in fact used by First Battalion, Sixth Marines on the battle's second day (D+1). Beaches on the island's south side, designated Black, were not used. Landings were made on the north side because the Japanese defenses were weaker there. The defenders had anticipated a landing on the south.

9   Guiding the *Heywood's* portion of the fourth wave was Lt(jg) H.P. Cole, USNR.

10   These two destroyers worked inside the lagoon, starting shortly after sunrise, which would have occurred about 0610 and therefore almost three hours before the Marines went ashore. They did good work on the Japanese heavy artillery, coastal defense guns which otherwise would have played havoc on the assault waves of landing craft.

in range of the island. The naval gunfire had knocked them all out. There were still smaller weapons, and the closer you got to the beach, the heavier the fire was. By the time we were aligned for departure and began the run to the beach, we were well within range of these smaller artillery weapons. My four boats with my teams were spread out over 40 or 50 yards. It was broad daylight.

I had instructed the boat teams that everyone except one man would be lying down the whole time. The squad leader in the boat I was in was a red-haired boy named [Corporal Robert J.] "Red" Rotchford. One of our replacement marines was hearing all this gunfire, shells exploding around. He said, "Red, is them theirs or ours?" About that time a shell exploded real close to the boat, and fragments came through the sides of the boat and water came over. He said, "Never mind."

When we got to the reef, the boats hung up. At the same time I looked and I saw the first wave of amtracs hitting the beach.[11] With another foot of water, the boats would have been able to go over the reef. But they hung up, and I wasn't a bit surprised when that happened.

We pulled the guns off the boats into water that was anywhere from mid-thigh to mid-chest, and we started in. Machine gun fire really began after we crossed the reef. I had no idea how long it took us to go 800 yards, but I know that's how far

---

11   Because of the delay in the landing process, it had been delayed from 0800 to 0900, the first wave of amtracs carrying the Second Battalion, Eighth Marines (Elrod's battalion) did not land until 0917. Elrod's wave was not far behind. It "landed" at 0920 according to the Action Report of the *Heywood*. Of course it had not really landed. It had hit the reef and began unloading troops. This coincides with what Elrod says, that the first waves of amtracs were coming ashore just as he began unloading at the reef. USS *Heywood* Action Report.

we went. Crowe's battalion going onto Red Beach 3 had the longest walk from the reef. We had been issued maps, and it showed the reef. I was able to measure it and knew it was 800 yards. We could see the pier to our front and to the right. The navy boat officers had put us exactly where we were supposed to be. I understand that a lot of the infantry units in later waves gravitated to the protection of the pier.[12] We held our distance between squads. As we moved in I could see that the Japanese machine guns were firing in the textbook, interlocking fire pattern. They were firing in bursts of a few rounds and then pausing. I had the idea that we would wade right up to where I could see the bullets hitting the water, and then I would hold up my hand: stop. The sergeants were all watching me. We would go right up to where the bullets were landing, and when it stopped I'd wave them across. We actually crossed three lines of machine gun fire. But there were all kinds of mortar shells and so forth that hit the water all around us. The water seemed to be boiling with fire, splashes rippling and stirring the water. In many places it was colored red with blood.

There was supposed to have been an air strike come in as soon as the naval gunfire lifted, just immediately before the first waves were to land. It never took place. During the time they were supposed to be striking there was not a single plane in the air. I don't recall seeing any of our aircraft overhead as we moved into the beach. As we waded in there was no naval gun-

---

12   This pier extended from the island to the edge of the reef was the only protection marines might avail themselves of as they waded ashore. It touched the beach where Red 2 and 3 came together. Naturally, it was tempting to move toward it. Elrod's platoon, however, maintained their position and moved directly toward their designated landing spot on Red 3.

fire. In these LVT-2s there were a few of them that had 40-mm cannons on them, and those were firing. The other LVTs had .50-caliber machine guns and they were firing. We could see all that and hear it as we came in.

My marines were pulling our 37-mm guns, their wheels were rolling. As I mentioned I had ropes, slings, and hooks that harnessed a couple of marines to the gun to pull it. In addition a couple of others were pushing against the rammer staff that had been inserted through the lunette rings on the trails, one man on each side of the gun. So, four marines were pulling and pushing on them at any one time. With these two men pulling with the ropes, they were out in front, and if there was a hole in the coral, they would pretty well fall in first. Every once in a while one of them would step into a hole, and it could be quite deep, but another marine grabbed his pack strap and would pull him up. But this kept the gun itself from falling in, sometimes it might have dipped down, but enough men were pulling it to keep moving. Really, the guns were under water almost the entire way in. Sometimes we actually could see the coral under us and sometimes not. It just depended on how many shells were landing and had stirred up the sand or coral. The coral was very, very rough. It had big holes, little holes, so you couldn't just go straight, you had to move back, forward and sideways, to get around the holes. A lot of times you were just wading blind.

There were two 75-mm halftracks. The front end of one fell in a big hole coming in, and it never got ashore. It was going in about the same wave. It had to land in an LCT [landing craft tank], which is like a Higgins boat but at least twice the size. Those two halftracks were the only ones in the regiment. The other one got ashore and stayed in action the entire time. It was used much the same way we later used the 37-mms, firing against gun emplacements and such. It was roaming around. It was amazing to me that it wasn't knocked out, but it kept operating the whole time, although it was hit numerous times with rifle bullets and so forth, but no large caliber round ever hit it.

Everybody was scared, but we kept moving. Very few people showed any problem about moving. Nobody in my unit did. I've heard that over 300 marines were killed going through the water. The marines on Red One and Red Two really took a beating. The wading in through the surf is really the one part of the Tarawa battle that I still think about. I remember how we felt. Frankly, none of us thought we were going to get ashore.

When we reached the beach, I saw where Crowe was. Actually, we came in almost directly behind where he was. There was one of the amtracs that had attempted to go over the seawall. When it turned belly up, the motor was knocked out by enemy fire. It was at a 45-degree angle on top of the seawall, and Crowe was there. That's where he established his headquarters. Crowe was very good about making sure everybody went over the seawall. He kept his finger on things very well. A time or two during the battle he would send a runner up to me, and he used his executive officer, Major [William C.] Chamberlain quite a bit. Those were the only two senior officers that I had any contact with in the whole operation.[13]

---

13 Lt. Col. Crowe was impressed with his marines' performance at Tarawa. He confided to an interviewer: "Of course, we old-timers, what we worried about was the kids. Wondering that they would just have the stamina and the guts to go in there and take it on the chin like we knew they were going to have to. We felt that their life back in this country had been an easy thing, rode everywhere; they

The seawall where we landed was anywhere from three to five feet high, and there were already casualties on the beach and bodies floating in the water. There was a Japanese officer's body there. He had his pistol in his hand. You could tell he had emptied his magazine because the slide was back. I had laid down the law to my marines that there would be no souvenir hunting. I would have like to have picked that pistol up but I didn't do it. I was going to abide by my own rules.

Once on the beach I was able to check my platoon and get a head count. I didn't lose a single man going in. I think I was one of the few platoons in the assault that got ashore with everybody. I did lose men later in the battle. There were all kinds of small arms fire and mortars hitting around the beach area, and this continued throughout the battle. It was never safe on the beach, or actually anywhere else on that island.

Crowe had told me before the landing, and he told me again once I was on the beach, to get over the seawall and start moving in. Swing to the left, move south and east. These were the only instructions he gave me. We had to physically lift these 1,000-pound guns over the wall. Other marines assisted in getting the guns over the wall and I'm sure we got some help from the troops that were there.[14] When we went over the wall, we

weren't tough at all. But I can say without reservations that there's never been a group of men that fought any more gallantly or gave their lives any more willingly than those kids did. I tell you it's just at times it worried you, the reckless abandon with which they would go into these things. They were good marines! The best! The best!" Col. Henry P. Crowe interview with Ben Frank, April 1979, transcript, p. 140–141 (Oral HistColl, History Division, Quantico, VA).

14   This event is written about in Hammel and Lane, *Bloody Tarawa*, p. 131: "Fortunately for Crowe, four 37mm antitank guns were on the beach. As soon as word of the arrival of two tanks was passed to the antitank platoon leader, the

had to pull our guns by hand across the sand. We didn't get far because of the fire.

It is hard to describe how much fire was taking place, or how loud it was. It was constant, a deafening roar. Every kind of weapon seemed to be firing and explosions occurring nearly simultaneously. The marines were shooting, the Japanese were shooting. Gunfire came from all directions because the island was essentially flat, there was nothing much to stop a bullet. Buildings were burning or in wreckage. I don't recall any building still standing. Palm trees were shattered and down; it was just a complete mess.

We didn't actually start shooting until over the seawall. We could knock out pillboxes. The gun was accurate enough that we could actually shoot at the firing ports. Our armor piercing rounds or high-explosive rounds could penetrate some of the smaller pillboxes. The Japanese had done a magnificent job of building emplacements. These emplacements were generally oriented to the south; that was the most likely landing direction. We had landed from the north, though. They had about thirty minutes when the naval gunfire had lifted and the air strike did not come in that allowed them to shift to facing north and move troops and weapons into position and dig out

---

guns were rushed to the seawall. The crews were momentarily stymied, for there was no passage through the wall. The tanks were still coming forward, although neither had fired. At length, as the tanks closed with the frantic gunners, Sgt. John Hruska uttered the simplest solutions, 'Lift them over.' There were more than enough free, eager hands to manhandle two of the 900-pound guns over the wall and forward to the southeast flank. A few well-aimed rounds stopped one of the tanks, and the other turned tail."

fighting pits or get in shell holes created by the naval gunfire or bombs. They were ready to fight us.[15] Once over the seawall I connected with executive officer of F Company, Captain [Orlando O.] Palopoli. I was going to be on their right. One of Crowe's other companies was on my right. I didn't have much connection with them. They were mainly facing right [south] against the edge of the airfield. They hadn't reached it but were attacking in that direction. Palopoli was mainly attacking east. My platoon ended up being right along the front. We started right in with my 37s, firing at gun ports on pillboxes and emplacements, primarily using high-explosive ammunition. I don't remember any target the first day that we used canister on. My men worked rapidly in firing at targets, even though they were under almost constant fire.

Platoon Sergeant Ramsey was a man I had known since we were both enlisted men in the company. He had come in with the replacements that we received in Samoa. I put him in charge of the number three and four guns, and they were facing more south. He should never have made the landing at Tarawa. He had apparently gotten elephantiasis to some degree, and his scrotum was swollen up as large as a grapefruit. He had to be in great pain, but he didn't complain at all and did

---

15   Elrod is referencing what happened due to miscommunication in the pre-invasion bombardment plan. Naval gunfire was supposed to lift at 0542 and navy aircraft were to attack the island. Both could not be blasting the island at the same time for fear that some of the ship-fired ordnance might hit a navy aircraft. The aircraft did not appear at this time. The admiral waited for them until 0605 when he resumed the naval bombardment. The aviation force misunderstood the directions and believed they were to attack at "dawn." This twenty-three-minute window when no fire was hitting the island is what Elrod is referring to. At 0613 the aircraft finally appeared, the naval gunfire stopped and the planes attacked for about ten minutes at which time the naval gunfire resumed.

a magnificent job. We were almost at right angles. He ran two of the guns, and I ran the other two. Mine were oriented to the east. We split the command because of the difficulty of moving around from one area to another. We would check in with each other a couple of times a day, but we operated independently. With our guns twenty or thirty yards apart, we covered a space of about seventy-five to 100 yards. There were a few riflemen from one of the companies scattered around in there, but we were pretty much the front line, sort of in the elbow of the battalion's [Second Battalion, Eighth Marines] line where it bent back to the west. I restricted my firing to the south or the west. I admit that a couple of times we fired to the west when we had a target but we generally did not. We knew that there were people from the Second Regiment over there.

Everything was compressed. We probably didn't move in more than fifty yards that first day. It was just a close quarters brawl really, and a small unit operation. So many officers and NCOs had been lost that individual marines would move forward or attack a position on their own. Sometimes a few marines would get together and attack. They might not have even been from the same unit. Communications to a rear headquarters was almost non-existent. Any that was done was by runner. It was so dangerous to send people that I wouldn't try unless it was really necessary. Movement was very slow, and there really was never a front line. Again, the firing never stopped, and it seemed to come from all directions. I told my people not to take more than three or four steps in any direction, hit the deck, and then when you get up, take off in some direction other than the one you were on. So, you didn't go straight to any place. If you stayed standing up for very long, you were going to get hit. It was a sure thing.

We had a lot of rounds: machine gun and rifle rounds that hit the shield of the guns. It would turn small arms fire. It was about a quarter-inch thick and a good grade of steel. The main problem was that it wasn't high enough to protect the heads of the gunner and loader. One of my marines, Joe Ault, was hit by a round that came over and into his helmet.[16] It knocked a piece of his skull out as big as the palm of your hand, leaving the brain exposed. He was my first casualty. I knew he didn't have a chance, and I wasn't going to risk three or four other guys to carry him back behind the seawall. They had to stand up to carry him. I just covered him up with a poncho. He lasted about thirty minutes and never regained consciousness. Later the same day another of my gunners was hit in the helmet. The bullet hit the helmet over his left eye and was at an angle. It went around the inside of the helmet and exited back behind his left ear. It just put a nice little indentation in the helmet and tore the helmet liner into a thousand pieces. Actually, it was close enough to his head that it made a red mark right around his head and didn't actually bleed much. But that was a close call. That was "Little Beaver" Burgess.

We were always finding targets, or they would be pointed out to us. A rifleman would contact us and ask us to shoot at some particular thing. My guns stayed in action pretty well, and fortunately I had plenty of ammunition. There was only one time I sent back for more ammunition, and that was for canister. We used it a lot the next couple of days. I estimate that

---

16 PFC Joseph E. Ault remains, as of 2016, missing in action.

my guns killed 200 to 300 Japs. Supplies by the end of the first day were coming in. The pier, by the time the operation was over, was loaded almost to the point of collapse with a mixture of every kind of supply imaginable. The beach area was so small that there was no place to store the boxes and cartons. That's why the pier was buried in supplies. It was dangerous. Anyone that went out on the pier was fully exposed. I'm sure we were taking a lot of casualties there by people handling supplies. I don't know of anyone that was short of ammunition or the necessities except water. It was barely adequate.

It was hot so the water shortage became a problem. We had two canteens each. I sent somebody back to the beach with all the canteens to fill. On the second day, they started bringing in five-gallon cans, so I would send somebody back to get a five-gallon can. My platoon was drinking about a five-gallon can a day. The entire time on the island I don't remember ever eating. We did land with two or three days of C rations or K rations in our packs. I probably did eat a can once in a while, but I don't have a recollection of it. I remember just perpetual thirst though, so maybe that's why I didn't eat much. We had to really conserve our water because we didn't want to be completely out. Where we went to the bathroom, I don't recall. I don't remember ever crapping. If we did I guess we just covered it over with sand.

It was difficult to handle the wounded. Along the atoll side of the log seawall, sometimes at high tide there was no beach at all. Even at the widest I saw, there was probably not more than ten or fifteen feet of beach. There was not much that the medical people could do there. To try to evacuate people you had to either use one of the half-dozen amphibious tractors that was still there or one of the rubber boats. I never did see one of the rubber boats that had a motor on it, so somebody would have to row or wade and push it. The casualty going out that way was under fire just as much if not more than they would have been if they stayed on the beach. As I mentioned, I had severe reservations in my mind of asking two, three, or four people to carry a wounded man because to carry him they had to stand up, and if you stood up there was a very good chance you would get hit. Many wounded stayed right where they were hit. We'd pass wounded marines, and they would ask for water, and everyone would give him water. But I don't remember any wounded crying; they were stoic, very stoic. I suspect a lot of people died that otherwise might not have. That was just a problem at Tarawa because of the all around fire coming in. My instructions to my marines were to let the corpsmen help the wounded. Your job is to man your guns and keep moving forward.

Near nightfall, the sergeant that had my guns that were on the left of my line spotted a Japanese tank that was inside a covered emplacement, but the side toward the inside of the atoll was open. They had covered it and camouflaged it to the south, but the north side was open. We could see that tank. He put it out of action with armor piercing ammo. As near as I could tell, it wasn't running. We were probably not more than a hundred yards from it and able to see it real well. He fired five or six rounds of armor-piercing into it. So, we knew we had killed the tank.

The attitude of the marines was that we were going to win. We never thought that we weren't winning. There were more Japanese bodies lying around than ours. General [Julian] Smith made the famous statement that the outcome was in doubt.[17] I have never talked to another marine that was there that didn't feel the same way I did. We were there to stay. Nobody had any intention of going back. We were there to stay, we were going to win or we were going to die there. I wasn't about to walk back out through that surf with all the rounds that were coming there.

Near nightfall I had my guns dig in. Every time we would stop for any length of time, we'd dig in. It was easy to dig there as it was loose sand. That first night and really every night, there was no let-up in the fire. There was no large caliber fire from our side but rifle, machine gun, and mortar fire. The Japanese never quit firing either. They had these small mortars, called knee mortars. They were like grenade throwers, but the round was larger than a grenade, maybe like three or four grenades. They had a gun, we called it a mountain gun—a very short-barreled artillery piece.[18] They also had regular mortars, so it was just as noisy at night as it was in the daytime. I don't think I slept during the entire operation. The Japanese used darkness to sneak around, and because there was no real front line, they often would crawl back into a pillbox the marines had cleared out in the day. If marines were still in the pillbox, then there would be some hand-to-hand fighting.

---

17   Col. Joseph Alexander wrote in an article entitled, "Tarawa: The Ultimate Opposed Landing," *Marine Corps Gazette*, November 1993, that "Julian Smith did not hesitate to call for help. At 1331 [of D-Day] he sent a message to [Major General] Holland Smith [commander of the troops ashore] reporting 'Situation in doubt.' This was alarming news to all who overheard." Holland Smith responded quickly by releasing the reserve troops [Sixth Marines] to the fight ashore.

18   This was Type 94, 75-mm cannon used by the Japanese throughout World War II for general support.

The closest call I had during the whole operation was that first night. Myself and another lieutenant who was in charge of the halftracks spent the night in the same hole. A knee mortar round came in and landed in the hole with us.[19] Actually, it hit right between us. We were squeezed in there, and the only thing that kept it from exploding was the force of our bodies that kept the striker that was on the tip of the round from hitting. The nose of the round had to hit something hard so that it would force the striker back enough to ignite the charge. He, Lieutenant [Cecil] Brown, grabbed it and handed it to me and said, "Here!" I took it and threw it as far as I could, and apparently it still didn't land on the nose because it didn't go off. If it had exploded in the hole with us, it would have disemboweled us. As it was, because it hit between us, it only bruised our ribs.

On the second day we were able to advance about 100 yards out to where that tank was that Ramsey's guns had knocked out. Apparently, the crew was inside the tank because it was beginning to smell—they were definitely dead. That armor-piercing round had an explosive charge, and when it pierced the skin and inside the tank it exploded. With tanks also, if you were lucky and hit the magazine with the ammunition, you would get a nice secondary explosion inside.

I didn't know it at the time but there were fourteen Japanese tanks at Tarawa. On the second day, we spotted a tank mov-

---

19   The Japanese "knee mortar," technically, the Type 89 Heavy Grenade Discharger, that fired fragmentation grenades or a more powerful impact-detonated shell. Allied soldiers nicknamed it the knee mortar because it had a curved base plate that suggested one might hold it against the thigh to fire it. This would cause serious injury, and one U.S. soldier broke his thighbone doing this. It actually was fired from the ground with the gunner holding the tube at a desired angle.

ing around farther back to the east a few hundred yards where there was a two-story Japanese headquarters. Both of my guns took it under fire. They stopped it. Smoke came out of it, and I could tell that the turret had been dislodged—it was at an angle. I learned later that they interrogated a Japanese warrant officer that had survived who said that we had knocked the motor out of the tank. I didn't realize it at the time. I thought we just destroyed the turret. The tank did stop moving. In fact there are pictures of it showing a wrecked tank right by the side stairway going up in that command post. So, my platoon killed two of the fourteen tanks.

On the second day the Japanese tried a counterattack. In Crowe's after action report, he said that two of my guns stopped an attack of 100 to 200.[20] Also on the second day, we began to try to do something about a large emplacement in front of us to the east. We had seen it earlier and took it under fire on the first day. It looked like a small hill actually. Machine gun fire was coming out of it to the south and east. It wasn't possible for any marines to move east because they would get enfilade fire all the way to the shore on the south side of the island. Marines couldn't advance along the south shore because the beach was too narrow. No more than two or three could go abreast. On the airfield it was wide-open, smooth, level ground for the taxiways to operate on, but no place for a marine to hide. These machine guns could sweep anything moving along there. So, this big emplacement had us bottled up. When I first saw the

---

20   This report is from Crowe to the commanding officer of Combat Team 2, Major General Julian C. Smith, entitled "Report of Tarawa Operations," and dated 13 December 1943. Copy in possession of author, Quantico, VA.

emplacement, there was a piece on the corner where concrete was exposed. At first I thought this was where the machine guns were. I fired five or six rounds there, armor piercing. It was just like chipping a hole in the concrete, it did little good. I realized that it must be very thick.

The next island to the east, Bairiki, had our artillery on it, the Tenth Marines.[21] This was one of the few times in the war that friendly artillery was firing from our front. We considered calling artillery fire in on this emplacement, but if any rounds were too long they would hit our lines. So, in this case we did not use artillery. The two navy destroyers were still out in the lagoon, the *Ringgold* and the *Dashiell*. We talked to them through an artillery spotter that was in our neighborhood. We asked for five-inch firing against this emplacement. The *Ringgold* began firing direct fire at a range of not more than 1,000 yards. We had to be very careful there because the shrapnel from those rounds came right back over us. Everybody got down and got in holes when the naval gunfire was going. What it did was blow away sand, blow away camouflage that was over the building. Then you could see ventilation ports sticking up. We realized a substantial structure was underneath all that sand.

Several times marines tried to get up close enough to throw a grenade at this machine gun facing east. My corpsman went out and picked up one of these fellows and was bringing him back to the position where my number one gun was. Then a rifle bullet hit him in the chest. Apparently, it was nearly spent, though. When he got back he gave first aid to the man he'd

---

21   This unit landed on the second day on Bairiki and fired 75-mm pack howitzers.

picked up, and then he instructed me what to do to patch up his wounds. He stayed right there, and I didn't try to probe and get the bullet out. It obviously hadn't gone into his chest cavity; I guess the sternum stopped it. I recommended him for the Silver Star, and he was awarded it.

It was the morning of the third day that Alexander Bonnyman, who was the lieutenant in charge of the engineer platoon, saw these ventilation shafts or pipes sticking up out of that building—the bombproof. He got the idea that we would drop explosives down these. We knew we were not going to do any good with this thing firing naval gunfire at it because the sand just absorbed the explosives. We were anxious to get on with it, go after that big power plant [bombproof]. Bonnyman went back to Major Crowe and presented his idea. Crowe got Chamberlain, his executive officer, and said, "You and Bonnyman get with Palopoli and Elrod, and come up with some kind of plan and put it into effect." While we were conversing and deciding on what we were going to do, a rifle bullet hit Palopoli right over the left pocket of his camouflage uniform and killed him instantly.

Bonnyman was going to tie four or five sticks of dynamite together and drop then down ventilators. I was going to cover the south side where the machine gun was. The machine gun firing out of the east side was going to be handled by F Company men. Sometime in the forenoon was when this action took place. Bonnyman had two, three, or four of his people who went with him and went up on top; they dropped these bundles of dynamite into the ventilation ports. Once they were up on top of this thing they could be seen from all over the island and they drew an awful lot of fire. They were using cigars to light the fuses, just one after another. After the first explosive round was dropped down, Japanese began to run out of the south and east entrances. We fired at them with my two guns with canister and that brought a lot of them down. I didn't actually see Bonnyman's situation as I was working the two guns. One of the Japs ran straight at my guns. We fired point blank, and he got all the balls of a canister round, and his middle just disappeared. Why he ran that way, I don't know. There was still his head, shoulders, and arms, then his hips and legs and nothing in the middle. These Japs were strung out. I would say the string of bodies was twenty-five yards long. None of them ever got away, everybody was firing away. Around on Palopoli's side, F Company, they had two flamethrowers, plus people with BARs and rifles. Other marines were firing away, too.

I didn't know until the operation was over that there were probably fifty or sixty bodies out in each one of these areas. I later heard there were like 150 people in there. When they stopped running out, the machine gun on the south side was still firing. It wasn't until after we had wiped out pretty much everybody who was coming out that we actually got to where we could take a look. When I crawled up there, there was a place between two walls of log timbers standing vertically with sand pushed up against them where this machine gun was set up. There were two gunners there, still on the machine gun. I was able to get up to them without the other machine gun shooting. I got up close and shot them both between the logs with my pistol. I left two of my marines there to make sure no one else came out. I guess they were the last two people, and they were going to die there with their guns. By this time Seabees and engineers had gotten armored dozers ashore. I went back and got one of these armored dozers to come up and push logs and dirt up and bury that door and this left it free for the First Battalion Sixth Marines to move east. Later, I found out that this emplacement was really a power plant that the Japanese had fortified and covered with sand, it looked like a big hill until the naval gunfire had exposed its concrete walls.

We saw several times Japanese moving around in the vicinity of a headquarters building, which was farther east a few hundred yards. We fired high-explosive rounds at it. Our high-explosive rounds had to hit something solid to make them explode. It wasn't a timed fuse; it was an impact fuse. They didn't explode when we fired at this headquarters. Actually, high explosive shells were not very effective at Tarawa. The Sixth Marines moving on east took out this position. The *Ringgold* fired five-inch rounds into it, and that I'm sure is where the Japanese admiral was killed.[22] Those destroyers did magnificent work. The *Ringgold* is the one that came in almost to the reef. That captain really stuck his neck out.[23] They turned broad side, so they were firing direct fire at short range.

After the operation Crowe gathered up what was left of the Second Battalion, and we waded over to Bairiki, the first island east of Betio and where our artillery had been set up. I had planned to take my guns over there, and as we were preparing to do that, a lieutenant colonel came by and told me to leave them. I told him, "Colonel, I don't know who you are, but one thing you have to know, these guns are my guns and they

---

22   This was Rear Admiral Keiji Shibasaki, who commanded all Japanese troops at Tarawa.

23   This was Commander Thomas F. Conley, USN.

go where I go." I just flipped my rifle off my shoulder, and the colonel walked away. I was still tightly wound. Everybody was tired. We were wired; we were really, really uptight. It had been just a continuous melee. This lieutenant colonel just turned and walked away. I guess he thought that crazy lieutenant is going to kill me. Crowe later instructed me to leave them, and I did. My guns eventually found their way to me on Hawaii where we were sent to rest and recover. We had to replace the barrels in them; they were burned out.

The Japanese had actually moved all the natives out. I didn't see a single native on either island. Some of the rest of the division cleared the other islands of the chain, but when Betio was secured, that was the end of the operation as far as we were concerned. In fact, all the units that were in that initial landing were badly shot up and exhausted. We had been fighting for almost seventy-six hours and there had been no sleep or rest.

I put Ramsey in for a Silver Star and he received it. I also recommended [Sergeant Thomas B.] Vann. He was the section leader of the first section. So, I had three men that received the Silver Star [including the corpsman mentioned earlier].[24]

On Bairiki there was an open shower arrangement. It was just a pipe with water, but we all were able to bathe and change clothes. We also got a hot meal there. In fact, we got two hot meals. We spent the night and then had breakfast. The next day we loaded and went back aboard the same ship that had brought us in. I returned to the stateroom on the *Heywood* I had left four days earlier that now seemed forever ago. My pla-

24   The author could not verify whether these men were ever actually awarded the Silver Star.

toon suffered eight or ten casualties, out of thirty-six. We were lucky. A lot of units were hit a lot harder than we were. We were all very thankful.

> *At Sea*
> *Nov 25, 1943*
> *Dearest Mom,*
>   *Here I am back aboard a ship, and believe me the ones that are, are sure glad to be here. By the time this letter reaches you all the news of our fight will have been in the paper. I was in the action on Betio, Tarawa Atoll from beginning to end. The thing only last four days but believe me that was enough. Our destination is unknown now but we know we are going to a rear area somewhere, maybe I will be able to tell you after we arrive.*
>   *We had a Thanksgiving service on the ship yesterday, this is one that I really had a lot to be thankful for. My luck was still good and I got through without a scratch. A news photographer took a picture of me that he thought might be used in a paper, you might watch for it. It won't be very good looking though as my face was pretty dirty.*

CHAPTER EIGHT

Hawaii: Recovery and Preparing for the Next Show

After the Battle of Tarawa, the Second Marine Division, instead of returning to New Zealand, went to the island of Hawaii for a period of recovery and rebuilding. The marines who had survived settled into a marine camp on the western slope of the dormant volcano peak of Mauna Kea. The campsite was a 441-acre piece of the expansive Parker Ranch that had been leased to the Marine Corps. The 20,000 plus marines of the Second Marine Division overwhelmed the sparsely populated region. The nearest town, Waimea, was a mere village without electricity or a dependable water supply. That all changed as the marines came in. It "leapt into the twentieth century because of the technology and plenty that seemed to follow the marines into town."[1] Marines brought electricity, running water, and a hospital to the local community and even established an icehouse that produced thousands of gallons of ice cream for marines and locals alike. There was some fear

1   Gordon Bryson, "Waimea Remembers Camp Tarawa," *Waimea Gazette,* http://www.waimeagazette.com/mar95_waimearememberstarawa.htm

that the marines fresh from the horrors of Tarawa could be a danger to the locals, many of whom were of Asian heritage. This proved not to be the case as the marines and Hawaiians developed a friendly relationship from which, both benefited. Hawaiians were employed to work on the base or support the marines in one way or another. Despite its tropical location this camp was far from being a sunny, warm tropical paradise. It was wind-swept grassland, often dusty and cold due to its high elevation. This became Camp Tarawa where the Second Marine Division recovered from the Tarawa battle and trained and prepared for its next big fight, Saipan.

They didn't tell us where we were headed, but we found out sometime along the way. We landed at Hilo on the big island of Hawaii. We loaded off the transports into boats and were ferried ashore. That was really the only port where we could land. Once we were offloaded we moved by truck from Hilo to the camp on the northwest side of the island that we came to call Camp Tarawa. We took the mountain pass road to reach it, a very primitive road that went from Hilo between the two volcanoes, Mauna Loa and Mauna Kea. Some trucks took the long way around a road that followed the coast to the other side. Our camp was to be on the western side of the island, actually on Parker Ranch.[2] The heir to the Parker Ranch had made available a section of the land for the marine camp.

---

2   Parker was a large ranch on the big island, started in the early nineteenth century by sailor John P. Parker. Under his descendants' stewardship the ranch grew to 500,000 acres by the mid-twentieth century. http://parkerranch.com/legacy/history-of/modern-history/

Our campsite was at a village called Kamuela [also Waimea]. At the time there were only about three buildings there: a little accommodation telephone and post office and a couple of small buildings. It really was a nothing kind of place.

> *Dec 19, 1943*
> *Dearest Mom,*
> *There is time to get off a letter this morning be-fore we go to church. Most of the boys go a lot more since we have been out of Tarawa, that show won't be forgotten by the ones who were there for a long time.*
> *Most of the Christmas cards and packages have been delivered. Mrs. McGee sent cookies and candy, etc. Unkie [Aunt Helen] and Grandmother sent some things too, handkerchiefs and eats. There have been several cards from people back home. I hope that it will be possible to write you about our present location before long, it is a nice enough place but I liked N.Z. better. This Christmas will be much better for me than last, we were in the lines and had been for over a month, nearly two in fact. One of my boys was wounded on Christmas Eve.*

After Tarawa I think a lot of us reflected on our own mortality. We were thankful to be alive after seeing so many others who did not make it out of there. Many of us turned to our religious roots during this time. There was a lot more interest in spiritual matters. Also, Hawaii was not like New Zealand. There were no victory parades, no parties with lots of girls. It was cold, austere, so really it was different all together, and I think in a way it helped us sort through what we had just been through and reflect on life and death. For me, I had settled this issue at Guadalcanal after seeing so many killed randomly, with no reason why him and not another. I believed that a man's days were determined by an all-powerful being. For me that was God. There was just no predicting who was going to be killed and who wasn't. Like the death of Palopoli; why was he hit and not me or Bonnyman? We were right there together. So, I had decided it was not really in my hands. Yes, I took due care, just like before. I was not foolish. I resolved to do my job the best I could and let the chips fall where they may.

> *Jan 2, 1944*
> *Dear Cozie and U Wayne*
> *Yesterday and today I have been Officer of the Day so there wasn't much opportunity for me to celebrate New Year. There isn't much to do here anyway. I did get to hear the last part of the A&M-L.S.U. game, too bad A&M had to lose. This younger generation must be getting soft.*
> *We are having a regular Muleshoe sandstorm and does that make me sore.*
> *The last campaign was quite an experience. Believe me, I am sure lucky. . . . Quite a large number of Muleshoe people sent me Christmas cards. The draft seems to be thinning them out a lot back there. It is going to take lots of them because I believe it is going to be a long war. For the life of me I don't see how we can finish it before 1947 or 8. Must close now it is time for my relief to be here. Give my love to all the family. Love, Roy*

When we arrived our camp consisted of piles of rolled up pyramidal tents dumped out and scattered around the landscape. So, our first job was to erect the tents. General [Julian

C.] Smith knew we were going to be up on the side of Mauna Kea at about 4,000 feet. This is December and he knew it was going to be cold. We had come up out of the tropics, and the marines had very little of their belongings with them. What they had been able to take away when we left New Zealand was lost at Tarawa. So, General Smith went to the army lieutenant general named [Robert C.] Richardson [Jr.], who was the army commander on the island and ordered some blankets. General Richardson said, "Well, these blankets are for emergency." General Smith was a small, mild-looking man, but he knew what he wanted. He said, "Well, I believe this is an emergency. I'm going for a tank and if the doors of that warehouse are not opened when I get back, I will open them." He returned with a tank, the doors of the warehouse were open. We got two blankets each. That tells us a lot about General Smith. Shortly after he was promoted and put in charge of the marines in the Pacific [Commanding General Expeditionary Troops].

We were very busy the first week or so—putting up our tents, getting the camp organized. I, being an old carpenter, soon scrounged up enough material to put strong-backs and a floor in our tent. My tentmate was the same fellow that I had bunked with in New Zealand, [Melvin D.] Seltzer, a Jewish boy from New York City. He was later killed at Tinian.

After getting our tents up and getting situated, the first few weeks after were primarily a rest and recuperating time. Everyone was emotionally beaten from Tarawa. Not only did we exert lots of energy in that battle, but we had not slept at all. Fighting went on day and night. It was hard to really rest on the troopship, the *Heywood*, especially for the troops. They were in the same cramped, hot, stinking, compartment that they had going to Tarawa. We were just beat down, physically tired and psychologically drained. Nobody complained about it though. We just felt extremely lucky to be one of the ones who came back.

We were depleted in manpower, too. There was very little actual training for several weeks when we got to Hawaii. We had to adjust to the climate and the difference in altitude. It was cold enough at night to require a jacket and our two blankets. Fortunately, we weren't too far from the beach. There was a very nice beach almost within walking distance, downhill from the camp.

> *January 15, 1944*
> *Dearest Mom,*
> *I am answering your letter of Dec. 27 and Jan 1. No Mom, I won't be coming home for a while yet. I am not in the least bit patriotic but I am proud of the Marine Corps and what it has done. It is my career and I intend to do everything I can to make a good officer. This is my outfit here and I don't want to leave it. It isn't just a matter of doing your share as all the papers, magazines, etc., say. This is going to last for years yet and unless everyone does his <u>share</u> and everything else he can it is going to mean unnecessary casualties. It isn't right for some to get knocked off while so many others are getting rich back home. That is the reason we are sore at the people that strike. They are just as much our enemies as the Japs and I think just as much of one as I do the other. That is what the civilians can't seem to understand. All the hardships and restrictions that every person in the States undergo, isn't worth the life of one man. These men live at the very best far worse than anyone there . . . I am not sore but*

this just about explains how most of us feel. Give
my love to all the family. Lots of love, Roy

I got the impression that the folks back home thought we
were fighting for the flag or the good old U.S.A., and, of course,
we were in the long run. But that was about the last thing in my
mind at Tarawa when peril and death seemed all around. I tried
to explain to them that the most important thing was my unit
and doing all I could to help accomplish our mission and helping other marines. That is all that mattered, and that is what
kept us so determined to defeat the Japanese. We knew the
only way we were going to survive was to kill all the Japanese
on that island, and every marine was determined to do that.

After Tarawa the concerns of the home folks seemed almost trivial. We had a hard time understanding why there
could be so much discontent and complaining. We heard the
news about strikes occurring. We could sort of understand it in
New Zealand; it was not the U.S. But it upset me quite a bit to
hear about the labor strikes then occurring in the U.S.[3] I tried
to help my family put it in perspective. I also tried to keep up
with marines who I had known or served with.

Feb. 5, 1944
Dearest Mom,
    Say Mom, did Hubert Clark lose his arm in the
Solomons or just where? That is too bad, he was a
nice kid, only about 19 I think. You remember the

---

3   Labor strife was rampant in World War II; there were thousands of strikes
in 1942 and 1943. The year 1944 set an all-time record for the number of strikes.
http://theden.tv/2013/11/29/hidden-history-labor-strikes-during-wwii/;
Robert Sherrod in, *Tarawa: The Story of a Battle* writes of the marines'"savage attitude" toward unions, pp. 114–115.

> boy [Harvel L.] Moore that I had my furlough in
> the States with? He was killed at Tarawa . . . He
> was one of the three boys I recommended for Lt.
> all of them made it and all got hit at Tarawa, two
> wounded and Moore killed.
>
> Mom, a Lt. I know who was wounded at Tarawa
> is being sent back to the State. He has your address
> and will drop in to see you if he is in Diego. His
> name is [Aubrey K.] Edmonds. He can get around
> but isn't ready for duty yet.

Harvel Moore was shot and killed on the third day at
Tarawa, very near the end of the battle. He had been in my
platoon at Guadalcanal. He did not like to wear a helmet and I
had to stay on his butt about wearing one. He was shot through
the head at Tarawa in a foxhole while cleaning his weapon. He
was not wearing his helmet.

The army had quite a few soldiers there [on Hawaii]. I never
did know how many. They had a nice big hospital and other facilities. They acted like they were right on the edge of the war—
they were driving with blackouts and so forth. We felt like we
were back in civilization. Those of us that had gone out originally with the Eighth Marines had now been out over two years.
We had seen a little bit of civilization in New Zealand. But we
could not take those army regulations seriously. We drove with
our lights on; we ignored them entirely, and other regulations.
Quite often marine officers wore their pistols into Hilo, which
was against army regulations. We wouldn't salute army officers
either. Actually, we were very disrespectful towards the army.

One of the Army Military Police [MP] sergeants had copied down the license number of one of our Jeeps that was driv-

ing with the lights on. He came to our camp and was wanting to arrest the driver. The major [George D.] Rich turned to the first sergeant and said, "Throw this man out of the camp." The first sergeant had a couple of clerks grab an arm and a leg of the MP and carried him to the edge of the camp, and "1 ... 2 ... 3!" pitched him into the street. As a result no one else came around our camp. Major Rich was a very hard-nosed kind of fellow. He didn't take very kindly to the army coming around and telling him what to do.

We still had a bad impression from the army at Guadalcanal, all except for the 164th Infantry, the National Guard Division from North Dakota. They were impressive and we considered them honorary marines. Other than them we had no use for the army. Of course, we didn't have the same attitude toward the army nurses.

> *Feb 5, 1944*
> *Dearest Mom,*
> *I have been going with a couple of nurses here (American) one civilian and one Army. We don't have as much time off as we did in N.Z. though. These are the first American women I have seen since leaving the States. The Army one is pretty nice, she is from Virginia. The first of next week another officer and I are getting a three-day leave. We are renting a car and plan to see the points of interest here. We are taking a couple of the Army nurses with us.*
> *Mom, I am feeling fine, I am staying nice and fat and getting balder every day. By the time we get home, I will be combing my hair with a wash rag.*

Right away Seltzer and I began shopping around for some young ladies. Women were very scarce there at that time. Men probably outnumbered them hundreds to one. Somehow we managed to make connections with two army nurses. We got a seventy-two-hour pass. Kona was a nice beachside town on the western side of the island. It wasn't anywhere near what it has become now. It was probably a fifty-mile drive around the island to it from where we were. We rented a car, and we took the two nurses to Kona. There was only one hotel there, and it was more like a motel. It was called the Kona Inn. Now at that site is a fabulous hotel. The morning after we arrived, I got a phone call from the regimental adjunct, who said, "Get back to camp." And I said, "We just started a seventy-two-hour pass." He said, "The Colonel wants to see you, so shut up. Pack up and get back here." So that ended the seventy-two-hour pass and all of our great plans we had for the trip. When I got back, I found out that I had been called back to be promoted to captain. That took some sting from having my seventy-two [pass] shortened.

After I was promoted there was some discussion about what was going to be my next duty. Major Rich had been told he was going to have a battalion. He and Crowe each went to the regimental commander and asked that I be transferred to their battalions as a company commander. There was some discussion. Then I was called in, and the regimental commander told them, "Either you two agree on this or I'm going to make him an assistant three [operations officer]." I said, "Please Colonel, don't do that to me!"

Somehow about that time, it was decided that the Regimental Weapons Company would be beefed up. We were given four 75-mm halftracks as a platoon. This was a captain's billet, so I was given that assignment. I had a lieutenant as an executive officer and about fifty enlisted men in the platoon.

I was excited about that. I liked the idea because I knew that with the 75-mm guns that I would be able to do a whole lot more damage than we were able to do with the 37s.[4] The half-tracks also mounted a .50-caliber machine gun on the center of the rear part of the halftrack at its rear. It also had .30-caliber machine guns on each side. So, we were capable of putting out lots of fire. I looked forward to that. This 75-mm gun had a fairly wide traverse, too. The halftrack had good communications equipment. Each halftrack had a driver, a unit commander, a gunner, and three or four men in the back who manned the machine guns and prepared the ammunition and passed it forward. The gunner could communicate with the driver, and he had controls that allowed him to turn the vehicle. The driver had the section or squad leader with him in the front.

This halftrack platoon was almost like a battery of field artillery. It had a lot of power for supporting infantry. The halftrack was armored well enough to resist rifle, machine gun, and probably shellfire. There was a shield that came up and covered the windshield and another shield over the front part where the gun

---

4 The M3 75-mm gun motor carriage halftrack was developed in 1941 to serve in an anti-armor role. The marines found it most useful in an infantry-support capacity in dealing with Japanese bunkers, caves, and other defensive positions. Characteristics: combat weight: 27,350 pounds, height: eight feet, two inches; Crew: five; Maximum speed: forty-five mph; fording depth: thirty-two inches; cruising range: 200 miles; armor protection at 500 yards: 3.2 inches of steel plate; maximum range: 9,200 yards; ammunition stowage: fifty-nine rounds; weight of complete round: 18.8 pounds; rate of fire: six rounds per minute; maximum elevation: +29 degrees; minimum elevation: −10 degrees; traverse: 40 degrees; engine: 147 HP, six cylinder gasoline power; communication: TCS radio system. http://www.ww2gyrene.org/weapons_GMC_75mm.html

was so the gunner and loader had a little bit of overhead protection. It was very well protected in the front. The rest of the halftrack was open. We were vulnerable to grenades or any overhead-type threat. The halftrack had been mounted on a standard truck chassis. They were mobile but really the weight of the prow was too much for the rear axle. We had to be very careful how we started and how much acceleration was applied to keep from splitting the axle. While we were training the drivers on how to operate them, we broke two or three axles. Fortunately, the motor transport people were able to replace those right away.

> *April 8, 1944*
> *Dearest Auntie and U. Rob,*
> *It is a rainy windy morning and there isn't much going on. We are listening to the radio and writing letters. The pecans got here about a week ago. Thanks a million. We are going back up in the mountains tomorrow and are all dreading the cold. We've heard that the 8th Marines was awarded the Presidential Unit Citation for Tarawa. That makes two of them for us who were attached to the 1st Marine Division in Guadalcanal. The only other outfit in the armed service to get two was Torpedo Squadron 8. We are very proud of it. The sun seems to be coming out. If it clears off I am going to the beach for awhile this afternoon. All my love to both of you, Roy*

We were pleased that the Eighth Marines got another Presidential Unit Citation. It seemed to be special recognition for our battles at Guadalcanal and Tarawa. Of course, nothing could really replace the marines we had lost, no medal or special recognition. The Eighth Marines began very rapidly to receive replacements and to be brought up to strength. We started with small unit training because we had so many replacements.[5] It didn't take long though before we were conducting company-level training, then after that battalion and regimental-level-type exercises.

We were permitted to move further up the side of Mauna Loa where we fired our 75s. We spent a lot of time up there. In that area it was cold enough at night that we had to put our canteens inside our blankets with us to keep the water from freezing. There was snow on the tops of both volcanoes. We did lots of live firing and toward the end had lots of realistic training, which included practice amphibious landings on Maui.

One time I was made the march officer for the movement of the entire company from Camp Tarawa, up the side of the mountain to where we were going to do live firing. The 37-mm platoon, my old platoon, was up there also. The area was large enough that all three platoons of the 37s, and my four half-tracks could operate independently. So, it was actually a wonderful place to train.

---

5   Replacements flowed into the Second Marine Division once it had settled at Hawaii. These marines were generally fresh from their initial Marine Corps training, which would have included boot camp and a follow-on infantry combat course. The veteran marines generally had little regard for the replacements because of their lack of experience, especially combat experience, a great measure of stature amongst grunt marines. The replacements generally stayed quiet, observed and tried to learn from the "salty" combat experienced marines. "As each Marine destined for assignment to a combat organization in the Pacific left the United States, he was aware that his was the same path taken by fellow marines who had fought at such now-famous places as Guadalcanal, Bougainville, and Tarawa. His sole consolation, if one was needed, was the knowledge that, although he had not participated in the beginning of the fight, he might possibly be there to help end it." Benis M. Frank and Henry I. Shaw, Jr., *Victory and Occupation: History of the U.S. Marine Corps Operations in World War II*, Vol V (Washington: Historical Branch, G-3 Division, Headquarters, U.S. Marine Corps, 1968), p. 27.

The engineers had this plastic explosive that had just come out. It was called C2. We experimented with that up on the side of the volcano. We discovered that we could take a pocket-knife and ring out a cone-shaped hole in the bottom of a block of C2 and set it off. We could actually blow a hole or split a rock with it, whereas if you let it explode without this conical shape, it would just blast the top. We came to understand about shape charges and got some realistic training in attacking fortified positions. The engineers would take the paper canister that held a hand grenade, take the lid off and put some plastic explosive in it and a cap and a short fuse. It made a sound a whole lot like a hand grenade, and the weight and size was similar. It gave the infantry units realistic training on throwing hand grenades, but it didn't make shrapnel so it was safer. You still had to be careful with it. One day on an exercise one of the engineers was sitting on a rock. Suddenly there was an explosion. We determined later that he had one of these practice grenades in his hip pocket, and the combination of his weight, body heat, and the pressure by sitting on the rock caused it to explode. It literally blew him to pieces. I think the largest portion that they were able to recover was his head. He was picked up in buckets. It was a pretty sad experience. Explosives and people together, pretty soon you have accidents.

Our main mission for the 75-mm platoon was fire support for infantry units. In training we worked with the infantry units, battalions, and companies. We could support them if they had to attack fortified positions. The engineers created simulated enemy positions and we tested our weapons against them.

The halftrack was not an amphibian. We would have to go in the LCM, landing craft mechanical-type ship. They required about the same amount of space as a two-ton truck. With our main mission fire support, we wanted to have plenty of ammunition available, and each halftrack carried a good bit of ammunition. There were compartments built into the vehicle, and I stacked ammunition inside the bed where the troops operated. With that ammunition loaded, we only had room for our own crew. We did not haul infantry; there was no room for other troops. The halftrack crew had to have room to fire the machine guns and work the ammunition to keep the 75-mm ready.

As far as tactics and battlefield employment of the vehicle, we had no formal operational plan. My halftracks were the only ones for the entire regiment. The only command I got for Saipan was from the regimental commander, and he told me: "Go where you can do the most good." So, once ashore at Saipan, I tried to find out which battalion was going to operate against emplacements and where 75s were needed, and in terrain that we could operate the halftrack in. It was somewhat of an unwieldy vehicle. You didn't have to have absolutely flat ground, but it had to be negotiable by a truck type vehicle. We weren't tanks. Sometimes the battalion commanders would be stressing one or two companies as being their main effort. We would coordinate with them. They were always happy to see us and we moved right up into the middle of the action.

We got along well with the people of Hawaii. There were a few Japanese around us there, but the Japanese in Hawaii we believed were transmitting to the enemy. Bill Cardiff had a straight razor that he had taken off a Japanese soldier at Tarawa. It had Japanese inscription on it and he showed it to a Japanese barber there at Camp Tarawa. She read it and said, "You're mean!" She never told him what it said; she just said "You're mean."

While in Hawaii, we were fairly free on the weekends. We often went to the Naniloa Hotel in Hilo, about forty-five minutes away. I had a few Jeeps and trucks assigned to my platoon for hauling supplies and extra ammunition. On weekends we drove them like personal cars. The Naniloa Hotel was another place where we butted heads with the army. The army felt pretty much like that was their place, but we outnumbered them or out-lucked them. Whatever it was, we took over the Naniloa. They quickly acknowledged defeat, and we weren't bothered by them anymore.

We got a new regimental commander there in Hawaii, Colonel Clarence R. Wallace. He came up one time to watch the practice firing; he was particularly interested in one 37-mm gun manned by the marine I called "Little Beaver" [Leroy McM. Burgess]. When the practice firing was over, the gunner stood up, and the colonel congratulated him. He noticed that he was wearing the helmet that had the bullet holes in it that he had received at Tarawa. The colonel said, "Oh, that was close, wasn't it corporal?" Beaver looked at him with a sort of strange expression on his face and said, "Colonel! Close don't count!" Colonel Wallace got a big kick out of that. Actually, I think we were looked on very favorably by the higher command, the entire weapons company was.

As I mentioned General Smith had been promoted and moved to Oahu. We received a new general, nicknamed, [Thomas G.] "Terrible Tommy" Watson. No one knew much about Terribly Tommy. The only time I saw him was when we were having our final inspection before loading out—we were going to load ship to go to Saipan. I looked down the ranks of my troops, and the sergeant of the second section had a peculiar desire for knives. He had knives hanging all around him and a machete sticking out of his pack. I never knew what he was going to be wearing for head cover. I looked and he was wearing a New Zealand woven auxiliary hat with the one side turned up with a Marine Corps emblem pinned in it. I thought, "Uh, oh. Here comes Terrible Tommy." He stops in front of this marine and starts asking him questions. I hear the sergeant say, "General, my grandfather was a thirty year marine, my father was a thirty year marine, and if those damn Japs don't kill me first, I'm a thirty year marine!" Terrible Tommy broke into a smile. He turned around and patted me on the shoulder and said, "Captain, it looks like your outfit is ready to go." I think he realized that this was a real tiger of a marine. This sergeant had been at Tarawa and at Guadalcanal. He was very salty. He was good enough that I overlooked his idiosyncrasies. It seemed that some of the better people had picked up nicknames of one kind or another. In those days everybody felt that if you were good, you were allowed to have a little peculiarity in some way if it obviously didn't interfere with what you were supposed to be doing.

We felt that we were well-trained and at this time, all our sergeants, corporals, and officers were battle-hardened. We were a pretty salty outfit to tell you the truth. In the spring of 1944 we knew we were going to be leaving very soon, but we did not know where. We got a copy of *Newsweek* magazine during this time, before we left Hawaii, and it showed Saipan with a big red arrow pointing toward it.[6] This made us all very unhappy. How the press got wind of that, I don't know. It just reinforced my distrust of the press that I already had to some extent.

---

6   This appeared on pp. 22–23 of *Newsweek*'s 8 May 1944 issue.

We packed up and sailed for Pearl Harbor aboard an LSD [landing ship dock].[7] The plan was for us to be there one night. That night though one of the LSTs loaded with mortar ammunition exploded in the harbor.[8] It was some explosion. We wound up being at Pearl for about six days. They had to fly additional mortar ammunition from the States and it cost extra days.

I took advantage of the delay. I found out that you could join the Pearl Harbor Officers Club for five dollars, and with your new membership they gave you two bottles of liquor. I joined five times, every day while in Pearl Harbor. I ended up with ten bottles stashed in my halftracks. It was against navy regulations to have booze on a navy ship. This had been the situation since Josephus Daniels had been Secretary of the Navy.[9] Rules get bent once in a while, very quietly and very carefully. After that we sailed west, we knew the next operation was near.

---

7   His platoon sailed on the USS *Frederick Funston* (APA-89). This was the newest transport he yet boarded. This ship supported amphibious operations by carrying vehicles or artillery pieces. When it was time to unload its cargo, it could ballast down, its doors would open, and a ramp extended that could connect with a landing craft to allow vehicles to roll into the landing craft.

8   This explosion occurred on 21 May 1944, caused by a 4.2-inch mortar round that ignited during unloading. It caused a conflagration that destroyed six LSTs, and caused ninety-five casualties among Second Marine Division Marines and 112 in the Fourth Marine Division. Henry I. Shaw, Jr., Bernard C. Nalty and Edwin T. Turnbladh, *Central Pacific Drive: History of U.S. Marine Corps Operations in World War II*, vol. 3 (Washington: Historical Branch, G-3 Division, Headquarters, U.S. Marine Corps, 1966), p. 252.

9   Josephus Daniels was Secretary of the Navy during World War I, and supported the temperance movement then powerful in the U.S. He mandated that there would be no alcohol on navy ships beginning 1 July 1914. It officially remained that way until 1980 when Secretary of the Navy Edward Hidalgo allowed that sailors and marines on board a navy ship could have a ration of two beers for every forty-five days served at sea. http://news.usni.org/2014/07/01/hundred-years-dry-u-s-navys-end-alcohol-sea

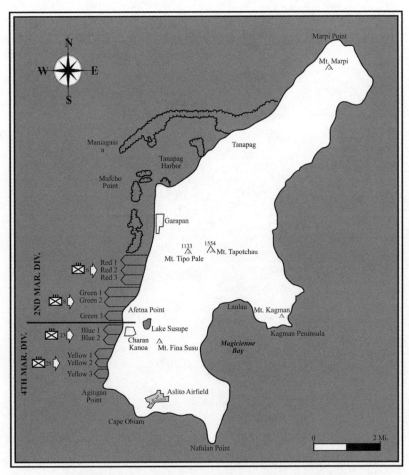

D-Day at Saipan: Initial Landings

CHAPTER NINE

Saipan: "We Were There to Kill Japs"

Even while Roy Elrod and the Second Marine Division fought at Tarawa, the leaders of the Allied nations were meeting in Cairo to lay out war strategy for the upcoming months. At the SEXTANT Conference (November–December 1943) they determined that an aerial assault on Japan, combined with submarine warfare already being waged, would bring Japan to its knees. This would obviate the need for an actual invasion of the Japanese home islands, thus shortening the war and saving countless lives. Capture of the Mariana Islands, which included Saipan, 1,250 miles from Tokyo, would put Japan within bombing range of America's new bomber, the powerful Boeing B-29 Superfortress. In light of these considerations, Operation Forager, the code name for the invasion of the Mariana Islands, was laid-on for October 1944. Unexpected success in the preceding Marshall Islands campaign caused Forager to be moved up to June 1944. The Second and Fourth Marine Divisions along with the Army's Twenty-

Seventh Infantry Division were given the task of conquering Saipan, the first of the Mariana Islands targeted.[1]

Japan had occupied Saipan since the end of World War I. A sizeable native population of Chamorro inhabited the island. In addition a number of Japanese civilians had migrated to the island and settled. Japan had also brought in hundreds of Korean laborers. What the marines were concerned about were the 31,000 Japanese troops who were ready to die fighting to keep Saipan in the Emperor's hands. The Japanese understood what was at stake. Saipan was within the Japanese inner defense perimeter, and they knew about the B-29. Its destructive power posed a terrifying threat.

Saipan was a markedly different island battleground than what the Eighth Marines fought over in its previous campaigns. Whereas Tarawa was a small flat atoll and Guadalcanal a tropical jungle, Saipan was a large volcanic island of forty-five square miles with varying terrain, swamps, sugarcane fields, jagged mountains and ridges, and a few developed towns. The Japanese were well dug in, hiding in prepared defenses, often in dense foliage. They had artillery on Saipan's high ground, pre-aimed and ready to hit marine formations. They also were ready to operate at night, probe marine formations and conduct mass formation assaults, banzai charges.

---

1 This chapter relies heavily on Henry I. Shaw, Jr., Bernard C. Nalty, Edwin T. Turnblaugh, *The Central Pacific Drive-History of U.S. Marine Corps Operations in World War II*, vol. 3 (Washington: Historical Branch, G-3 Division, Headquarters U.S. Marine Corps, 1966), p. 231–351; Capt. John C. Chapin, *Breaching the Marianas: The Battle for Saipan*, World War II Commemorative Series (Washington, D.C.: Marine Corps Historical Center, 1994).

The Eighth Marine Regiment was assigned to fight through probably the most difficult terrain: the island's middle. It was comprised of rugged ridges and peaks covered in dense tropical foliage. Caves pocked the ridges, and the Japanese reinforced and networked them so that they had multiple openings. From any they would suddenly appear, fire at marines, then quickly disappear back into the caves. It was a treacherous fighting ground. The marines never knew from where the next shots would come. Elrod's kept his platoon of 75-mm cannons right at the front. The marine riflemen were most appreciative. The 75mms had the blasting power to wallop Japanese positions and kill or stun the defenders or collapse the cave opening.

Captain Roy H. Elrod along with 17,000 other marines of the Second Marine Division departed their Hawaiian camp in early May, bound for Saipan by way of Pearl Harbor and Eniwetok in time for a 15 June 1944 amphibious assault on Saipan. This was Elrod's third time in combat; he knew what awaited him. He and the marines were ready to accomplish the mission: seize and secure Saipan. That was their job and it was accomplished by killing as many of the enemy as possible.

June 9, 1944 [six days before D-Day]
Dearest Mom,
    You have most likely been wondering about the gap between letters. For several days we have been at sea. In the next few days we will be back in action. As usual this won't be mailed until the ship returns from the target area. So you will have read about it before the letter gets to you. This is the largest operation we have ever been in and all of us are very determined to make it a successful one. Please

don't worry about me anymore than you have to.
This is where I want to be now and I am doing
what I am best fitted for.

This has been a very nice cruise, fine weather. . . .
Most of the time has been spent sleeping, reading
and sunbathing on the deck. . . . Lots of my time is
taken to give the final instructions to my boys and
giving them all the dope about the show ahead. All
in all time passes very quickly.

I have been taking off a little weight, now 182 as
it is better to be a little on the slender side, it gives
me more endurance and the heat won't be so tiring.
It doesn't bother me much. As you know I have
always liked hot weather.

There may not be a chance for me to write again
until after we are ashore. Give my love to all the
family and God bless you all. I love you, Roy

We sailed through Eniwetok. We stopped there, and that's where we tied up with most of the other divisions, with the Fourth Division and some army troops. Eniwetok had been beaten right down to the sand.[2] There were a few stumps of palm trees standing up. We spent the night there, and I didn't leave the ship. It was just a place for the other ships to join the convoy and for the ship's captains to find their positions in the armada. The next morning when we sailed, I was amazed at the number of ships

---

2   The battle for Eniwetok had occurred about four months earlier, in mid-February, and was undertaken, as was the case for other islands seized in the Marshall Island group, to support the U.S. invasion of the Marianas by providing airfields and fleet anchorages.

that were there. I heard it was something like 800. You couldn't possibly see them all; they went from horizon to horizon in all directions.[3] Our ship was somewhere in the middle of them all.

From the time we left Eniwetok until we arrived we zig-zagged and followed the avoidance procedures for Japanese submarines. It was several days cruising to reach Saipan. I spent a lot of time with my troops talking about what lay ahead, what our mission was, tactics, Japanese tactics, what to expect from them. The living conditions aboard this ship were the same as all troopships. They were crowded to the max, hot, sweaty, stinking. We exercised as much as we could, and every day we went down in the hold and looked over our vehicles, to make sure they were fully serviceable and ready to do the mission we were there for. I thought I had done everything I could to get my marines ready. I ordered everyone to cut their hair very short, only about 1/4 of an inch long. It was more sanitary. I told them if you get shot in the head it would help the corpsman. He wouldn't have to dig all that hair out of your brain. Mainly it was for sanitation. I knew we would not have a chance to take a bath, much less get haircuts, once the campaign began. My platoon was ready for the show to begin. For some it was their third operation, we were seasoned warriors. We had quite a few replacements. They didn't say a lot; they just watched and listened.

We had some British army people with us. I shared a state-room with one, a lieutenant colonel. He and I had some interesting discussions. He was there as an observer. You hear

---

3   This estimate is a good one. There were about 800 ships in the attack force. Chapin, p. 7.

that the British don't have a sense of humor. They do have one, but it's not like ours. A couple of these Brits put on a skit on the fantail one day, and they were mimicking how marines talk, and every sentence there would be at least one 'f-word.' That was their impression of marines, liberal use of the 'f-word.' I never saw them again after the landing.

Also, for the first time, we had Navaho talkers, not in my platoon but in the regiment. We referred to all of them as "Chief." The movie "Windtalkers" left the impression that we intended to kill them if they were about to be captured. That wasn't true at all. As a matter of fact, the marines would have fought hard to protect them. They fit in quite nicely. They were able to transmit messages in real time, directly between units on the front lines, without going through a lot of codes. We also had a Chamorro [native of the Mariana Islands] man on board. He had lived in Hawaii and was going back with us as a translator. He was wearing a green uniform that had a big American flag sewn to the front and one on the back. He was very Asian-looking. Though he said he was Chamorro, I think he also had a quite a bit of Japanese blood.

The assault was going to be with the Second and Fourth Marine Divisions abreast, landing on the west side of the island; the Second Marine Division on the left and the Fourth Marine Division on the right. There was a pier that went out from Charan Kanoa that was the boundary line between the two divisions. There was also a reef and a lagoon, like Tarawa. This was the first time that I heard of the underwater demolition teams or UDTs. They were about half-marine, half-navy. They were nothing like the SEALs [sea, air, land units—the modern day navy special operations teams], all they had for equipment was flippers, no snorkel or scuba gear. They went ahead of us and marked the channels for the landing craft to take into the lagoon. I also heard they blew passages through the reef.

This was my third combat operation. Tarawa caused me to think about what was about to happen. Everybody was scared. You would be an absolute idiot if you weren't scared. I found that fear was very useful because it brings up instincts and reflexes that you think civilization has taken away. They're there. You become very, very aware. Your senses just sharpen up. My own personal feeling was you're either going to make it or not. So why fret about it. I saw it as a job that had to be done. I was determined to fulfill my duties. I believe most marines felt the same. I never saw a marine in any of these battles running for the rear. I knew we were well trained. I hoped to survive, and I wanted to protect my men. But I had long determined that my fate in combat was really something I had no control over. I had also decided that I would not survive the war.

Invasion day we were up early. The ship was a beehive of activity with announcements over the bullhorn, organized chaos. We got a good breakfast of steak and eggs. I ate in the officers' stateroom; the troops ate in the galley in relays. After breakfast, I organized my platoon. It was a matter of loading our halftracks into the LCMs [landing craft, mechanical—a larger variant of the Higgins boat and built to carry vehicles to the beach]. This was considerably more difficult than getting the 37-mm guns into LCVPs. The ramp on the LCD [landing craft dock, the ship that Elrod sailed on to Saipan. It's a large ship that carried troops and vehicles, including Elrod's four halftracks] had to connect with the LCM's ramp and then the halftracks driven aboard, backwards, because we wanted the front of our halftracks facing the ramp of the LCM to drive off when we landed on the beach. There were sailors directing this activity. They watched the waves and told the marine driving the halftrack when to go and when to stop. These sailors were really good. They knew what they were doing. Some of them by this time had eight or nine operations under their belts. One aspect of this loading was easier. We didn't have to go down the rope nets or ladder from the side of the ship into the landing craft. We just rode in our halftracks. Going down the nets, like we did for the Tarawa landing, loaded with gear, when both the ship and landing craft are pitching and bucking was not easy. Some marines fell and were killed. They either drowned or were crushed between the transport and the Higgins boat. I had four 75-mm halftracks so my platoon was loaded into four LCMs. We also had a tank platoon attached, commanded by a first lieutenant. They had four Sherman tanks.

Unlike at Tarawa there was not a delay in H-hour. I was again in the fourth wave, landing mid-morning, a couple of hours behind the first waves.[4] When we started in, I used the

---

4   Elrod does not mention it but he was surely aware of the massive pre-invasion shelling that the Japanese defenses were receiving. Actually the hammering began on 11 June by a massive airstrike by navy aircraft from the sixteen aircraft carriers of Task Force 58. The air attacks continued for three and a half days (on all the Mariana Islands). Then the surface ships went to work blasting the island beginning on 13 June and continued the following days with increasing ferocity. On 15 June, the day of the initial landings, two battleships, two cruisers, and six destroyers blasted Japanese positions along the landing beaches. The shelling was lifted for thirty minutes beginning at 0700 for a furious aerial attack by navy planes from TF 58 carriers. Once the airstrike ended, the navy began shelling the island again and reached a crescendo as the landing craft approached and did not cease until the first landing craft were within 300 yards of the beach. Aerial attacks had also resumed with bombing and strafing on going along the beaches. These

chimney of the sugar mill at Charan Kanoa as my guide on the right. In this position, I was probably landing on the extreme right-hand side of the Second Division. The Second and Third Battalions were in the early waves, and the First Battalion followed in about an hour.[5] As we moved toward the beach, Japanese artillery was hitting. Some of the LCVPs got hit, but no shells came close to us. It was nothing like the shell fire that we received going in to Tarawa. There was very little machine gun or rifle fire. Their artillery was very active though. They had all the high ground, and they could see us.

I was in the right hand boat. I had an executive officer, a lieutenant, and I was very unhappy about him because he reported in as sick and didn't land. I did not know what happened to him, I assumed he was in the fourth boat, but he never made the landing, and I never saw him again. I never forgave him for that, and I didn't understand it. He had been at Guadalcanal and Tarawa. If I hadn't have been wounded and evacuated later, I probably would have asked for a general court martial. You'd have to be awfully sick to make that an excuse not to land. I had a good platoon sergeant, Staff Sergeant Edwin D. Knight. I leaned on him as I would have done with the lieutenant.

---

airstrikes continued even after troops were ashore, but were careful to keep at least 100 yards in front of the troops.

5   Elrod's platoon landed with the Eighth Marine's regimental reserve, which was First Battalion. It was ordered ashore at 0950, which was ninety-eight minutes after the first wave made its run for the beaches. The two battalions that landed earlier had landed about 600 yards north of where they should have due to strong tides and enemy fire. Therefore, there was a gap between the Second Division's right flank and the Fourth Division's left flank. It was in this gap at Green 3 Beach, that one company of the First Battalion landed and evidently with Elrod's platoon in support. Shaw, Nalty, Turnbladh, pp. 263–271.

My main concern going in was trying to hit the beach in the right place. The coxswain of my boat was a little hesitant; he kept drifting, not heading toward where I thought we should be going. I passed word up to my sergeant to put a pistol in his ear if you have to; "Head him straight to the beach!" My other three LCMs were guiding on my boat so it was important that we go to the right place. I did not know why the first sergeant, [Richard J.] Baker was riding with me, but he was. He was quite a character actually, a French Canadian and very French in his attitude and looks. Whenever he got a bit too much to drink, he would jump up on a table and sing the "La Marseillaise" in French! We had been together a while. In fact, he had been my first squad leader. Now I was the captain, and he was the first sergeant of the Regimental Weapons Company. This time, unlike at Tarawa, we were able to go right up to the beach. The LCM plowed into the beach, and when the ramp dropped, we drove our halftracks ashore. Expecting total chaos and overwhelming noise like at Tarawa, I found that not to be the case. Japanese resistance was nothing like that at Tarawa. In fact it seemed like a piece of cake compared to Tarawa. Of course, for the marines who were making their first landing, it was pretty rough. There was some scattered small arms fire, but almost everything that was hitting the beach was artillery and mortar fire. It hit near but not close enough to harm my halftracks. I was able to think how best to maneuver my vehicles. At Tarawa you only thought about staying alive.

We got the notion that they had a forward observer in the smokestack of the sugar mill, so every so often I had one of my gunners use his .50-caliber machine gun to rake the top of that stack, just to be on the safe side. We were able to move in several hundred yards that first day. It was difficult because of the terrain. Where we landed the beach was sandy, but as we moved in the ground was covered with a lot of little lakes and ponds. I was more concerned about finding a way through the bogs and soft land than anything.[6] I had my marines out looking for the best paths to move the halftracks forward. I didn't want them to go in trail of one another that would make them an easy target for Jap artillery. I wanted them spread out. We had to be very careful because the rear axle was a little weak for the weight. One of the halftracks broke an axle that first day. Part of the problem is that I had them overloaded, but I wanted to be sure we had plenty of ammunition. I didn't know how well the supply system was going to work, but as it turned out it worked fine. It was good enough that we got a replacement axle for this halftrack in only a couple of days. If this had been like Tarawa or Guadalcanal, there would have been no way to get a replacement axle. There were no shortages during the time I was on Saipan except water, and that was because the Japanese bombed one of the desalinization sites. I left two men with the broken-down halftrack. I gave direct orders that one of them remain with the halftrack at all times. It had in it some personal equipment and various gear; it also had a couple of bottles liquor I had stashed. The halftrack was repaired and rejoined us about the third day.

There was something like 30,000 Japanese troops on the island. There was another wave [Japanese reinforcements] on the way, but they didn't make it because of the Mariana's Turkey

---

6 The ground was wet because Elrod's platoon had moved into a swampy area near Lake Susupe. Shaw, Nalty, Turnbladh, p. 271.

Shoot.[7] The navy pilots didn't get them all though because it seemed like every night the Japanese planes would come in and harass. On the second or third night they hit one of the desalinization plants. For the rest of the operation, our drinking water was barely drinkable. Because there was only one plant instead of two, they had to short cut the desalinization process. They took just enough salt out of it to make it possible to drink it, but it tasted horrible.

We didn't have many targets until toward the end of that first day, and we didn't do a lot of shooting. I moved my platoon up very close to the front line infantry. The only order that I had received came directly from the regimental commander, and he had told me to go where I thought I could do the most good. He knew quite a bit about me and that I had a little bit of an aggressive attitude.[8] At night I made contact with one of the infantry commanders, and we set up in the perimeter with his company. I told the lieutenant of the tank platoon that I wanted him to stay down in the beach area because along the beach line on the coast road was the only area that armor could

---

7   Elrod is referring to the Battle of the Philippine Sea, a great sea battle that occurred 19 and 20 June 1944 when the Japanese fleet moved out to challenge the American invasion of Saipan. The fight was largely an air battle, thus its name. The Japanese lost about 476 aircraft to the U.S. Navy's 130, most of the U.S. Navy's losses however were operational losses, not by enemy action. The operational losses were incurred when the U.S. pilots tried to recover aboard carriers at night, and low on fuel. Much more effective in interdicting Japanese ships bearing troops and supplies than navy aircraft were navy submarines. This action had been on-going well before the marines approached Saipan. James D. Hornfischer *The Fleet at Flood Tide* (New York: Bantam Books, 2016), pp. 230–232.

8   The regimental commander was Colonel Clarence R. Wallace. Elrod apparently was given a lot of latitude in how he would fight his halftracks, as he notes his reputation as an aggressive battlefield leader assured his superiors that he would "go to the sound of the guns."

move about easily. I was impressed with him and felt that he would go where he was needed. I never saw him again after the first day. I heard that he participated in stopping a Japanese attack, a big banzai attack.[9]

Crowe had been wounded early in the fight, actually the first day. I was greatly concerned because he was a mentor and someone I looked up to. I heard that he took shrapnel straight through the chest. Doctors later told me that he was breathing through the hole in his back rather than through his mouth. Apparently, when the stretcher bearers were carrying him into the aide station, a shell hit and injured a couple of them. This doctor told me that he figured he couldn't live, so he put him with other people who had no chance. An hour or so later he looked, and Crowe had worked with his elbows and was leaning against a tree looking around. So, he figured, "Well, if he's done that, I'll patch him up." They put some type of patch over the hole in his back.[10]

---

9   Elrod explained that the tanks were attached to his platoon mainly for organizational purposes while on the LSD and like Elrod's platoon were not really attached to a specific battalion. Elrod said that it would have been very difficult for him to work the tanks into his platoon during the following land campaign. There was a lot of terrain where the halftracks could go that tanks could not. The lieutenant commanding these tanks evoked confidence, and therefore Elrod had no qualms in leaving him to manage his tanks and employ them well. As he explains, they were more useful along the coastal road. For instance on the night of D-Day the Japanese counterattacked fiercely, intending to throw the marines back into the sea. There were other Japanese counterattacks, and they sometimes included tanks. Marine tanks did good work in repelling these attacks. Interestingly, both the halftrack platoon commander and the tank platoon commander were given a good bit of latitude as to how, when, and where they would fight their vehicles.

10   Crowe, who commanded Second Battalion, Eighth Marines, was wounded soon after landing, on the battle's first day. He said he was hit by a 13-mm machine gun round that went through his chest and, "grooved the cardiac muscles" on the way through. He said his life was saved when the round was deflected off his

There was a road that ran from Charan Kanoa to Magicienne Bay. I pretty much followed that road, and I stayed with the First Battalion [Eighth Marines] for the first several days. That was the area that I could maneuver in the best, and also [Lieutenant Colonel Lawrence R.] Hays [Jr.] was a very aggressive battalion commander, and he made good use of our halftracks.[11]

After the first day, I began to get lots of targets for the halftracks. A lot of this area was in sugar cane production. The cane

---

pistol holster before it entered his chest. After being hit he and another marine, who had also been wounded, lay within thirty yards of the Japanese machine gun position that had hit them. He recalled, "I thought I was dying. And this is serious business. I had read where if you're dying you think of music or hear music or you feel that you're going blind or something. So, I thought well, I'll soon be hearing 'Tales of the Vienna Woods,' which was my favorite piece. That didn't happen so I thought well, my eyesight, I'm going blind, but that didn't happen. And I thought, lying there on my back I couldn't have been [dying]. And I thought I must be bleeding. Well, I wasn't bleeding here but very little. I thought that bullet, I didn't know where it was, whether it had gone through or what. But I thought maybe I'd better take a little interest in things. So I put my carbine in my hand, put my fist in this hole [in my chest]; the doctors said that is what saved me. Once in a while I took this carbine around and shot at this emplacement over there, which was thirty yards from us. [Bill] DeNatale, my corporal, lying there, pulled his left arm up and looked at his wristwatch. I said, 'Why are you looking at your wristwatch, Bill?' He said, 'Sir, I want to see what time I die.' Eventually Crowe was moved to an aid station on the beach, but he was not out of danger. As a navy corpsman rushed up to give him medical attention, a shell struck nearby. Crowe recounts: "The shell hit down around my knees . . . and it just laid him [the corpsman] wide open. Just like you take a knife and cut him wide open, and everything in him flew out against me. The doctor got hit [also], I got shrapnel in my leg. Then a shell came up and hit a tree right at my head and I had my helmet on my face, my poncho on my chest, and my pack down on my stomach. Well, that poncho, fortunately, that was a good move because four pieces went through that poncho and the rubberized thing slowed it down a slip, I'm sure and I just got bleeding cuts, no real punctures there. I got it in my arm and wrist. So, I got up and left. I wasn't going to stay there any longer, that was too hot a spot."

11   The battalion commander of First Battalion, Eighth Marines, Lt. Col. Lawrence Hays, Jr. He was wounded the first day but remained with his battalion. Hays had been in command of this battalion at at Tarawa also.

was at various heights because at Saipan they didn't have any real off-season. They allowed some of the land to lay fallow, but some of the cane was being harvested, some was growing, and some was being planted at any one time. The visibility in most areas was pretty good though the Japanese did have all the high ground at that time. We were able to operate over a fairly wide area because of the cane fields. We could also handle fairly difficult terrain; I wasn't really road bound. The Japanese had begun to learn some lessons [from previous battles], and they had dug in like moles. They used the same tactics at Iwo [Jima] and Okinawa later. Everything that had some overhead cover seemed to have Japanese in it. Some of the caves were natural and some were dug. That's where our 75s came in. We used armor piercing and high explosive shells, which direct fired into these cave mouths did outstanding work. The Japanese had also created hundreds of concrete emplacements at some time or another. They had apparently been preparing Saipan for who knows how long.[12]

This was the first time we had flame-throwing tanks. Those were extremely useful against Japanese dug-in positions. Almost all of them had more than one entryway or opening, and they were mutually supporting. It was just a continuous

---

12   The Japanese had been preparing to defend Saipan from the beginning of the war, but as their forces moved further east into the Pacific they paid less attention to Saipan's defenses. When the Allies began to roll the Japanese back in the Pacific and the Japanese realized Saipan was in danger, they worked on defenses there with greater urgency. By this time, however, it was almost too late. Late 1943 and early 1944 the American submarine threat was such that a good many Japanese ships carrying troops and materials for creating more elaborate defensive positions were sunk on the way to Saipan. Nevertheless, Elrod remarked that he was "astounded" at the heavy equipment and guns that the Japanese had emplaced in the ridges and hills. Without improved roads it seemed virtually impossible to get those guns in those positions.

struggle on the part of the front-line units to get close enough to throw a satchel charge inside or for us to fire in there. Sometimes this would make the Japanese come out; sometimes they would open fire from the other edge. When they would come out, they were very quickly dispatched. Our days were taken up by shooting caves. We discovered some and others the infantry pointed out to us. We got good support from them because we needed them to keep the Japanese troops away, and they liked us to be there with the machine guns and the heavy guns. It became a very cooperative and a mutually supporting operation. The routine became: we'd find a cave, shoot into it until the Japanese inside were either wiped out or wounded, then a marine tossed a charge into the opening, and this would cave it in, trapping any survivors inside.

Some of these caves went back very deep. I never did go inside any of those.[13] They had been designed and laid out very cleverly. Their entrances often were positioned to be in the shade. With brush and rugged terrain and a shadow, it made it very difficult to find the opening. You would receive fire, but you couldn't tell where it was coming from. We had to maneuver around and try to get the right view so we could see the entrance. This is what the section leaders, the squad leaders, and I did. We walked or drove our Jeeps in front of the halftracks

---

13 Elrod observed that, "Some of these positions are still intact on Saipan to this day. I explored in some of them when I returned to Saipan in 2011. It was amazing how many of those structures actually survived the war; they were just so heavily built. There was one that had been a major ammunition storage unit for their heavy artillery and for their airplanes. It had three sets of steel doors that were about six to eight inches thick. It was totally untouched. Some had been designed in a very clever way. They were rounded so the average shell would just ricochet off."

trying to locate Japanese caves and finding the best places for the halftrack to maneuver and position. Of course, this made us pretty good targets.

Lieutenant Bill Cardiff was one of the 37-mm platoon leaders. He was a great fan of Shakespeare, and he was always quoting Shakespeare or reading a book on Shakespeare. He had contracted malaria very seriously at Guadalcanal, and when he would have a serious attack, he would hide out in a tent for fear he was going to be sent back to the States. I think his high fever affected his judgment a little bit. One day, when his platoon came upon a Japanese machine gun, he tried to get his 37s to hit it. They couldn't see it though so he said, "I'm going to walk toward it. When it starts firing, you fire." Well, they told me that the machine gun virtually cut him in half; the 37 knocked it out, but it was too late for Bill.[14] He had been selected for captain but never got to pin the bars on.

Everything, as far as I was concerned with, was a repetition. Every day was just like another day. I stayed right along with the front line infantry units. We occasionally had a chance to use the machine guns when we would see a Japanese soldier somewhere in the open, which was pretty rare. The road that went directly across the island from Tapotchau to Magicienne Bay was almost a straight road. It had been surfaced with crushed coral. As we moved along that road, we looked up the road and probably 1,000 yards ahead was a Japanese soldier walking with his back to us. There was a warrant officer, Spoon. He and I had been together on the officers' screening program at Samoa. He made marine gunner [warrant officer] at the same

---

14   First Lieutenant William Lee Cardiff was killed in action 29 June 1944.

time I was made a second lieutenant. Warrant Officer Spoon reached over and grabbed a BAR from a marine. A BAR is not a light weapon; it weighed about fifteen pounds. He made one off-hand shot, and the Jap threw his arms in the air and went down. When we got up to the Jap, we saw that he had been hit directly between the shoulder blades. Spoon made a big deal out of it, but it had probably been an accident, a lucky shot. Everyone got a charge out of that.

Once the Fourth Division reached Magicienne Bay, they were to reel to the south and clear the south end of the island. When the Second Division reached the line of the Mt. Tapotchau and that ridge line down the center of the island [a distance of about two miles], we were to swing north there, and the army infantry division, the Twenty-seventh, was going to move in our the right.[15] It took several days for us to move into that point. After a few days the Fourth Division reached the other side of the island, swung and started south. I don't know how long it took them to clear the southern part. The heaviest fighting was all in the northern part of the island because it was suitable for these caves. That's where we [the Eighth Marines] operated. The Japanese were incredibly persistent and difficult to root out. You could shoot at them, and they'd pull the guns back, and as soon as you stopped shooting, they would come right back out again. We often had to make two or three at-

---

15   The island of Saipan is dominated by Mt. Tapotchau, a 1,500-foot peak. Actually, the entire center of the island was a mass of extremely rugged hills and ridges into which the Japanese had ferreted themselves. The Eighth Marines reached their turning point—orienting their attack direction from east to north— in less than a week. The push north by the entire Second Marine Division began on 22 June.

tacks. There were a few cases where the Japanese used the concrete tombs that were on the island, but not that often. I don't
think I ever shot at a tomb. When we started moving up that
ridge toward Mt. Tapotchau, we could look down into the valley where the army was.

The army wasn't moving. It was probably about the eighth
or ninth day when Hays told me that he had one entire company tied back to his rear to maintain contact with the army.
The army seemed to be following this business of artillery bar-
raging and then moving, but they were not too pressed about
making a move. It all came from the division commander.[16] He
just wasn't pressing his subordinates. They would pound with
artillery and then not move. You could see there wasn't anything left there. You could look right down in that valley, and
if there were any Japanese around you could see them, and I
didn't see any.[17]

16 The Twenty-seventh Infantry Division commander was Major General
Ralph C. Smith, USA. During the Saipan battle a controversial inter-service battle
arose over the perceived lethargy of the Twenty-seventh Division. General Ralph
Smith was relieved of command by the overall commander, Marine Lieutenant
General Holland M. "Howlin' Mad" Smith, who commanded the V Amphibious
Corps. After Maj. Gen. Ralph Smith was relieved, he was replaced by Maj. Gen.
Sanderford Jarman, USA.

17 Elrod here is addressing an issue that in actuality became quite a con-
troversy. The overall commander of the Saipan battle was a marine, Lieutenant
General Holland M. "Howlin' Mad" Smith. In his view the army's Twenty-seventh
Infantry Division moved too slow, was not aggressive enough as it fought through
the central part of the island, which as Elrod notes, was to the right of the marine
lines. Major General Smith relieved the army division commander, Major General
Ralph C. Smith. Rear area army generals were furious, although H.M. Smith had
the complete support of his own commanders, Admirals Raymond A. Spruance
and Richmond K. Turner. The episode blemished relations between the army and
marines for years after.

Later on, the army did a good job clearing the north end of the island. They had one real hard fight as the battle was almost over. The Japanese attacked at night, and it was in one of the areas that was very overgrown. They handled themselves very nicely, and the Japanese did not get through.[18]

When we got to Mt. Tapotchau, I drove two of my half-tracks nearly all the way to the top. There was just a narrow road, very rough almost like a trail going up. That actually was sort of foolish, but we made it. I looked out and walking across one of the cane fields—the cane was about knee-high—was a Japanese soldier. He had no idea that we had seen him. I grabbed a rifle from one of the marines. I didn't know if it was zeroed in or whatever. I prided myself on being a prime rifle shot, so I raised it up. It was probably a 1,000-yard shot, and I fired. I allowed for the distance, but I didn't realize the plunging fire wiped out a lot of that. The shot went right over his head and hit right behind him. There was a coral outcropping about half the size of an office desk and he dived behind it. My pride was injured that I had missed. I told a gunner on one of the halftracks to "Get a high-explosive round and get that Jap." Well, he made the same mistake I did; the first 75-mm round was long. The second round, though, got about half the rock and all the Jap. He went flying through the air. So, then the marines all took a few shots at the dead Jap just to make sure their rifles were working properly.

Generally, the fighting would go all day, but at night things quieted down. That didn't mean we could take it easy. The

18 Elrod here is referring to a massive banzai charge by approximately 3,000 Japanese, a last ditch and desperate effort on their part that occurred before dawn on 7 July along the Tanapag plain northeast of Garapan.

Japanese would be out moving around. This was particularly true in the beach area because the terrain down there was much more maneuverable. There was one night that it was really pouring down rain, and it was so black that you couldn't see anything. I always slept in my hole in a sitting position, or a semi-reclining position, and I would put my knife in the bank where my elbow was on my hip, and I could grab my knife in the dark. I had a shoulder holster, and I had my .45 loaded and locked. That was not a particularly safe thing, but it was very peaceful for sleeping. In the middle of the night First Sergeant Baker, who had a hole next to me, said, "Captain, I have one in here with me!" So, I crawled over there, and I couldn't see anything. He knew that I was kind of quick to shoot, and he said, "Please don't shoot! I'm down under this guy." I just happened to touch an entrenching tool that was lying there and picked it up. I reached down and put my left hand on this Jap's forehead, he had lost his helmet. I raised up the entrenching tool and smacked him real hard in the back of the head. All the back of his head just turned into marbles. His skull broke up just like safety glass.

The Jap had actually just fallen in the hole, and Baker grabbed him and wrapped his arms around him and pinned his arms, squeezing him in a bear hug. We didn't know whether he had a grenade or what. By the time we pulled him out of the hole, a couple of other marines had responded to the noise and crawled up to the hole and stuck him a few times with their knives—just to make sure. When daylight came, we could see that when he stepped in the hole he must not have had the chinstrap hooked on his helmet, and his helmet had fallen forward, and so had his rifle. That was the closest I ever came to hand-to-hand combat.

At night we always set up in a perimeter with one of the infantry companies. On about the seventh or eighth night, we had set up a perimeter with a circle-the-wagons type of defense. Our halftracks and 37-mms were in the perimeter, with our guns facing outward. The Japanese attacked that night and actually got up to and inside the perimeter. There was a tremendous amount of firing. My marines were firing away with the machine guns, and everyone who was not on a gun laid under the halftracks and fired through the tracks, so we had that for protection. A lieutenant named Smith, who had a 37-mm platoon, was killed in that attack along with several other marines. There were numerous Japanese bodies found the next day, many inside our perimeter.

After we had some marine planes ashore, we frequently saw spotter planes. These were for directing artillery fire. This was the first campaign I was in where the air support was pretty effective. It seemed there were aircraft always overhead, and they did quite a bit of bombing right along the front line—dive bombing.[19] Artillery was outstanding. In that big banzai attack down by the beach, one of the artillery batteries had to finally fire point blank into them. That's really where the charge stopped. So, the artillery did a fantastic job. I don't know of any

---

19   The Marine Corps had very few aircraft ashore, actually only two squadrons, VMO (Marine Observation Squadron) 2 and 4 which did good work in marking and directing artillery fire. Air support at Saipan was of questionable quality, with many arguing that it could have been better. Colonel David M. Shoup, however, Chief of Staff for the Second Marine Division, remarked that the air support he saw at Saipan was almost all navy aircraft, and was the "finest" he saw in World War II. The aircraft were generally all U.S. Navy planes flying off carriers nearby, although there were also army squadrons of Republic P-47 Thunderbolts operating from Aslito Field. No marine dive bombers were present, as at that time no marine squadrons were aboard carriers. Shaw, Nalty and Turnbladh, p. 584.

case where we had anyone hurt by friendly fire. There could have been an occasional accident, but I don't know of any. For the artillery people, this was third operation, too. We functioned pretty efficiently.

It was amazing how, because of the volcanic nature of the terrain, natural caves existed even in areas least expected. One time we were going through one of these cane fields. The cane was about hip-high. I heard some shooting. It was one of my sergeants, John [H.] Morgan. He called out to me, "There's one that's just gone in a hole here." I got over to him and he said, "I know I hit him a couple times." Morgan was carrying a .30-caliber carbine, which was really a useless weapon. It just made you think you had a weapon. We looked around and found a small cave in the middle of the cane field. I looked in there, and I could see a leg. It looked like someone was standing up in there and I could see the leg to about halfway up the hip. About this time, the major that was theoretically my reporting senior got there. I was getting ready to shoot this guy in the leg, and he said, "Oh no, it might be a civilian. Tell somebody to crawl in the hole." Well, this really set me off. I said, "Major, I will not give such a damned fool order!" So, I just flipped the safety off my pistol and crawled in the hole myself. Just as I was almost back to this guy, something hit my right hand and knocked off part of my thumbnail where it gripped my pistol. I figured it was a grenade, and he was going to share it with me. I grabbed his leg with my left hand and pulled him down and pulled him up to me and then out the cave. What he had done is throw a rock at me; that's what hit my thumb. It was a civilian all right, and he still wanted to fight. The marines that were there took him down and turned him over. And sure enough, the sergeant had hit him in the right shoulder, but it was a glancing penetration. It had gone about eight or ten inches across his shoulder blade and then exited, so he had a wound there. He was still agitated at us and wanted to fight, so I had one my marines smack him with the butt of his rifle. This addled him, and we were able to tie him to a stretcher. The corpsman set about treating him.

In the meantime, his wife and a two-year-old boy came out. We made the woman lift her dress to make sure she didn't have grenades. Then some of the marines offered the boy some water and a piece of what we called an iron ration bar. This was a chocolate bar that had been designed to not melt in the heat and had oatmeal in it. It tasted pretty good because it had chocolate. Apparently, they were desperate for food and water. When the mother saw how the little boy was treated, she settled right down. She kept telling the husband to calm down. At least that's what we thought she was saying. Some marines from the rear came up right away and took them back to the rear.

I crawled back in the hole, and there was just enough room in there for them to stand up. It was just a natural cave. Apparently, they had been there several days and had been subsisting on sugar cane. They were very tidy people; they had the chewed-up pieces of cane stacked in little stacks around the cave. They were obviously of Japanese extraction and probably were farmers. He probably hid out during the day and would go out at night.[20]

---

20 There were thousands of civilians on the island, Chamorro, Korean laborers, and Japanese civilians. The Japanese were most reluctant to surrender and actively supported Japanese troops. They had also been instructed not to surrender to the Americans, that they would be brutalized and murdered. A well-known and tragic characteristic of the battle of Saipan is the mass suicide of Japanese civilians on the island's north end in the final days of the campaign.

When I had gotten out of the hole, this major that I had refused a direct order from was gone and I never saw him again.[21] I don't know what would have happened if he was there. He had joined us just a few days before we left Hawaii. He replaced [Major] Rich. I had developed a pretty strong distaste for him.[22] I don't know what would have happened if I hadn't been wounded later, because I had just flatly refused to do what he said. When I came out of the hole, he was gone. I think he realized I had been pushed a little further than was a good idea.

The only other time I had contact with civilians was a time when we came up on a group of about fifty or sixty; and they were mostly women or children. They were terribly confused, frightened, actually terrified, because here they were right between both forces. We didn't want to harm them. How they had made it that far without being killed I could not understand. One of them was a young woman who was very upset. She kept making a shooting-type motion with her hands. Apparently, machine guns, before we had seen these people, had fired into them and killed some. I couldn't tell a word of what she was saying, but I could tell she was talking about machine guns and firing into them. There was an old man who seemed to be the leader. Right away somebody realized that this fellow was speaking Spanish. So, I got one of my Hispanic

---

21   This was Major Robert L. Holderness.

22   Elrod explained: "He had been in the movie industry. He had a stack of full pictures, full-body nudes of young ladies. Apparently, when they were aspiring actresses, one of the things they did, they were made to strip off their clothes and have their picture taken. He said that what he would do when the boss felt like he needed companionship, he would give him two or three pictures and if the lady was sufficiently cooperative she would get a small part in the movie. I thought that was a pretty sorry kind of way to make a living."

marines over. It turns out before World War I Spain controlled Saipan.[23] When he was a teenager or young boy, the Spaniards had required them to learn to speak Spanish in school, and he remembered it. So, we explained to him that they should keep going back, that they had a separate camp for the Chamorro civilians and a different one for Japanese, both military and civilian. I never saw either one of these camps, so I have no idea what took place there. I never was back in the rear areas the whole time that I was at Saipan. They had marines following us that came quickly to take care of such situations as handling the civilians or wounded.

Apparently, there were more prisoners taken at Saipan than Guadalcanal. There was one marine who had been the son of a missionary in Japan. He persuaded some 280 Japanese troops to surrender, so there was some taken. I know in the areas where I was, no Japs surrendered and there was no effort to take prisoners. No marines ever thought about surrendering either, and none did. We were all of the mind that nothing good was going to happen to you if you were captured by the Japanese. I'm sure the people who came behind us and went in these caves found some wounded and so forth. I know we killed some 30,000 Japanese soldiers.[24] I never heard of any specific code or rules of engagement. We just shot every Jap we could get a bead on. We figured if they were dead they weren't a problem anymore, at

---

23   Saipan was a Spanish colony until the Spanish-American War; in 1898 Spain relinquished control of Saipan and it became a German colony. The Japanese seized the northern Marianas in World War I. Shaw, Nalty, and Turnbladh, p. 237.

24   Elrod is saying that for the most part, all the Japanese soldiers who were on the island were killed. In actuality, more survived than he thought; the official count of Japanese deaths was 23,811, Shaw, Nalty, Turnbladh, p. 346.

least not much of a problem. We still had to do something with the bodies. Nobody wanted to dig the graves for them. Once when there were several bodies lying around, somebody finally decided to pour gasoline on one or two and burn them. That didn't work too well. It just sort of cooked them, and it made an awful stink and lots of smoke. Finally, somebody hit on a real solution. Put all the bodies in a little house nearby, then burn the house down. That worked fine. I don't know anything official was ever said about it.

> *9 July 1944*
> *Dearest Mom,*
> *. . . A funny thing happened. Just before dark our company 1st Sgt. rode up on a Nip bicycle and handed me a paper all filled out like a singing telegram. There were a lot of the men around so they all sang "Happy Birthday" and the Co. officers gave me the most weird looking Nip shirt, they had picked it up somewhere that day. . . .*

The day of my birthday, the 23rd of June, it was pouring down rain. We got a lot of rain because it was right at the start of their rainy season. On this one particular day, I looked for a place to get out of the rain and eat. The only place I could find was a little shed over a pile of cow manure. I was sitting on this pile of cow manure eating a C-ration, and the first sergeant came up riding a Japanese bicycle. He had a very odd looking shirt on. It was a bright yellow kimono that he had "liberated" somewhere. He was singing a song, and then a bunch of my marines gathered around and sang happy birthday to me. This turned out to be one of the best birthdays I have ever had. The first sergeant turned to me and said, "Skipper, we've had a mail call and you have a letter." It turned out that the letter I had mailed to my long time, high school girlfriend, Malda, back at Pearl [Harbor] had reached her, and her answer reached me that day.

I found out just before we left Hawaii that Malda had divorced her husband. So I wrote the letter on the ship between Hawaii and Oahu and mailed it in Pearl Harbor. So this was her answer on the 23rd of June. She had learned to fly in San Antonio and bought a small plane. She made a living by renting her plane and carrying ranchers who hunted coyotes. Then she got a contract teaching young men to fly, getting them ready to fly in the army. This was at the airbase in Ft. Stockton, Texas. She got involved in the organization with Jackie Cochran.[25] She had applied to be a ferry pilot and had been accepted. One day five or six girls came into Ft. Stockton flying open cockpit aircraft from Ohio to California. Their faces were burned up from the wind and the sun. So she tore up her contract. But this letter was the first mail call that we had had. In this letter she opened the door a little bit toward us getting together again, so that was a pretty good birthday present. Well, it turns out we later were married and lived together for a little over sixty-three years, but that's another story.

We lived on C rations or K rations. Ham and beans was the favorite. Corn beef hash was the worst. I don't remember getting any prepared food the whole time. So, it was always either C rations or K rations. Since I made a policy of eating last,

---

25 Jackie Cochran was a pioneering female aviator of this era. Upon the commencement of war she was significant in the creation of the Women's Auxiliary Army Corps (WAAC) and Women Airforce Service Pilots (WASP). Elrod is probably referring to the WASP program here.

I probably ate more corn beef hash than any other marine in the unit because I got what was left. It tasted very greasy; it was like eating wet plaster. We would put powdered coffee on it, anything to try to mask it. Ham and beans, though, everybody went for. We would eat in lulls. If you had got a chance to eat, you ate. If you got a chance to sleep, you slept; if you got a chance to have a bowel movement you did it, because who knew when the next chance would come. I don't remember being hungry there like we were at Guadalcanal. I don't think anyone was. Apparently, the supply on the beach was much better organized. I had heard that they were using beachmasters for the first time; of course I didn't see any of that because I was never back in that area. But we had plenty of ammo, and we had plenty to eat. It just was a very irregular type of existence.

Like I said, I believed that officers should eat last. Privates ate first, NCOs next, and then officers. That was my policy the whole time. I had a real objection to officers living better than the troops. I had no formal schooling or whatever as far as the military was concerned. My theory was I didn't tell my marines, I showed them. I didn't send my marines, I took them. In retrospect I realized that after we got this major who replaced Major Rich, right before we headed to Saipan, I became for all practical purposes the company commander. The platoon leaders would come to me, the troops would come to me. During the fighting on Saipan, I saw this major one time a few minutes, and I never saw the captain who was the executive officer. I had been a private, a PFC, a corporal, a sergeant, and I had an idea of good officers and bad officers. Incidentally, I remained in the same unit, the Weapons Platoon of the Eighth Marines, through all of these ranks; I had been in this unit since boot camp graduation. I don't think many marines had moved up through the ranks like that and remained with their original unit.

Somehow at Saipan I wound up with the scout-sniper platoon attached to me. The platoon sergeant of the scout-sniper platoon was an older fellow, probably thirty-five years old, and had been a police sergeant in the St. Paul police force. He was Hungarian and named Stephanus Bostic Klopcsik. We called him "Steve" for short. He told us that that his last name meant stone fish in Hungarian. He was very, very conscientious. One day there at Saipan, probably after we had been there eight or nine days, I realized he was nearing exhaustion. I said, "Steve, crawl in your hole and sleep." The platoon leader of the scout sniper platoon was a character, and a good platoon leader. He had been a professor at one of the California colleges, and his name was Finneran. He used to go around saying, "Finnero, Finnero, the French matinee idol!" He had been promoted from the ranks and was a second lieutenant. He had motivated his marines in the scout-sniper platoon to hone their accuracy. To increase their enthusiasm, when they got a little bored with practice firing at paper targets, he devised something more exciting. He took a half block of composition C and put it on a stake, and if they hit that there would be a nice little explosion.

One of the marines, Corporal Burgess, "Little Beaver," one day had a rifle bullet hit his right foot and knocked the heel off his shoe. Four or five days later, he came to me and said, "Captain, it is getting almost impossible for me to walk around. I want to go out and get a pair of shoes." I knew what he had in mind. When dark came he took his knife and crawled out. I told the marines along there, "When 'Beaver' comes back in, if any of you shoot him, you're going to have to answer to me." And he came back with a pair of Japanese military shoes tied together by the string hanging around his neck. He wore those shoes the rest of the time because he had very small feet. I don't think he weighed more than 135 or 140 pounds. At Tarawa he had taken a bullet through the helmet that did no real harm, and at Saipan a bullet knocked the heel off one of his shoes.

Leadership in combat is a difficult thing, though. The most difficult thing for me was writing letters to the family of one of your men killed. I wrote to the families of all the marines lost in my platoon. I was not able to do that at Saipan because of being wounded. There were probably a few that I didn't get to write. I hope that one of the other officers did. A very difficult task, I would almost rather do anything than write those letters. I usually said that they were very brave, which they were, and that they didn't suffer too much, which in some cases was not true, they did suffer. If they were killed, I said his death was instant, which in many cases was not true. I knew it wasn't going to be a pleasant thing, no matter which way. I was concerned about the family, as I was my own family. I never wrote about the miserable conditions, the dangers, and suffering I experienced in letters to my own family. I just didn't want them to worry about me. But writing letters to the family isn't an easy thing to do.

I remember one marine, Marvin Sheppard, who got hit in the leg. When we cut his pants legs open, he was bleeding severely. It looked like a chunk of his thigh had been torn out. He wound up in a hospital in San Diego, and I wrote my mother to go and see him. She did and would write back telling me of his condition and that he was doing okay.

I would try to give my marines a break whenever we could. I had mentioned earlier that I had joined the Navy Officer's Club five times before we left Hawaii. Lieutenant Colonel Hays knew that I had some special rations, so he sent a runner over with a canteen cup for some of that special fruit juice. Hays had been wounded early in the battle. Shrapnel hit him in the buttocks, but he was not evacuated. He stayed with his unit. Maybe he wanted some whiskey to ease the pain, I don't know. But I put about a half-cup of gin in Hays's canteen cup, and I told this marine jokingly, "Now I don't know if I should tell you this, but the battalion commander said if you spill so much as one drop of this, he was going to have you shot when you got back." Anyway it arrived safely. But on a particularly hard day of fighting, we passed a bottle around, and everybody could take one drink.

We were getting ready to pass to the army control of the north end of the island. I didn't understand that. The battalion I was operating with, Hays's First Battalion, Eighth Marines, had been told to make a 90-degree left turn. The other two battalions were pressing north, so it was a pincer actually against the town [Garapan]. By 9:00 that morning, we had been attacking about an hour. Suddenly Japanese artillery fired a round. I had gotten out of the halftrack and was walking over to talk to the company commander. A round hit in front of me probably about fifty yards or so. I realized that there probably would be at least three more because the Japanese habit was to fire at least a four-round volley. They obviously could see us because it hit right in the line with the attacking unit. I started to bend over to run over to a hole where one of my halftracks had just knocked out a machine gun. Just as I bent down the second round landed right behind me, just about 7:00 from me, and that's the one that wounded me. It felt like I had been hit across the back with a baseball bat or a two-by-four. It hit very, very hard. The blast probably knocked me six or seven yards, and I was lying on my stomach. I had no sensation of my left leg, and I thought it had probably been blown off.

CHAPTER TEN

Death Came Near: Wounded and Recovery

The battle of Saipan, which lasted twenty-four days, pro-
duced almost 17,000 American casualties, about 700
Americans killed or wounded daily. On 2 July, a week be-
fore Saipan was secured, Captain Roy H. Elrod was seri-
ously wounded. Like so many of the casualties, the Japanese
fire that struck him came suddenly, virtually out of the blue.
An artillery blast broke next to him. There was no boom
of a cannon prior, just a sudden maiming explosion. His
medical treatment began immediately, provided by a navy
Corpsman assigned to Elrod's unit. Elrod was evacuated
and his medical care continued for the next six months.
This ended the war for Elrod, but the rest of his life began.

I was wounded on the 2nd of July, the same day that the
Second Division was taken out of the line. The entire
Saipan operation was over on the ninth. So, it was right at
the end of the operation. When the artillery shrapnel from
that second round hit me, like I said it was really a hard blow

to my back, and I believe it sent me flying a good ways, then a numbing pain. It sent shell fragments through me in several locations. I have shell fragments to this day in my spine, one in the right cheek of my butt, and one in my left hamstring. There were others, quite a number of them, removed later. One was just down from my right collarbone, six or seven inches or so.

I don't know what happened to my unit after that. I didn't know at the time that there were thirty-two marines either killed or wounded with the four rounds that landed there. I could see quite a bit of blood, so I thought well I had better get my belt off and get a tourniquet on what was left of the leg. I was able to turn my head enough, and to my great relief I saw that my leg was still there. About that time the corpsman came, and they just ripped my uniform off until I was stark naked. He must have given me a shot of morphine because my memory goes in and out. I remember I had to be carried on a stretcher by two marines about 75 or 100 yards to a Jeep. I remember one of the marines saying, "This SOB is really heavy!" The only thing I was able to take away with me, I had a little notebook in my breast pocket of my utility jacket. Apparently, I put it in my pocket that morning before the attack to take notes. There wasn't anything written in it. I still have that notebook. A shell fragment had gone between my arm and my side, because when I leaned over my jacket was hanging down, and there's a cut from a shell fragment that is an inch or an inch and a half long. All my other things I never saw again. They laid me cross-wise over the back of the Jeep. They had a man with a really serious wound lying cross-wise on the hood. I think they had one or two that were sitting. I could see their heads sticking out from behind the stretcher. I was right behind the driver just stretched out across there.

They had taken all the battalions and regimental surgeons of the units and set up a triage place down on the beach in tents. That's where the Jeep took me. I don't know how long I was there. I don't remember how they put me to sleep. I just remember waking up. I don't remember actually arriving because I guess I was going in and out from the morphine. In that triage place they dug some of the shrapnel out. When I began to come up from the anesthetic, it turns out the surgeon that had worked on me was our regimental surgeon. He and I had become fairly good friends because he was from Lubbock, Texas, which was only about seventy miles from Muleshoe where I grew up. He looked me over good, examined me, and when he was finished, he said, "They're going to have to take you off the island." Then he said, "Now wake up and listen to me. People are going to want to work on your back. Tell them to keep their hands off—keep their goddamned knives out of your back!" In the first two or three hospitals, there was discussion of them operating on my back, and I told them I didn't want any surgery going on there. They respected my wishes. Pieces of shrapnel continued to fester up later.

Sometime late in the afternoon I was taken down to the beach and put in a LCM. The whole floor of this landing craft was covered with wounded on stretchers. It was to take us to a hospital ship, the *Solace* (AP-5). I was stark naked, but I had insisted on keeping my pistol and my knife and had those curled up under my hip. I had my hip turned slightly to the left, and I could see the marine in the stretcher next to me. He was lying on his back, and as I looked at him I saw that his face was turning blue. I realized he was probably strangling. I just reached over with my left hand and put my index finger down in his mouth and pulled his tongue back. Right away I could see the color coming back. He was totally unconscious, but I lay there holding my finger in his mouth, holding his tongue down.

When we got to the hospital ship, a Japanese air attack came in, so the hospital ship had to get underway. We stayed in the LCM until it returned. We bounced around in that thing until after dark. Just how long I don't know, but it was a long time. I think there was a corpsman on the boat with us, but I don't remember for sure. When we did get back alongside the *Solace*, they dropped down a wire basket, and they took us off the stretchers and loaded us in the basket. Then they hoisted us up into the ship. I had watched the marine next to me and had my finger in his mouth just about this whole time. As they loaded me into the basket, I told the corpsman, "Watch him, he's going to choke." I never found out what happened to him.

When I got on the ship, the master at arms took my pistol and my knife. I was placed in a stateroom in a lower bunk, and I was on my stomach. Sometime in the night I woke up and was very, very sick to my stomach. I guess it was a reaction to the morphine. That's when I decided I was allergic to morphine. I realized I was going to throw up, and I didn't want to throw up in the bed. I managed to get my head over the side and throw up on the floor. The nurses came in after that and berated me, but I could not have cared less. I didn't pay the least bit of attention. I was just sort of in and out anyway. The next thing I recall, I was in a different stateroom and on some sort of bunk arrangement in the middle of the room. There were four or five other wounded officers in bunks along the side. There were two of us lying on this thing in the middle. It was about the height of a table, where they could get to us. This other marine turned out to be Lieutenant Verner "Pop" Austin, one of the 37-mm platoon leaders from my company. We had been together in California; he was my squad leader when I was a PFC. He had been selected for commissioning. He had taken a very serious wound in his right thigh during the same artillery barrage that got me. The piece of shell that hit him was probably about two inches long and an inch in diameter and had shattered his femur. He was in a half-body cast from his navel down below his knees.

We were on that hospital ship about seven days because they took us all the way from Saipan to the Russell Islands [about 1,200 miles south, southeast]. I guess it was about the third day on the ship the nurse came in with a pair of pajama pants. She threw the pants on me and said, "I'm getting tired of looking at you. Put these pants on." I said, "You know damn well I can't put these pants on." I couldn't sit up. So I said, "If you want them on me, you put them on me." So she did.

There was a lot of chit chat back and forth among the officers in that room. People had different degrees of wounds. By this time we're all talking. This officer that was lying beside me I think was becoming addicted to morphine because he was always begging for another shot. I was making sure that nobody ever put another morphine needle in me.

July 9, 1944
Dearest Mom,
You have most likely been worried about me so I will try to put your mind at ease. You may have received a telegram from the Navy Dept. saying I was wounded, or you will receive one in the near future.

I am not hurt bad and it is nothing that won't heal
up in a fairly short time. I was hit about the mid-
dle of the morning of July 2. . . . I am now aboard
a hospital ship and will soon be in one of our base
hospitals out here. Up until the time I was hit I was
fine. I will not say my luck ran out because I could
have been hit bad.
Lots of love, Roy

I knew we had to pass Truk, and I was quite concerned
about that because we knew the Japanese had a big base there,
or at least we thought they did. I suppose the route was far
enough away that we were not in range of the Japanese planes
from Truk. We had formulated in our own minds that Truk
was a very strong base.

I was in sort of a navy equivalent of a MASH [mobile army
surgical hospital] on the island of Banika in the Russell Islands.
The officer casualties were in a Quonset hut. I was happy I
wasn't dead, but actually I don't think I thought much about
anything. They sort of kept me sedated to some extent. For
example, I don't remember how we got from the ship to this
Quonset hut. They probably knocked me out some way. But as
I was going to be taken off the ship, I asked for my knife and
pistol back and the master at arms was reluctant. I used my full
rank then, I said, "I'm not leaving the ship without them." So
they produced them. I still have the pistol and the holster. I got
back to the States with the knife, and after I was retired I had
it in my tool box and somebody stole it from there, so I don't
have it. These things and the small notebook I mentioned earlier were the only personal things I had left when I left Saipan.
The notebook with my notes and all my records of addresses

and so forth were in my pack with all my other belongings. I also had a few souvenirs. I had a Japanese *Hari Kari* knife, a 1,000-stitch belt, and the yellow kimono shirt my marines gave me on my birthday.[1] I never saw those things again. I could only remember my mother's and my sister's address. I also remembered the address of the young lady that I had dated most of the time in New Zealand. But it took quite a period of time before I could write to different friends and relatives, only after I received letters from them.

July 12, 1944
Dearest Mom,

> *There is plenty of time on my hands this afternoon so I will try and put it to use. I am feeling fine and getting along alright. The last letter I did not tell you the nature of my injury. Several shell fragments hit me in the lower back and left leg, none of them are serious.*

> *The hospital here is nicer than I had expected it to be so all in all everything is fine. Its location is in the Solomon Islands, so it isn't really new territory for me.*

> *As you have already read in the papers we were fighting in Saipan. The 2nd Div. manages to get in on the most exciting operations. I was hit on the 18th day of the fighting so I almost lasted until the finish.*

---

1   Merriam-Webster defines *Hara-kiri* or *Seppuku* as ritual suicide by disembowelment practiced by the Japanese samurai or formerly decreed by a court in lieu of the death penalty.

They had four Quonset huts, side by side and end to end, and in the middle of each were shower and toilet facilities. I had the bunk nearest the door, and there was a little hallway that connected to the other four. There were probably fifteen or twenty other officers in the Quonset hut I was in. I think I was the senior one. A navy lieutenant was there. He had been hit by a shell fragment or some kind of explosion; I'd guess in a kamikaze attack. One of his elbows was completely missing. There was flesh that held the arm together. He was the most mobile person there. I think his name was Ellis. He claimed he was the heir for a lumber company that operated in Louisiana. He gave us the impression that he was a very wealthy man. There were two nurses that looked after us. They were regular navy nurses and were both lieutenants. That was pretty much the glass ceiling for nurses in those days, although the head nurse there was, I believe, a lieutenant commander or commander. The two nurses that worked our Quonset hut were wise to the ways of the military and military men. They didn't put up with any foolishness. I remember the name of one, a tall slender girl named Nurse Stuckey. There were several corpsmen that worked there also. The doctor always appeared sort of over my right shoulder. It was about the second or third day he came in and pinned a Purple Heart medal to my pillow.

We were all restless and generally bored. Of course, I was bed bound. Most of us were bed bound. They brought our meals to us on a tray. I was given sponge baths by a corpsman. There was a lot of chatter amongst us. Everybody entertained himself by telling tales and listening to the others tell their tales. We were woken up real early one morning by a lot of commotion. They brought in a young navy pilot, and it seems that his

Corsair had hit the top of the palm trees when he was taking off. As we began questioning him—worming it out of him—it seems he had forgotten to unfold the wings of the Corsair. The tower was shouting at him but he was determined to get the thing in the air and kept giving it full throttle. He managed to get enough power on it to lift it high enough to hit the top of the coconut trees. He had a real hard time with everybody after that. We were always making up funny questions to ask him about his flying ability and so forth. One other interesting incident—there was a commotion one night. The next morning we found out there was a Russian woman in one of the bunks. So, we queried the two nurses. She had been on a Russian ship that had come in there and complained that she had been attacked and raped by one of the crewmen. One of the nurses said, "I suspect what she was really complaining about was she wasn't paid."

I had been there probably four or five days, maybe a week or so, when a marine lieutenant colonel came in. He said that he was the G-1 of the First Marine Division [Lieutenant Colonel John W. Scott, Jr.], which was on the island right next to ours, Pavuvu. We were on the one named Banika. He said he was the division intelligence officer and that I was the senior casualty there from Saipan. He wanted to ask me questions about the type of defenses we had faced at Saipan. I told him it was quite different than what we had experienced either at Guadalcanal or at Tarawa. The Japanese were purposefully dug into caves and had built heavy concrete bunkers. This required digging them out, one hole after another. After he had finished asking these questions, he said, "Well, what do you drink?" I said, "Well, Colonel, I'll drink most anything. If I had one, my preference would be scotch." I didn't think I'd hear any more about it. The next day he came back again, and he had a bottle about three-fourths full of scotch. He said this was every drop of scotch there was in the First Marine Division. It turns out that they were going to Peleliu, and later I heard he lost a leg there. I never did see him again, but he was very pleasant to talk to and treated me very well.

I began to improve somewhat. I could move my leg a little more. I was probably there a month, maybe longer. Toward the end of my time there I was able to get up, with a corpsman helping, and go to the toilet with corpsmen standing on both sides of me to help. The very last few days I was there two corpsmen would take me in a wheelchair to the shower and put a stool down so I could shower. I had been getting sponge baths for weeks.

> *August 1, 1944*
> *Dearest Mom,*
>   *This is a nice cool morning so I will use it for writing. Some of us have moved over to a new ward, seven of us to be exact. It is much cooler than where we were and there is more room. We also have a table for writing, cards, etc.*
>   *Last night a chaplain from Texas that I know came over and took us out to his camp for chow. We had barbeque, and was it good. He is from San Angelo and knows the bunch [part of Roy's family] down there. He went to the University [of Texas]. There is another officer who has been seeing me a lot. Maury Maverick, Jr., the Senator's son.[2] He is*

---

2   Maury Maverick, Jr., was the son of Texas politician Maury Maverick, who was a Democratic Texas Representative to the U.S. Congress, serving 1935–1939.

*a friend of Sid's and I have known him since N.Z.
Every place I go now in the Corps I find people that
I know or have served with before.*

*I am feeling fine, all my wounds have closed ex-
cept one in my back. The left foot is still on the blink
but will get alright. These other places are still ten-
der and get sore when I move around but all in all
everything is going well.*

*The Lt. [J.M.] Westerman who was hit with me
is married to a N. Zealand girl. She was to have a
baby about the 20th of last month, he is sure anxious to find out the outcome.*

I don't remember how I was transported from Banika over
to Guadalcanal. Apparently I was sedated, so I don't know if I
was flown there or if I was taken over in a boat. I just went to
sleep on Banika and woke up in a Quonset hut on Guadalcanal.
Guadalcanal by that time had become a big supply base for marine activity in the South Pacific. We were in a much larger
Quonset hut and a bigger, better hospital. I would say there
were probably forty or fifty beds there. I had progressed to the
point such that with the help of the corpsman I could be taken
down to the shower room to shave and taken to the toilet and
so forth. I couldn't walk on my own, but I could with the help
of a corpsman. There was a time—I suppose I had been there
maybe a week or so—one of the corpsman said, "Oh, another
captain from the Eighth Marines was flown in last night."

Maury Maverick Jr became an outspoken champion of unpopular causes in the
years after the war, as a liberal lawyer, legislator and editorialist. This Maverick
family descended from Texas Founding Father Samuel Maverick, whose unbrand-
ed cattle generated the term, "maverick."

I said, "What was his name?"

The corpsman said, "Mel Seltzer."

I said, "You know, he and I were bunkmates in Hawaii and also in New Zealand."

So, the corpsman put me in a wheelchair and wheeled me over. I tried to talk to Mel, but all he would do was shake his head and point at his right leg. His leg was amputated about halfway between his knee and his hip. He had been wounded at Tinian.[3] He probably survived for a week or two and should have been getting better because the worst was over by surviving the shock period. It was obvious to me that he wasn't the least bit interested in surviving. He was very vain. I was told he died that night.

Later on, Bob Hope came down with his crew.[4] I wasn't taken to go to the show, but the morning after the show Bob Hope, Jerry Colonna, and two or three of the girls came to the hospital area. The girls were in their shorts and skimpy tops, and they sang and kicked their feet for a bit. Hope and Colonna exchanged jokes. Then the girls went around to each one of the beds and gave each one of us a kiss. One of the mornings while Hope was still there, I was in my skivvy drawers shaving, and he was in his skivvy drawers at the sink next to me shaving. It was impressive to me how respectful he was and how grateful he was for what we were doing. He was just a great man. I learned later that he and the other entertainers did not receive any pay for these shows.

---

3 The Second Marine Division assaulted Tinian, an island near Saipan, and part of the Marianas group on 24 July 1944, shortly after Saipan had been secured.

4 Hope and his troupe visited the Russell Islands in early August 1944.

I remained in that Quonset hut on Guadalcanal until October. I was gradually able to move around a little better all the time. I kept pushing myself. From the very beginning I was pushing myself to become mobile. I wanted to get back to the States or back to duty. In my own mind, I knew that I wasn't going to do this very quickly. It turns out I was hospitalized for over five months from 2 July to 8 or 9 December.

From the beginning the doctors told me that I probably would not walk again. I was determined that I would. I didn't have sensation in the left leg from the hip down, and the right leg from the knee down. I think a piece of shrapnel actually nicked the nerve right where it splits in the back of my leg, and that's what caused the paralysis and the loss of sensation in my leg.

All through my stay in those hospitals, little pieces of shell fragments festered up. The corpsman or one of the doctors would lance it and fish out these little chunks. This happened a number of times. It was not too painful. Before they poked around, they always deadened the area with multiple shots.

There was lots of jokes and talking back and forth between us. I still took all my meals sitting on the side of my bed and eating off a tray on the side. I didn't leave that Quonset under my own power until I was ready to be taken back to the States. We began to hear rumors in late September, early October about how we were going back, whether we were going to fly or if we were going by ship or so forth. It turns out that I was taken back on a jeep carrier. They were using those jeep carriers to ferry the planes from the factories in the states down to the various aircraft carriers and islands in the Pacific. On the return they would carry the wounded back to the states, as well as other personnel headed home.

I don't know how many casualties went back on the ship. There were five in the stateroom I was in. There was a navy lieutenant commander and three marine lieutenants and I was a captain. This lieutenant commander was a real smart aleck. None of us really cared for him. He claimed he was highly connected with professional baseball and swore that he was a friend of Babe Ruth. None of us believed his stories. There was one other officer whose name was Dodd. He was skin and bones. He ate but apparently his body just wasn't processing the food. He ate as much as we did, but he was just a skeleton practically. I never knew what happened with him. I always thought that the navy commander was faking his condition just to get back to the States. There was a marine major in the room that had been wounded by a submarine shell while he served on a navy ship in the Atlantic earlier in the war. The shell had cut into the rectum and the lower back. That was causing him problems, so he was being evacuated. His name was Alan Levi.[5] He was a reserve officer, and he and I became pretty good friends. We were able to eat up in the wardroom with the crew. Everyone that was in the stateroom with me was able to get into the wardroom.

It was the 18th of October when we reached the States. We were loaded in an LCM. It was another amphibious landing, my third. This time we were going home instead of going into a fight, but there was still danger. We landed at Oxnard, California. The coxswain hit the beach at a little too high speed and nearly knocked all of us off our feet. Some of us really

---

5 Alan Levi had been injured 12 November 1942 while serving with the marine detachment on the USS *Erie* (PG 50). The *Erie* was escorting a convoy of U.S. ships near Caracao when it was torpedoed and sunk by a German submarine.

weren't too sturdy to begin with. Fortunately, I was hanging on to the gunwale. Ambulances were waiting at the landing site. I sat up front with the driver on one of them. We didn't go very far before we saw a bar. We demanded that the driver stop, and we all got out and went in and had a drink. That was an appropriate welcoming back, to me. But it was a very strange sensation being back. It took me months actually to adjust to life in the U.S. and being around civilians. I felt detached, and that I just didn't fit in. It was pointless talking to people. They didn't understand.

I went to a hospital in Long Beach and stayed there probably until sometime in November. I began to be able to move around pretty well then. We had been given fifty dollars when we were leaving Guadalcanal. At that time you couldn't be paid unless they had your pay records. Everything was done from actual documents. I hadn't been paid for at least four months and probably more. For uniforms while in the hospital, we had been given two pairs of khaki pants, two khaki shirts, a navy officer's belt, a little canvas fore and aft cap, and a pair of navy shoes. When I was sufficiently ambulatory to get out, the first thing I wanted to do was get a marine uniform. I felt a bit insulted walking around in that navy khaki.

I went into town, and I went into a restaurant. I ordered a glass of milk and two raw eggs. I broke those two eggs into the milk, put a little bit of sugar and some vanilla in, stirred it with a spoon, and drank it. I had never done this before, but it just seemed like it would be good. A waitress had been standing there watching me. She shook her head and said, "You marines come back from the Pacific like animals. You're not even civilized." It tasted real good to me and sat real well on my stomach. I had had stomach problems virtually since Guadalcanal—a steady case of diarrhea and some dysentery. In fact it was years after the war before these digestive problems went away.

I went to a Bank of America. I had a bank account in a Bank of America in San Diego that I had been putting money in. Actually I sent it to my mother, and she put it in. I wanted to get $300. The bank officer that I was talking to looked at me, saw how I was dressed, and he must have thought that this couldn't possibly be a legitimate thing. We argued back and forth. Of course at that time, they had no electronic means to find out about deposits. I kept telling him that I had the money in my bank in San Diego. Finally I said, "Well, let me make a deal with you. You get on the telephone and call your branch there in San Diego, and if I don't have the account then I'll pay for the phone call." With that I plopped down the money I had left of that $50, which was only four or five dollars. Sure enough, he went ahead and of course I was right. I got a check and then I went right over to a uniform shop and ordered a Marine uniform, a set of "greens." In only a short time they were delivered. I think they had a ready-made suit and did some alterations.

I had managed to get word to my mother in San Diego that I had returned to the States. So, she and my sister came up to visit me one afternoon. I made sure to walk as normally as possible into that reception area where they were waiting. I had been telling them all along that my wounds were not that serious. I also wore my new marine uniform. We had a great reunion. They seemed to be real pleased that I was home and I was really happy to see them.

Alan Levi was in the same hospital, but not in my same ward. I had a room all to myself there. I had my own head [bathroom], and it was a pretty nice room. One morning Levi came in and said, "Another officer and I were out last night, and we picked up three pretty girls. We got a date tonight, and we told them we had just the fellow for Lena, the other girl." So, I went and it turns out that two of these girls were widows from navy pilots.[6] The other one was a sister of one of the girls. They had pretty much set their minds on the two other girls, the two sisters, so that left the other one for me. We went out and had a pretty good time: had drinks and dates and browsed around. We had a date almost every night after that. I guess it was after the second or third night this one sister that wasn't a widow announced that her husband had been some place up in the mountains and was coming home. So, this one fellow now was without a girl. He really got ugly with me because I still had one and he didn't. I said, "You made the selection." I don't think he was ever real friendly toward me after that.

About this time, I discovered that the navy had a policy that if there was a naval hospital near where you had a family, they would transfer you there. I asked to be transferred to the hospital in San Diego. So, I got moved to the navy hospital in San Diego. I was getting around pretty well by that time. I had my own room there also, a nice room. The reason I was getting separate rooms was because I was fairly senior amongst the wounded. Most officers who were wounded were the troop leaders, the lieutenants and captains. Few field grade were wounded. After I had been there a week or two, I was pretty

---

6   Elrod said these were widows of men from Torpedo Squadron 8 (VT-8). The men had been essentially wiped-out at the Battle of Midway, June 1942, as its aircrews flying obsolete Douglas TBD Devastator torpedo bombers, heroically attacked Japanese warships. Out of the fifteen aircrews there was only one survivor, Ensign George Gay.

much left on my own. I think I had to appear at sick call every other day or something like that.

I went before what was known as a "profile board." They had a lot of discussions about my case. They wanted to retire me at 100 percent disability. I wanted to stay in. I was a regular officer then, and I wanted to stay in the Marine Corps. All the officers on this profile board were Navy Reserve doctors except one, who was a Reserve Marine Major. I had to convince them to let me come back to duty. They said if I could pass the physical after a year I could remain on active duty. I was released from the hospital on limited duty, and I went to work trying to get a set of orders. This went on for probably two weeks before orders finally came. Also about this time, my records caught up with me. My citation for the Silver Star was there, so a navy captain had a formation and pinned the Silver Star on me. I had been wearing the ribbon ever since Guadalcanal, but apparently the medal had been following me from one place to another. I also started getting mail. One day I got over 100 letters that had been moved from one place to another. It's hard for people today to understand that at that time, everything had to be physically carried from one place to another; the only electronic communication was telegraph and radio.

Coincidentally, Lieutenant Colonel Crowe was in the same hospital, but he was on the floor above me. While I was there a newsman from *Time* magazine came in and wanted to interview Crowe. He told the reporter, "If you want to find out about me, go down and ask Captain Elrod." The reporter came down, and I made a pretty long comment to him about Crowe. Later I was flipping through a *Time* magazine, and his story was there. It was almost verbatim what I told him. Crowe had been hit very seriously. It took him longer to get well, but he eventually went back to duty.[7]

This widow that I had been dating at Long Beach found another widow of a man from the same squadron at North Island. So, she had followed me and moved down there. These gals were really hunting for a husband. There were four of five of them there in San Diego that we encountered from time to time. I dated most every night. Since she was living with one of the girls over on North Island, I had to take the ferry back and forth. The ferry stopped around midnight. I remember there was one night I missed the last ferry, so I spent the rest of the night there in my car waiting for the morning ferry.

Sometime around the first part of December, I finally received my orders to duty. I was supposed to be stationed at the naval gunfire support school there in Coronado.

Since my mother now lived in San Diego, after a while I started staying over at her house. I also decided that I needed to buy a car. They hadn't made any new cars since the war had started. I went to a car dealer and found an old, but pretty, little Mercury coupe. It ran well, but the tires were pretty bad. Actually, the reason they had decided to ration gasoline in those days was to save the rubber because the Japanese had captured all the rubber plantations. This was before we had synthetic rubber. After I got the car, I went to the ration office to get my gasoline ration. I don't remember what it was, but it was just a few gallons a month. I made some comment about this, and this little gal that was issuing the ration cards said, "Well, there's a war on you know!" I'm standing there with my uniform on, my

7   Crowe remained in the Marine Corps until 1960 and retired as a colonel.

ribbons, and all. I said, "Amazing! I wondered what all the commotion was about." She didn't even pick up the idea. We could get an extra ration of gas that would take us from wherever we were living to where we were going to be stationed.

By this time I was really wanting to get back to Muleshoe. I also wanted to go see Malda. She and I had been corresponding during the time I was in the hospital. The army had closed down the base at Fort Stockton where she had been a civilian flight instructor for flying cadets. She had moved to Galveston and was a contract monitor for the navy at the Galveston shipyard. I wanted to go see her.

I was given leave but I was wondering how I was going to be able to get to Texas because it was impossible to get a space on a plane, train, or bus as they were absolutely crowded with service people under orders. I happened to encounter a young navy officer in the officers club one night. He had been a pilot on the carrier *Bunker Hill* [CV 17]. It had been hit by a *kamikaze* during the Battle of Okinawa and limped back in to Bremerton, Washington. The navy was transferring some of those experienced pilots to Pensacola to be instructors. If you were being transferred you could get sufficient gasoline to take you from where you were to your new duty station. He and I were sitting at the bar having a drink in the North Island Officers Club, and I found out that he was from Sudan, a town sixteen miles west of Muleshoe. His name was Petey Boyle. I said, "Petey, I'll tell you what I will do. You give me your gasoline ration to Pensacola, and I'll drive you to your front door." I was going to be going through there on my way to Galveston anyway.

Well, we made that deal and off we went. The second-hand car that I had bought was a pretty good convertible coupe, but the tires on it were really rotten. Well, I had one flat after another, and it was even difficult in a town to find a place to get the flats fixed. By the time I got to Odessa, Texas, I had had six flats. I had an uncle who was a rancher there, and he was sort of a mover and shaker there in town. I had planned to spend one night with him, and he said the Chamber of Commerce is meeting tomorrow, and I'd like for you to stay an extra night and speak to the Chamber of Commerce. I was probably the first marine officer ever in Odessa. All the people were there, and after I finished talking all the people were standing around patting me on the back, and they asked, "Is there anything we can do for you?" I said, "I sure could use some tires." They had an emergency meeting of the ration board right there on the spot. Within an hour I had four brand-new tires and tubes on the car. So, that problem was fixed.

When I got to Galveston it had been about five and a half years since Malda and I had seen each other. But we picked up right where we left off, almost like we had never been separated. I think it was the second night that I asked her to marry me. She said, "Okay but it's going to take a while." I said, "Well, we have nine days, so use as much as you need." We managed to get married on the 21st of December. George Mitchell, one of my former Aggie schoolmates who was in my battery at A&M, was there.[8] Right after the reception we were going to leave to start to San Diego because I had to report in to my new job assignment the second of January. I had asked the preacher to get our

---

8   George P. Mitchell, a billionaire Texas oilman, graduated in 1940 from Texas A&M. This would have been the same class as Elrod if he had remained at A&M. Mitchell, considered the father of "fracking," died in 2013 in Galveston.

marriage recorded because I knew if we didn't get it recorded there, it might never be recorded. He mumbled something, and I slipped him a couple of $20 bills, which at that time was a lot of money. When we got to the reception, he was there with the recorded documents. So, we made the trip back to San Diego. The night before our marriage, I was sitting in my hotel lobby reading a newspaper. I was in my uniform. The hotel manager began a conversation with me. His son was a marine and had even been at Saipan, so we had a lot to talk about. He asked me what I was doing in Galveston, and I told him, "Getting married." He asked to do me a favor—to line up hotel rooms for Malda and I for us to stay on the trip back to San Diego. He could not be dissuaded, so I agreed. So, as we drove back to San Diego, there were rooms waiting for us along the way, and they were all paid for. This impressed Malda. She told me that, "This life in the Marine Corps is not going to be so bad."

Epilogue

fter their wedding in Galveston, Roy and Malda drove cross country to San Diego, staying in the rooms that the generous and patriotic Galveston hotel manager had provided. In San Diego Roy resumed his job as an instructor, teaching navy officers the intricacies of naval gunfire in support of troops fighting ashore. This was something he could put his heart into because of the powerful effect of naval gunfire he had witnessed at Tarawa and Saipan, especially at Tarawa where the two destroyers fired from the lagoon, close to shore, and "really saved our butt!" as he proclaimed.

When the war ended, the flow of officers entering training diminished. Malda and Roy were transferred to Guantanamo Bay, Cuba, where he commanded the Marine Guard Company. As he transferred from Guantanamo to his next duty station at Quantico, he ran into Kenneth C. Langness. He had been a corporal in his platoon at Guadalcanal and Roy had recommended him for commissioning and aviation training. Now he was a lieutenant and wearing pilots' wings, qualified to fly the F4U Corsair. Roy was extremely glad to see that things had turned out well for this young marine, who had endured

Guadalcanal and Tarawa. They had a couple of beers together and talked at the officers club at Jacksonville.[1]

On several occasions throughout his career and after, Roy encountered marines who had served with him or under him on those Pacific battlefields. It was always a special occasion. They shared experiences unique to men who have been in combat, experiences they shared with no other and that forever bound them together.

During his Marine Corps career he served a number of tours of duty at the Marine Base in Quantico, Virginia, sometimes known as the "schoolhouse of the Marine Corps." Roy often served as an instructor teaching marine officers fundamentals of combat. He knew what awaited his students, and he was dedicated to giving his students skills they would need to succeed in combat and survive. He also served in a number of operational billets. One tour for Roy was especially memorable. This was with the Third Marine Brigade at Camp Pendleton, California. Its commanding officer was the iconic marine Lewis B. "Chesty" Puller, who even in the early 1950s had a sweeping reputation among marines as a tough, no-nonsense fighter. He seemed to encapsulate what it meant to be a marine. Elrod found "Chesty" to be not only a motivational leader but also a sensitive and personable character. Roy recalled that he never raised his voice. He would approach and ask, "Hello, old man, tell me about (this or that). Did you ever think about another way of doing it?" That to Elrod (and others) was considered an order chiseled in stone. On a glowing fitness report (an evaluation of performance) that Puller wrote on Roy, in his own

---

1   See footnote Chapter 5 in regards Langness.

scrawl, Puller commented: "I would particularly desire his services during war time."

Lieutenant Colonel Roy H. Elrod retired from the Marine Corps in 1961. He had actually wanted to retire a year earlier. The Commandant, General David M. Shoup, who had commanded the marines at Tarawa and knew Elrod, called him in for a conference when he received his request to retire. Shoup, when finding out that Roy was getting into the building business, remarked, "It sounds like you want out at a time that is convenient to you." Elrod replied, "Well, General, only an idiot would retire when it wasn't convenient." Of course, this did not sway General Shoup, and he refused Elrod's retirement request. The Marine Corps ordered him instead to Okinawa for a year. Malda joined him there and upon completion of that tour they returned to the U.S. They went the long way home, going west to visit sites in Asia, the Middle East, and Europe. Upon returning to the U.S. Roy retired at the Brooklyn Navy Yard.

After Saipan, he had never returned to combat. To an infantry officer, and a warrior at heart, this was a disappointment. He attested, "Frankly I was getting bored, if I had known that Vietnam was around the corner, I would have stayed in."

They settled in Northern Virginia where they started a construction and development business. This was going back to his first love that started when he was a teenager in Muleshoe: construction. He had built houses throughout his Marine Corps career at the various places they were based. It began when they were based at Quantico after World War II. The housing situation was awful. He and Malda were living in a cramped and primitive off-base apartment. Roy wanted better. Finally, he told Malda, "I am going to round up some tools, find us a piece of ground, and build us a house." In seven months he had erected their first house on an acre of forested land near the base. This was the first of many houses they built. When he retired they had six houses. The rental income from them exceeded his Marine Corps pay.

Their construction and development corporation was profoundly successful. Malda was an active partner in the business. They built housing subdivisions, commercial buildings, churches, and hospitals. Snow skiing and worldwide travel were their recreational pursuits. Roy also served in local politics and was a leader in a Methodist Church in Woodbridge, Virginia. In 1994 they retired from their building operation and downscaled to a smaller home in Fredericksburg, Virginia.

On Christmas Day 2005, Malda woke Roy: "Roy, there is something wrong with me." Roy hurried her to the hospital. The diagnosis was that Malda had suffered a serious stroke. She survived the stroke but was in for a long rehabilitation period. The medical people recommended she be placed in a nursing home. Roy refused. He told them, "I know this lady. I have the resources. You tell me what she needs, and I'll make it happen." And he did. He made the changes to their house to facilitate her recovery. She made remarkable progress, but in March 2008, she succumbed to the aftereffects of the stroke and an on-going struggle with COPD.

Roy remained in Fredericksburg, living alone but active. After Malda's death Roy, now 89 years old, made an epic trip to Alaska and back. He drove his Hummer to Winnipeg, Canada. From there he traveled by train, ship, and airplane across Canada and back to Winnipeg. He then drove his Hummer back to Fredericksburg.

He suffered a bout of prostate cancer in the late 1990s, which an aggressive routine of radiation cured. He still however suffered from the Japanese artillery shell that hit him at Saipan. The loss of hearing in his right ear impaired his balance and shell fragments near his spine and hip caused difficulty controlling his legs. In 2015, sponsored by Representative Ken King of Hemphill, the Texas House of Representatives formally recognized Roy's World War II service.

It all goes back to the Marine Corps to the World War II experience, a profoundly pivotal point in his life. "I am very proud to have been a marine. I felt that I always did the right thing for the right reason at the right time and never had a problem mentally for what I did in the war. There are bad things that happen in combat, I did some bad things but we all did them. I felt like I was acting in the best interest of the Corps and the country, and that what I did was justified because they contributed in some way to the success of the operation. This was a duty and I did it to the best of my ability."

Lieutenant Colonel Elrod passed away at his home on 17 December 2016.

Bibliography

Primary Sources

Documents

Casualty Cards, World War II. U.S. Marine Corps History Division, Reference Branch, Quantico, VA.

Crowe, Major Henry P. "Report of Tarawa Operations," to Major General Julian C. Smith, 13 December 1943. Archives, U.S. Marine Corps History Division, Archives, Quantico, VA.

Elrod, Lt. Col. Roy H. Official Personnel Record. National Personnel Records Center, St. Louis, MO.

Elrod, First Lt. Roy H. Memo to Major Henry P. Crowe. "Report of 37-mm Gun Platoon in recent operations," 28 November 1943. Author's files, U.S. Marine Corps History Division, Archives, Quantico, VA.

Greer, Dexter E. "My Military History, December 1942– December 1944." 15 January 2008. Author's Files, Archives, U.S. Marine Corps History Division, Quantico, VA.

Muster Rolls. U.S. Marine Corps History Division, Reference Branch, Quantico, VA.

Report on LONGSUITS Operation, USS *Sheridan*, 20 December 1943. U.S. Marine Corps History Division, Archives, Quantico, VA.

Tarawa After-Action Reports. U.S. Marine Corps History Division, U.S. Marine Corps History Division, Archives, Quantico, VA.

USS *Heywood* Action Report, 29 November 1943. U.S. Marine Corps History Division, Archives, Quantico, VA.

Oral History

Crowe, Colonel Henry P. Interview with Benis M. Frank, 4–5 April 1979. Transcript. Oral History Office, U.S. Marine Corps History Division, Quantico, VA.

Day, Major General James L. Interview with Benis M. Frank, 24 October 1989. Transcript. Oral History Office, U.S. Marine Corps History Division, Quantico, VA.

Elrod, Lieutenant Colonel Roy H. Interviews with Fred H. Allison, Mike Miller, and Allyson Stanton, 2012–2013. Transcripts. Oral History Office, U.S. Marine Corps History Division, Quantico, VA.

Secondary Sources

Books

Alexander, Colonel Joseph H. *Utmost Savagery.* Annapolis: Naval Institute Press, 1995.

Chapin, Captain John C. *Breaching the Marianas: The Battle for Saipan.* World War II Commemorative Series. Washington: U.S. Marine Corps Historical Center, 1994.

Frank, Benis M., and Henry I. Shaw, Jr. *History of the U.S. Marine Corps Operations in World War II,* Vol V *Victory and Occupation.* Washington: Historical Branch, G-3 Division, Headquarters, U.S. Marine Corps, 1968.

Frank, Richard B. *Guadalcanal.* New York: Penguin Books, 1992.

Hammel, Eric, and John E. Lane. *Bloody Tarawa*. Pacifica: Pacifica Press, 1998.

Hornfischer, James D. *The Fleet at Flood Tide*. New York: Bantam Books, 2016.

Hough, Lieutenant Colonel Frank O., Major Verle E. Ludwig, and Henry I. Shaw, Jr. *History of U.S. Marine Corps Operations in World War II*, Vol. 1, *Pearl Harbor to Guadalcanal*. Washington: Historical Branch, G-3 Division, Headquarters, U.S. Marine Corps, 1958.

Rottman, Gordon L. *World War II Pacific Island Guide*. Westport: Greenwood Press, 2002.

Shaw, Henry I. Jr, Bernard C. Nalty, and Edwin T. Turnbladh. *History of U.S. Marine Corps Operations in World War II*, Vol. 3, *Central Pacific Drive*. Washington: Historical Branch, G-3 Division, Headquarters, U.S. Marine Corps, 1966.

Shaw, Henry I., Jr. *Opening Moves: Marines Gear Up for War*. Washington: Marine Corps Historical Center, 1991.

Shaw, Henry I., Jr. *First Offensive: The Marine Campaign for Guadalcanal*. Washington: Marine Corps Historical Center, 1992.

Sherrod, Robert. *The Story of a Battle*. New York: Duell, Sloan & Pearce, Inc., 1944.

Stockman, Captain James R. *The Battle for Tarawa*. Washington: Historical Section, Headquarters, U.S. Marine Corps, 1947.

Updegraph, Charles L., Jr. *U.S. Marine Corps Special Units of World War II*. Washington: History and Museums Division, Headquarters, U.S. Marine Corps, 1972.

Articles

Alexander, Colonel Joseph H. "Tarawa: The Ultimate Opposed Landing." *Marine Corps Gazette*, November, 1993.

"Fighting Fronts." *Newsweek*, 8 May 1944.

Simmons, Brigadier Edwin H. "Remembering the Legendary 'Jim' Crowe." *Fortitudine*, Winter 1991–1992.

Smith, Lieutenant General Julian C. "Tarawa." *United States Naval Institute Proceedings*. November, 1953.

Websites

"100 Years Dry: The U.S. Navy's End of Alcohol at Sea." USNI News. http://news.usni.org/2014/07/01/hundred -years-dry-u-s-navys-end-alcohol-sea (accessed November 2016).

Bryson, Gordon. "Waimea Remembers Camp Tarawa." *The Waimea Gazette*. http://www.waimeagazette.com/mar958 _waimearememberstarawa.htm (accessed February 2015).

"M3 Halftrack Car." Tanks Encyclopedia. http://www.tanks -encyclopedia.com/ww2/US/M3_Halftrack.php (accessed January 2017).

"Muleshoe." Texas State Historical Association. tstps://tsha online.org/handbook /online/articles/hgm09 (accessed May 2015).

"Photo Galleries." United States Marine Corps History Division. https://www.usmcu.edu/historydivision/photo -galleries (accessed January 2017).

"Photography." Naval History and Heritage Command. https://www.history.navy.mil/our-collections/photography .html (accessed January 2017).

"US Forces in New Zealand." New Zealand History. http://www.nzhistory.net.nz/war/us-forces-in-new-zealand/yankee-boys-kiwi-girl (accessed January 2015).

"Who's Who In Marine Corps History." U.S. Marine Corps History Division. https://www.usmcu.edu/historydivision/frequently-requested/whos-who-marine-corps-history (accessed December 2016).

"World War II Labor Strikes." Hidden History, Labor Strikes During World War II. http://theden.tv/2013/11/29/hidden-history-labor-strikes-during-wwii/ (accessed July 2016).

Index

W

X

Y